D1377545

T57.5
I57
NO. 4

Management Information Systems

SELECTED PAPERS FROM MIS COPENHAGEN 70 — AN IAG CONFERENCE

Edited by

Walter Goldberg
Thorkild Herborg Nielsen
Erik Johnsen
Harald Josefsen

OCCASIONAL PUBLICATION NO. 4
IFIP ADMINISTRATIVE DATA
PROCESSING GROUP (IAG)

AUERBACH
publishers

princeton
philadelphia
new york
london

278589

Studentlitteratur · Sweden

NO LONGER THE PROPERT
OF THE
UNIVERSITY OF RI LIBRARY

© IAG
Studentlitteratur, Sweden, 1971

First published in the USA in 1971
by AUERBACH Publishers Inc., Princeton, N.Y.

Printed in Sweden
Studentlitteratur
Lund 1971

75806

CONTENTS

A conference on Management Information Systems, MIS COPENHAGEN 70, was held at Hotel Marienlyst, Elsinore, Denmark, between October 14 and 16, 1970, sponsored by IFIP Administrative Data Processing Group, IAG.

The 293 conference participants came from 23 nations and presented a total of more than 30 papers.

The program for the conference was a varied one that revealed the wide range of problems encountered in development and implementation of management information systems.

Although "MIS" continues to defy precise definition, professional managers, management scientists and data system specialists have problems in common, and these common concerns are the subject of the three parts of this publication.

Part 1 contains 10 papers on Managerial problems encountered by conferees in connection with development and implementation of MIS.

Part 2 contains 9 papers on system design with emphasis on procedures for system evaluation.

Part 3 contains 6 papers on data structure with emphasis on the different ways of organizing data bases necessary for implementation of a flexible MIS.

The Danish minister of economic affairs, professor P. Nyboe Andersen opened the conference. He gave an overview with examples from Denmark of the problems confronting government agencies in developing and implementing management information systems.

The papers included in this publication cover a very wide range of subjects pertirent to a university course on management information systems. Therefore, the publication might be used as a textbook or as supplementary reading material for such a course.

The IFIP Administrative Data Processing Group (IAG) generously provided the basis for its publication by including it in its Occasional Publication Series.

On the whole, the increasingly sophisticated understanding of the nature of management information systems is revealed in the various papers contained in this publication. It records one additional step in the advancement of the state of the art of management information systems.

Copenhagen

Walter Goldberg   Erik Johnsen
Thorkild Herborg-Nielsen   Harald Josefsen

OPENING ADDRESS

P. Nyboe Andersen, Minister of Economic Affairs

Denmark

The set of problems to be considered at this Conference are familiar enough inasmuch as it has always been a problem for decision-makers to get sufficient relevant and accurate information as a basis for the decision-making process.

The complexity of our modern society has made this problem greater than ever, but our ability to find data and to process them mechanically has also improved, especially by means of EDP technology, which has developed at a pace that opens up almost unpredictable perspectives.

In this as in many other fields, the technical problems have been solved much faster than expected, but it has been very difficult to change the attitude of present and potential users of the new techniques. These techniques have very often been used to solve problems in the old-fashioned manner in spite of the fact that the efficient use of the new techniques and their potentialities generally requires radical changes in the formulation of the problems.

From the list of conference papers I see that EDP technology will hold a prominent place in your deliberations. I realize, of course, that these problems are important and must be solved. I shall, for good reasons, refrain from discussing the technology of EDB. But let me add that I have the layman's unlimited confidence in the experts: I'm sure they will know how to solve the purely technical problems.

I can, on the other hand, speak with rather more weight about the consumer's side of the problem - more particularly about the public sector's needs and problems in this context.

It i often said that the public sector has much to learn from the private sector - if only the public sector wants to learn. The development of management information systems is, I suppose, a fairly typical example of a field where private industry has spearheaded a field which the public sector not only should but will inevitably have to enter.

Having said that, I must add that the problems are much more complex in the public sector than they are in business and industry. This is true of the formulation of specific aims as well as of the provision and quantification of data which are of relevance to the decision-making process.

In the public sector, the application of management information systems may be placed roughly under three main headings:

1) how to obtain relevant data for use in legislative work and in the government's formulation of policy in important fields, such as economic policy;

2) how to plan and implement administrative functions, such as the collection of income tax under the pay-as-you-earn system, and the operation of the central population register;

3) how to plan the organization and operation of individual government agencies.

I shall not deal at any length with the third group whose problems are fairly similar to those of industry and who can use the private sector's experience with the least modifications.

The major problems are in groups (1) and (2). These are also the groups that offer the widest scope for improvement. The two groups are interrelated in that the administrative operations in group (2) emanate from legislation adopted by group (1), but experience gathered through the operations of group (2) also affects decisions to be taken in group (1).

One example of this interrelationship is the newly-established EDP-register of all wage and salary earners and of all employers required to withhold income tax for their employees. This register is the result of tax legislation, while the information collected in this register offers new opportunities for compilation of statistics on economic fluctuations which, in turn, offer the government a better basis for its decisions on economic policy.

Several country-wide registers have been established in Denmark in recent years. In other fields, too, we have gathered experience which has been very useful and - I regret to say - also expensive. We have, for instance, established a centralized EDP wage and salary payments system for large segments of government administration. Let me deal very briefly with the most important aspects of this experience and discuss how very difficult it is to apply the lessons drawn from it.

To take the crucial problem first, the political machinery is inimical to the application of EDP techniques.

11

75806

Our laws are enacted in keeping with time-honoured democratic procedures; the outcome is a compromise between divergent political views which are reflected in escape clauses and exemptions from the law. I need hardly explain to you, Gentlemen, how this affects the application of EDP to the administration of laws.

It is, of course, unacceptable that the political content of laws should be dominated by considerations of EDP technique.

Here already is one very important obstacle to the consistent and rational application of EDP technique in governement administration. But this does not mean that we cannot and should not try to go much further into EDP that we have done so far.

I submit that politicians could give a wide measure of consideration to the exigencies of EDP without compromising the political content of laws. They could even learn something very useful from it. Close reasoning, which is a precondition for efficient data processing, will in my opinion be useful also to political life, for instance in the form of consistent and well-considered legislative work.

In order to achieve this, however, politicians must learn to assess the potentials of these new techniques. They must learn, in fact, to understand and speak the EDP language. Here, politicians are in the same boat as managers of private firms who want to apply EDP to management. Only if the relevant problems can be formulated and presented to the technicians in correct terms can technology become the servant and not the master.

Whenever bills are being drafted, one central consideration should be to provide for as much feed-back as possible about the effects of the laws.

Such feed-back will be useful not only in the administration of laws but also in the future work of the government and parliament.

Efforts have been made to achieve this by instructing the National Bureau of Statistics (Danmarks Statistik) to direct or take part in the planning and use of the central registers established by public authorities.

In practice, the results have not quite lived up to the intentions. The big public registers have to serve specific administrative purposes, and they were built up under fairly tight time schedules. As a result of these pressures, only moderate attention could be given to statistical considerations during the build-up phase. Extraction of relevant statistical data, if available at all, will therefore require extra runs involving disproportionate costs.

Management information systems have, as far as I can see, so far been concerned mainly with the management of individuel firms. The experience gathered and the progress achieved in the theory of M.I.S. can no doubt be used to a fairly large extent in government administration. But public authorities cannot, in their own interest, merely rely on the achievements of other sectors. The government must play an active role in this work in order to ensure that data obtained from private sources are consistent.

The many data which public authorities claim from the private sector can keep to unify or streamline the concepts and data used in the information systems of private firms. But this will be possible only if the government co-ordinates the collection of data for various purposes in a systematic manner and if the information required is of immediate relevance also to the internal needs for information in the individual firms.

The application od EDP to more and more fields of activity will certainly lead to great changes in management patterns, both in the private and the public sector. In my opinion, the dreams - or misgivings - that all problems can be solved by pushing a few buttons is not only unrealistic but, in fact, a stumbling block to progress. The problems must, as always, be solved by human beings. Machines cannot do it, but they can, if properly used, give us a better basis for our decisions, and they can ease the technical implementation of decisions. That will call for work and knowledge - knowledge about the potentialities of technology, and the limitations of it, and hard work to ensure that the machines will serve the purposes for which they have been designed.

This conference is an important initiative to that end. I'm sure that new light will be shed on many problems and keep to improve the general understanding of the problems of management information.

I wish you welcome to Denmark and trust that the results of your conference will live up to the expectations which the conference programme holds out.

I now declare the conference open.

CONCLUDING ADDRESS

Thorkild Herborg-Nielsen
The Århus School of Economics and Business Administration
Denmark

The program committee has specified the purposes of this conference as follows:

- To bring together an international professional group in order to stimulate a discussion among professional managers, management scientists, and data systems specialists on the problems of designing, implementing, and utilizing Management Information Systems.
- To produce a publication which will define the state of the art of Management Information Systems.

Let me begin this summary with some remarks on the background and the broader perspective for these purposes. Only a couple of years ago the conference FILE 68 was held at the same historical place where we are now. I was given the opportunity to welcome the conference with some remarks on the Management Information System as a basis for file considerations. Although I thought to pinpoint some realities behind the requirements of management as regards the building-up of a management information system, and introduced a distinction between information for decisions and general survey information, in the fall of 68 I was frequently met by the question: Isn't all the talk about MIS a chimera?

An initiative to answer that question was taken by N.D.U. - Nordic
Data Union - as well in the winter 68 as during 69 where meetings were
held between management scientists and professional managers. In the
same period quite a number of MIS conferences have taken place on the
international arena. Also IAG has given its contribution to this picture
by organizing a three days conference in September 69 in Stresa, Italy.

To be, or not to be another event? we can ask with a slight transcription
of Hamlet's words, well, it is my opinion that the result of our meetings
and discussions is that MIS has passed the stage of a chimera, also this
conference has convinced me that we are on the road enabling the management to make appropriate utilization of the resources of the enterprise.

This point of view has already been taken by the IFIP Council, which has
decided that the next IFIP World Conference - taking place in Ljubljana,
Yugoslavia, 1971 - among the technical areas* shall include an area concerning systems for management and administration. As chairman for
the committee organizing the technical area, I found it reasonable to discuss ways and means for a preparatory work to this event. The result
was this intermediate conference, and I am grateful to all of you for being
here and for the contributions given to this conference.

1: Numerical mathematics
2: Mathematical foundation of information processing
3: Computer software
4: Computer hardware
5: Systems for management and administration
6: Technical applications
7: Social sciences and humanities applications

It is obvious that the purpose bringing us together has been clearly realized, and to an extent I did not expect. But also to produce a publication worth
while to present for an international audience can be realized. In the following considerations I will not try to comment the papers we have been through,
but to present some viewpoints related to the main themes which have con-
stituted the structure of the conference program.

State of the art

If it is correct that the state of the art mainly had to be described in metaphoric considerations a couple of years ago, it seems as things have changed. The papers presented here demonstrate that the art can be described
by concepts, rules, and methods, and that the contents of these elements
have been clarified to some extent in the process of practical applications.
The MIS-concept has been considered as an approach both to the management decision and to the design of database. For the first point of view it
seems essential that the key-processes and the clarification of objectives
at different management levels have been brought into focus. Further it
has been pointed out that management approach to a structure of MIS can
be developed as well in a general architectural model as in a structure of
reports, and in the frame of the process which constitutes the management task.

The field of database-design is perhaps the best example of developments
in concepts and rules from this conference. The construction of hierarchical structures has been described in several papers with the help of clari-
fying concepts as the logical file and the pluto database, identifiers, and
attributes as well as structure mode and methods of control. These are
only examples. As a red thread goes through these parts of the contri-

butions the interest for simplification of the operation procedures in administrative handling of a database. This is a problem which is considered seriously by Danish researchers and I hope that people involved in the problem have found contact to each other at this conference.

The implementation of management information systems has been demonstrated in so different areas as cash management, management of a college system, and an approach for ship-building policy. In the last case the interplay between an overall system, the basic system model, and the concept of model-stages was descibed in a way which to me seems useful for pedagogical purposes. Furthermore we have received recommendations for the establishment of control groups, design groups, and implementation groups as means to an effective solution of the organizational asspects.

The problem of adaptivity

Charles Kriebel presented the classical control system with a very essential specification connected to the "mechanism of decision" indicated as "adaptive mechanism". He specified what to me was a main topic of discussion at a MIS conference: How do overall systems (organizations) react towards the new subsystems we put into them - or: How can the adaptive mechanism be described with the parameters we have the possibility to specify and control.

A metaphoric analogy will give you my point: The conditions of succesful surgery are - when hearts or kidneys are transplanted from person to person - that a very specific knowledge from tissue structure is developed and respected. The adaptive mechanism is here closely related to a set of tissue structure parameters.

From our organizational world, I can give you a fresh example. A small firm - called Denmark - has for the last two years tried to transplant a subsystem into its social body called "taxation at the source". This new function has till now been badly adapted. One reasonable explanation is that the old tax system had a very high variety - all taxpayers were involved in execution, and a stochastic process regulated how their taxes were paid over a period of time including late payments. The new system has a much lower variety (employers pay for their employees) and it is practically deterministic as the rules of payment.

Some conclusions about parameters could be drawn from recognitions of the type mentioned. But - what has been decided a couple of days ago - I refer to the newspapers - is to pay in the future considerably higher wages to the subsystems' topmanagers! I do not expect the adaptivity will rise.

I am not satisfied by our discussions related to this serious problem, and my conclusion is, that it would be useful to have an IAG conference in the future - a MAP conference: Managing Adaptive Procedures.

Let me finish this point by saying that the development of interactive systems seems to show promising possibilities to overcome some of our tissue structure problems. Let us start our analysis. The state of the art has shown that we do not master the art! I say so, also because I have found too much reflect from traditional organization theory in parts of the considerations presented. This judgement includes my own contributions, I am willing to add.

Methods of analysis and construction

The interplay between the decision model and the database has been described as well from a theoretical as from an implementation point of view. I wish to contribute to this discussion with the following remarks: The management requirements are affected through

a) a creation of ideas to which survey information is of essential importance
b) decisions (actual decision-making)
c) operations comprizing the application of sources to keep the enterprise operational
d) control to keep the operations of the enterprise under observation.

This means that there is an interplay of interest also between the survey data model and the database. Furthermore it must be emphasized that a well designed management information system not only comprizes the machine-stored data but also the information availabe from the human elements of the system more or less directly. The human factor in MIS has many aspects. One contribution to the problem of system construction has been concerned with the security problem and how to solve it by two types of mechanisms "static security locks" and "dynamic security locks". We have here touched upon a problem which has severe juridical aspects. Questions about legal regulations are discussed in all countries. In Denmark a new committee has just been formed and I appreciate that the question has been elucidated from a technical point of view.

The concept of profit visibility was new to me and seems to be a realistic approach from which we can expect new results in the future.

I must add to these statements that I am quite satisfied that we have not tried to use this conference to play with cristal balls, but really have discussed our actual experiences.

Managers' role in development and implementation of MIS.

This part of the program has been covered in several papers and the approaches to answers are two interesting - but different - questions.

A couple of papers start with the question: What should be understood by MIS? A conceptional as well as an operational analysis of the semantic content of the three words in "Management Information System" leads to the clarification of some fundamental relations.

Paul Dixon, our key note speaker on this topic, asks: What are meaningful questions in the role of a manager? From this starting point he reaches to the questions: The role of manager? At which level of the company? In which functional area? Which management information system should serve which purpose?

This type of approach has uncovered the concept of key processes for which planning, control and administration constitute the process of management. Contributions as "goal programming approach" and the "corporate planning strategy" seem to be based on the same philosophy and present the management tools to produce operational results.

A final remark

I am sure that we all have questions which have not been discussed. Some of them can be very fundamental questions. As an example I will mention Paul Dixon's axiom (or postulate) that goals and objectives need to be set and directed from the top down since a corporation cannot function as a democracy. It could take another conference to analyse and discuss the contents of this axiom.

22

Part 1 - Managerial Problems

METHODS OF ANALYSIS AND CONSTRUCTION;
THE INTERPLAY BETWEEN DECISION MODEL AND DATA BASE

Sam Sjöberg
The Gothenburg School of Economics and
Business Administration
Sweden

1. Definitions
2. Descriptive model of the firm as a controlled system
3. MIS/MCS – an overview of the decision structure
4. Some remarks on the corporate data base concept
5. In summary

In this paper I will give some aspects on a few of the complex problems behind designing Management Control Systems. I have chosen to give it the form of comments to some illustrations in the firm belief that one picture tells you more than one thousand words.

DEFINITIONS

The title of my presentation includes a few words that have to be defined. I am primarily thinking of the words Decision Model and Data Base.

I will let the expression Decision Model or perhaps better the Decision System refer to a component of what might be called a Control System. Other components comprising a Control System are the Data Collection System, the Information System and the Ordering System.

I will use the word Data Base in the sense of all the data that a specific Control System needs for its proper function. I want to stress immediately that this has no necessary connection with the expression Data Bank which I will use referring to a specific way of organizing data for computer use.

If we consider a firms total control system (equal to the Management Control System (MCS) to consist of several sub control systems, we could use the word data base in the sense of the total demand for data from these different systems (Corporate Data Base). The corporate data bank would then mean those parts of the total data base that are accessable in a specific way by a computer. I am not going any further into these definitions. Illustration No. 1 might give you an idea of the different sub systems of a control system and how they interact.

In illustration No. 2 you will find a somewhat less simplified model. I will touch upon these things later in my presentation.

A DESCRIPTIVE MODEL OF THE FIRM AS A CONTROLLED SYSTEM

Before we can design what might be called a MIS we have to analyze the situation in which this MIS is expected to operate. For such an analysis some kind of descriptive model of the firm is valuable or even necessary.

In the following, I will try to give you a rough idea of the descriptive model we are developing for this specific purpose. You will find it in illustration Nos. 3 and 4. First we have to recognize the necessity of knowing the goals for the firm's operations. It is on this knowledge we form the basis for measuring the efficiency with which the different control systems function within the firm. These goals can be formulated intuitively or by means of some more formalized method. We generally use what we refer to as participants analysis, i.e. a practical application of the theoretical model presented in Cyert-March: A Behavioral Theory of the Firm. We have designed formal rules for making such an analysis. There certainly still is very much to do to improve our methods in this respect but we find our attempts promising. The goals either derived in such a formal way or formulated intuitively have to be expressed very precisely in order to make possible the measurement of the goal attainment. The process of making vague goals more precise I refer to as goal analysis. For this purpose we are using the general means ends analysis where we have designed very strict rules for what is allowed in the break down procedure in order to avoid logical and other mistakes that can easily be done. We have paid quite a lot of attention to this problem. An analysis of this kind cannot be made successfully without being based on a thorough knowledge of the actual firms operative activities. The definition of what shall be considered to be the operative activities may sometimes involve Rather subtle delimitation problems, which it would lead too far to penetrate in this presentation.

Each firm operates in a certain environment. This can be looked upon as the frames (restrictions) within which the operative activities have to be kept. Some of these frames can be changed by the (long run) activities of the firm, some cannot. In the descriptive model of the firm we try to define both the operative activities and the activities that are necessary either to change the frames or to adapt the firm to the expected future values of the frames. This has to be done in such a way that the goal attainment for the firms operative activities can be kept at a high and even level.

Now, if we have defined the operative activities and the frames within which these have to be carried out we can define the necessary changing/adapting activities. The goals mentioned earlier can now be referred to these different activities. This means that we have both defined the activities to control and the goals (objectives) towards which they should be directed. This forms the basis for the further analysis and construction of the necessary decision systems from which we can derive our need for information. In other words we have established the basic knowledge for the construction of the necessary control systems both for the firm's operative activities and for its changing/adapting activities.

In this presentation I am supposed to treat the interplay between the decision systems and the data base. This prevents me from going any further into the continued process of designing these control systems. I just want to mention that the further formal analysis mainly contents treatment of the organizational consequences, studying and minimizing the interactions between different control systems, cost/revenue analysis for prioritation purposes, creating a suitable project administration and finally systems design starting with those with highest priority values. We are since a few years working in close cooperation with a couple of Swedish firms to develop such a formal method for attacking the firm's total need for information starting with an analysis of the management (control) process. The results are promising. The above described model of the firm has proved very useful both as an analytical tool and as a means for communication with management.

MIS/MCS - AN OVERVIEW OF THE DECISION STRUCTURE

We are discussing problems in the design of MIS. The development of the MIS-concept has to a great extent come from people with a thorough knowledge of data processing and computing. This has very much centered the focus of the discussions on the role of the computer in the firm's MIS. It is important that the data processing problems can be solved, e.g. good operating systems permitting a flexible use of different on line devices, effective ways of organizing data giving a real meaning to the frequently used expression data bank, etc. Much more attention has been paid to the problem of data handling within a MIS than to the development of formal methods of analysis of what the content of the MIS should be. I hope it is quite clear from what I have previously said that my opinion is that the MIS-problems have to be attacked starting with the process of management control.

What, then, is a MIS? With the introductory definitions in mind I would like to suggest the following answer to that question: By MIS we mean all the (data collection and) information systems that are necessary to provide all management levels in the firm (i.e. all decision systems in the firm) with the information they need for their proper function. In illustration No. 5 I have tried to give an overview of this in a slightly idealized situation.

The partitioning of management in top, middle and lower is conventional and arbitrary. I have suggested that top management primarily devote themselves to goal formulation, efficiency measurement problems and strategic planning. Within these frames middle management should primarily establish the necessary plans for the use of the available operative resources (tactical planning). Corresponding activities for lower management will be the execution of these plans in a direct contact with the operative activities.

The decisions at each of these levels are different in several respects. The most interesting differences from the MIS point of view could be the two following: The economic importance is much greater at top than at the lower management level. The same is true for the time range of each decision, leading to a raising frequency in the decision making when approaching the lower management level. The systems at each level must be constructed in such a way that they can meet the requirements from the decision systems. This would lead us to following suggestions: The output from the lower management information systems has a higher volume, is more detailed and must be able to meet very high requirements concerning the timely precision ("need for fast information") all compared to the higher management level information systems.

Some other remarks might be worth mentioning. The possibility of formalizing and hence automizing the decision systems is decreasing when we approach top management. Further, more advanced computer equipment especially on line devices should primarily be placed where time is crucial for the quality of the decisions, i.e. where the decision system cannot work properly without very fast access to information. This would lead us to the conclusion that the burden of proof should be placed with those who argue that an essential feature of a MIS is to provide top management with possibilities for on line communication. I will gladly accept the CRT-tube on top manager's desk

a) if we believe that the quality of his decisions depends upon fast access to information

b) if we have the necessary knowledge and techniques to organize our data in such a way that he can find what he wants for his often very unstructured decision situations, in other words - if we have a good corporate data bank.

c) if we have the resources to keep this data bank up to date so that he gets not only fast but also accurate information.

SOME REMARKS ON THE CORPORATE DATA BASE CONCEPT

Illustration No. 5 shows that most of the data needed for decision making at the different levels of management come from the same sources. The previous discussion indicates that different decision systems require different information. Some need fast, accurate and detailed information while others can work properly with summaries and much less time pressure. The cost of collecting and keeping data accurate is often very high. There are good reasons to believe that a coordination of the data collection and updating activities can lead to considerable reductions in these costs. This directs the attention again to the concept of a corporate data base, possibly organized in such a way that the expression corporate data bank is adequate.

In illustration No. 6 I have tried to give a highly simplified

overview of what a MCS could look like under these circumstances.
All data is registered only once ⌐ as distinguished from what often
is the case in conventional file handling systems ⌐ and via some
data collection system included in the corporate data base. Each
information system is built in such a way that it can access those
parts of the data base that can be of value for the specific decision system to which it belongs. In the more advanced information
systems we certainly will see a high degree of flexibility as to
what data to use in the different decision situations that may
occur within the same decision system from one time to another.
This idea of varying width of the data base was indicated in illustration No. 2. It might be argued that this is a first step towards
the concept of Management by Perception, especially useful when the
decision situation changes in a predictable way. This does of course
not exclude the use of management by exception in cases where the
boundaries for the desired result (ex ante) can be specified. The
actual result (ex post) is measured and decision parameters changed
if needed. This should be the ordinary situation for most decision
systems concerning immediate control of operative activities.

The above discussed concept of a corporate data base gives
freedom to solve the data collection problem isolated from the information systems, at least from the integration point of view.
This means that the immediate connection between data collection
system and information system is broken. Provided that the necessary
interfaces between these different systems is standardized this
could lead to certain advantages in the systems design procedure.
The development of software for keeping large data quantities up to
date and accessible to a computer is promising, even if some problems
still have to be solved before there is any real meaning in the
expression corporate data bank.

IN SUMMARY

I have been using the expression Management Control System
meaning all the control systems necessary for all management

activities in the firm. A control system consists of four subsystems: Data Collection System, Information System, Decision System and Order System. The data base of a control system is all the data that the system needs for its proper function. Data organized in a specific way and accessable to a computer are referred to as a data bank. A Management Information System consists of all the (data collection and) information systems that are necessary to make the decision systems work properly.

I have argued that information systems cannot be designed unless the decision systems are well known. Further, decision systems cannot be constructed if the relevant control processes have not been analyzed. The conclusion is that the construction of a MIS must start with an analysis of the management process. Too little attention has been given the problems connected to this analysis compared to the more glamorous questions of the role of the computer in the MIS. It is time to rethink and to research!

ILLUSTRATION NO. 1.

A SIMPLIFIED MODEL OF THE COMPONENTS OF A CONTROL SYSTEM

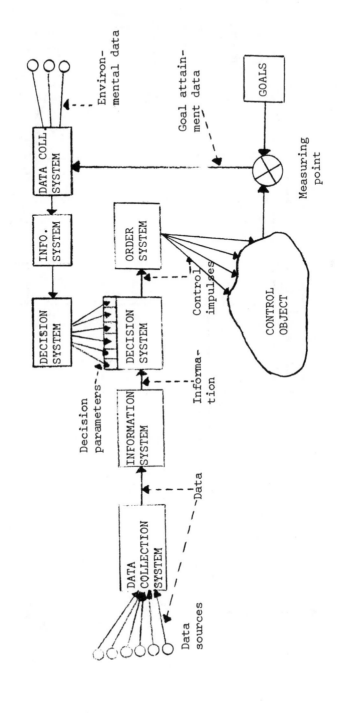

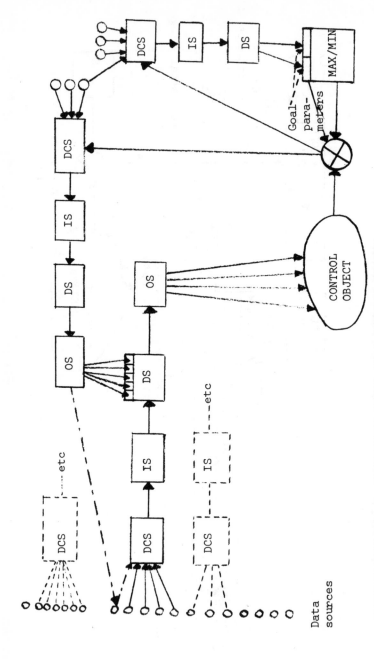

ILLUSTRATION NO. 2. SIMPLIFIED MODEL OF A CONTROL SYSTEM.

(INTERACTIONS BETWEEN THE DIFFERENT COMPONENTS)

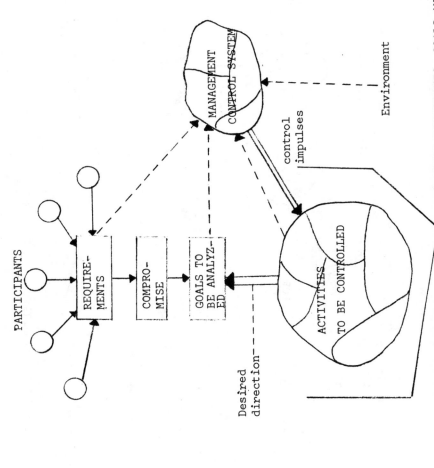

ILLUSTRATION NO. 3. SIMPLIFIED MODEL OF RELATIONS BETWEEN PARTICIPANTS, GOALS AND THE MCS

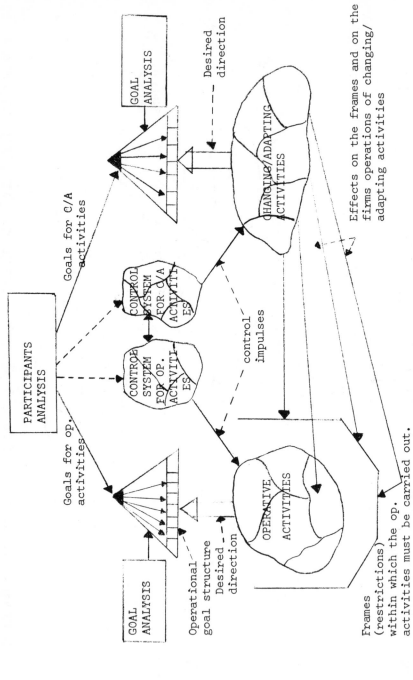

GOAL ANALYSIS

Desired direction

Goals for C/A activities

PARTICIPANTS ANALYSIS

CONTROL SYSTEM FOR C/A ACTIVITIES

CONTROL SYSTEM FOR OP. ACTIVITIES

CHANGING/ADAPTING ACTIVITIES

Effects on the frames and on the firms operations of changing/ adapting activities

control impulses

Goals for op. activities

GOAL ANALYSIS

Operational goal structure

Desired direction

OPERATIVE ACTIVITIES

Frames (restrictions) within which the op. activities must be carried out.

ILLUSTRATION NO. 4. SIMPLIFIED DESCRIPTIVE MODEL OF THE FIRM

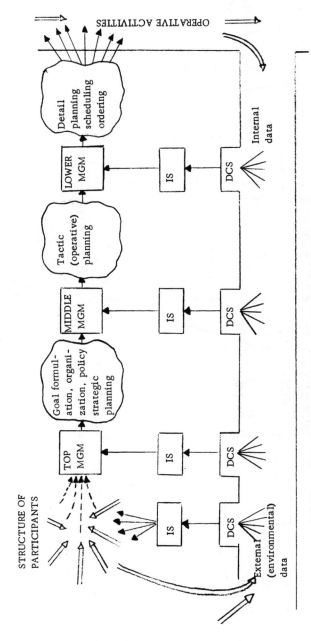

STRUCTURE OF
PARTICIPANTS

OPERATIVE ACTIVITIES

Detail
planning
scheduling
ordering

Tactic
(operative)
planning

Goal formul-
ation, organi-
zation, policy
strategic
planning

LOWER
MGM

MIDDLE
MGM

TOP
MGM

IS

IS

IS

IS

DCS

DCS

DCS

DCS

Internal
data

External
(environmental)
data

ILLUSTRATION NO. 5. SIMPLIFIED MODEL OF MANAGEMENT ACTIVITIES

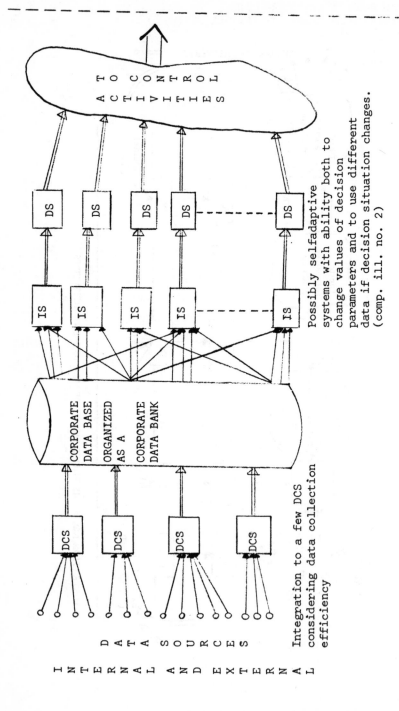

ILLUSTRATION NO. 6. SIMPLIFIED MODEL OF THE RELATIONS BETWEEN DATA COLLECTION, DATA BANK
AND INFORMATION SYSTEMS

MANAGER'S ROLE IN DEVELOPING AND IMPLEMENTING MANAGEMENT INFORMATION SYSTEMS

P. J. Dixon
Massey-Ferguson Limited
Canada

Recently, I have seen stated, that the introduction of a new information system will have as its benefit "better information for improved decision making." This is a kind of cliché which has aided a number of moderately competent or incompetent people to earn a good living in the information systems industry for years. As stated, it is meaningless. But all is not lost. Perhaps it can be, with a little discipline, used to come up with a meaningful formulation of benefits by asking a few questions. One of the roles of a manager, you know, is always to keep asking meaningful questions:

- How is the information going to be better and why?
- Decision making by whom for what purpose and when?
- How is this specifically identified decision making going to be improved?
- How is all this going to be translated into better (financial, marketing, manufacturing)performance?
- How are you going to prove all this has actually happened?

With such questions, when answers are forthcoming, one separates an ill conceived system serving objectives which have not been thought through from a project which has a hope of actually contributing to the on-going performance of a department, division, or a company.

Now let us ask a few questions in a similar vein about the title of this paper, so that we may hopefully remove it from the realm of a platitude, which it is in its present form, and find some guidelines for dealing with the topic in a more disciplined fashion:

- The role of which manager?
- At what level of the company?
- In which functional area?
- What Management Information System?
- Serving what purpose - Operational Control?
    - Financial Evaluation?
    - Tactical Planning?
    - Strategic Planning?
    - All of these?

As you can see, one could build a nice matrix, based on the title of this paper when exploded into a set of disciplined questions, and happily write a paper on each i,j square of the matrix. It might even make up a very fat book. So, while all these questions really need an answer we will try to look at the problem from another angle which should give us some of the answers, without doing it the hard way.

We shall look at some of the key processes which go on in a company; the planning, control, and administration of these processes constitutes the process of management of the company.

We shall look at the several levels of management involved in the management of these processes and see what role they play as managers.

Then we shall look at the types of information systems which are needed to support the planning, control, and administration of the processes which go on in a company.

Having done all that, perhaps we might get some insight into what role the various levels of management play, or should play in the design and implementation of management aiding information systems, if the resulting systems are to be any good in helping to improve both the manager's effectiveness, and the company's performance.

We shall do all this by example, because we do not have the time, and I do not have the competence, to define all the major processes and levels of management to treat a typical company exhaustively.

It will make our life easier if we assume that the company plans to grow, make a profit, plans to operate with good return on assets employed, and that it develops, engineers, makes, and sells several lines of products in competition with others.

There are a number of interacting processes which together represent a dynamic entity which we call the company. For example:-

 a) The Financial analysis and control process.

 b) The Market research--product definition--product introduction process.

c) The Sales monitoring--sales forecasting--provisioning
and manufacturing planning process.

d) The Purchasing--Provisioning--Manufacturing--
wholegoods distribution process.

Further, all of these processes need to be managed at Strategic,
Tactical, and Operational levels.

Each of these processes has to be supported by an information
system, or information flow which is the symbolic representation
of the process itself. The information system in turn needs to
provide the planning, control, and administrative data required by
management to plan, control, and administer the process.

Now we already have a clue to what the role of top management is
in the development and implementation of management information
systems. That role can be stated quite concisely. Top management
needs to recognize that:-

a) The company, over time, consists of on-going processes,
which interact, each of which has to be planned,
controlled, and administered.

b) The processes are represented and supported by
information needed to plan, control, and administer
the processes.

c) The processes, the information flows, and the planning,
control, and administrative activities, must be
recognized to operate over different time spans, and at
different levels within the company.

d) It is useful to think in terms of Strategic, Tactical, and Operational aspects of the processes--and information flows--to represent both the varying time spans and different levels of processes to be planned, controlled, and administered.

Having recognized the above stated aspects of management of the company, top management needs to further recognize that a formal mechanism needs to be established within the company which is charged with:-

a) Assisting management at all levels of the company with formal definition of the process that a particular management is accountable for planning, controlling, and administering.

b) Assisting with the definition of the information necessary to support, or accomplish the on-going planning, control, and administration of the process.

c) Formalizing the information into a disciplined data base and an organized information flow.

d) Assisting in the definition of the management techniques and reports which, if used intelligently, will result in the effective planning, control, and administration of the process concerned.

e) Assisting with the formulation of a management structure (organization) which will actively facilitate the organized flow of information, and the resulting formally designed planning, control, and administrative system essential to effective on-going management.

The "formally established mechanism" which has assigned to it
the responsibilities which we have just defined is the Management
Information Systems Department, or division--which, personally,
I prefer to refer as Management Systems Department. In order
to fulfil the role we have defined for it, it must be:-

a) Entirely service-oriented; i.e. its sole justification for
   existence is to serve the rest of the company by helping
   all other functions, via improved information systems,
   to plan, control, and administer the processes for
   which they are responsible more effectively on a
   continuous basis.

b) It must be independent of any particular function or
   department within the company, so that it may serve
   impartially all, and allocate its resources to projects,
   over the company as a whole, in accordance with the
   priorities set by the chief executive and the board of
   directors.

c) It must identify and bring about interfunctional
   information flows, and means for their systematic
   establishment and control, to assure co-ordination
   among all the functional processes which interact in
   achieving the goals of the company.

d) It should report to the chief executive and its director
   should be part of top management; he should function
   in a line capacity in a centralized company, and in a
   staff capacity in a decentralized company.

That, I hope puts into proper perspective the role of top management in the development and implementation of information systems, including that of the top management of the Management Information Systems function. To some extent, even though only partially, we have also incidentally described a portion of the functions of top management in a company, as they relate to bringing about effective planning, control, and administration by setting appropriate policies, and mechanisms for achieving these on a company wide basis.

In the general way in which we stated the role of top management in the development and implementation of M.I.S., relatively little has to be added when we look at the processes to be planned, controlled, and administered at other levels of the company, over different time spans. In each department, or function, the departmental head and the managers reporting to him must go through a similar disciplined thought process, with the assistance of the systems staff, namely:-

1) Define the process for which the function is responsible.

2) Define the information necessary to plan, control, and administer the process.

3) Design the information system which will provide techniques and reports necessary to plan, control, and administer the process.

4) Create, or revise, the structure of the function to facilitate the information flow, and to plan, control, and administer the process more effectively.

Let us take the process of acquiring raw materials, transforming them into finished product, and distributing the product, as an example. Let us examine it at Operational, Tactical, and Strategic levels, and then look at the implications.

At the Operational level we are looking at the following aspects of the process:-

1) Planning:

    a) Plan the receiving and progress chasing schedule for next day's schedule of material deliveries.

    b) Plan releases on suppliers to be processed next day.

    c) Plan machine shop schedule for next day.

    d) Plan assembly schedule for next day.

    e) Plan inspection, packing, and shipping schedule for next day.

    f) Plan minimum/maximum in-process inventories (short lead items).

2) Control:

Control all activities (processes) against documented plan prepared yesterday; report and take action on variances.

3) Administration:

Prepare and communicate all operational control documentation and capture for future analysis and extrapolation of historical performance. (Receiving Documentation Machining Orders and Instructions, Scrap Reports, Assembly Tallies, Packing Instructions, Shipping Documentation, Production Volume Data, etc.)

At the Tactical level we are looking at:-

1) Planning:

    a) Forecast of sales in code detail of product within lead time of matèrial acquisition.

    b) Translation into future build program.

    c) Determination of sourcing pattern.

    d) Planning of inventory levels of Raw Material, Work in process, and finished goods.

    e) Planning of purchasing quantities and orders on suppliers.

    f) Planning of utilization of existing facilities and available labour.

2) Control:

Monitoring of accuracy of all forecasts up to cut-off point determined by lead time of materials and components.

Continuous feedback in response to market changes and production achievement, modifying Tactical plan on a continuous basis.

3) Administration:

Maintenance and communication of all Tactical planning and feedback information. Acquisition, maintenance, and extrapolation of historical data.

At the Strategic level we are looking at:-

1) Planning:

   a) Determine future product line requirements and strategies.

   b) Estimate long range demand for existing and planned products by demand region.

   c) Determine production and warehousing facilities requirements.

   d) Plan management, administrative, and other resources required for planned growth.

   e) Determine capital requirements and financial conditions for successful growth.

2) Control:

   Control against predicted performance to adjust strategic plans on a continuous basis in response to:

   - Economic trend changes.
   - Inflationary changes.
   - Political situations.
   - Industry and competition.
   - Technological developments.
   - Current performance accomplishment.

3) Administration:

   Maintain continuously updated planning data base containing feedback from the tactical control system and monitoring of external environment.

It is evident that in the development and implementation of information systems in a company, when we view the problem as supporting planning, control, and administration of a major process, we have to define the Operational, Tactical, and Strategic requirements and considerations which permit optimal management of that process on a continuous basis.

Conversely, when we are looking at the Strategic, Tactical, and Operational management needs of the Corporation, we have to take into consideration and formalize the planning, control, and administrative systems necessary to manage the major processes.

We are now, I hope in a position to answer the questions into which we translated the title of the paper on the role of the manager in the development and design of Management Information Systems.

Firstly, at all management levels the manager must be accountable for formal definition and understanding of the process he manages, and he must be accountable for defining his requirements in respect of planning, controlling, and administering the process. Finally, he must be accountable for the results of a management system he agrees will meet his requirements, as designed with the assistance of management information specialists. He must also be accountable for controlling the development of such a system within agreed costs, and for tangible and intangible benefits he committed to his superiors.

At different levels of the company hierarchy the Strategic, Tactical, and Operational time horizons will vary. The Strategic horizon of a machine shop foreman may be a week, and his Operational horizon an hour. The Strategic horizon of the chief executive of a multi-billion dollar company may be 15-20 years, and his Operational horizon at most 6 months, more probably a year. It is the manager's responsibility to take into consideration in formulating his requirements in respect of planning, control, and administration of the process for which he is responsible the Strategic, Tactical, and Operational need of the process, using time spans and perspectives appropriate to his span of responsibility

It is obvious from the foregoing I hope that with this approach we are no longer talking about the Management Information System, which is a mythical beast like the Unicorn, but about an interlocking, co-ordinated set of management systems designed to optimize the planning, control, and administration of specific processes operationally, tactically, and strategically. Modularity is essential in our approach to management concepts as well as in our approach to system design.

Finally, one word on goals and objectives. In order to plan, control, and administer a given process, we have to do it with a set of accomplishments or objectives which the continuous operation of that process has to fulfil. Such goals and objectives, since a Corporation cannot function as a democracy, need to be set and directed from the top down. Management goal setting and control is an inherently top down process. However, if each executive in the company discharges his responsibilities in the development and implementation of management systems in the manner and within the concepts discussed in this paper, the chief executive and his management hierarchy can set goals using formal planning and control data anchored in a set of Management Information Systems directly used to plan, control, and administer each major process which has to function effectively on a continuous basis if the company is to flourish. In that manner, while the accountability and executive authority of top management is not diluted, Corporate goals and objectives become anchored in substantial reality rather than hope.

TRAINING FOR SYSTEMS WORK ON MIS

P.G. Raymont
The National Computing Centre Ltd.
England

INTRODUCTION.

In the United Kingdom it is common to use the terms <u>Systems Analyst</u> to describe a person who carries out any of the range of systems tasks from analysis through design to implementation; the term <u>systems analysis</u> has a similarly wide connotation: we shall use the terms with this wide meaning in this paper.

Suppose, then, that the systems analyst has a basic knowledge of systems analysis. We ask the question:

What additional knowledge does he need to acquire in order to carry out systems work on an MIS?

We define an MIS as:

> A system providing organized information
> to aid a manager in carrying out his
> planning and control functions.

This definition is deliberately vague in using the word 'organized'. Whilst feeling that the mere provision of some odd bits of information to managers does not qualify a system to be called an MIS, we are not willing to put any precise limits on the degree of organization required. In limiting MIS to helping in the <u>planning and control</u> functions of management we are making explicit something which seems often to be implicitly regarded as a natural limitation on the use of computer systems to aid managers. In point of fact other functions <u>can</u> be so aided e.g. staffing can be helped by the use of a computer based personnel information system.

We thus see that to work on MIS the systems analyst must know a good deal about management planning and control. It also transpires that the data processing techniques used in MIS sometimes acquire a rather novel aspect. Thus the systems analyst may need to review his data processing knowledge from a rather different point of view.

The knowledge required can also be classified as:-

Technical: concerned with techniques for
 accomplishing tasks,

Human: pertaining to human behaviour,

Organizational: concerned with matters

arising from the interaction of people in organizations.

We are thus led to the following matrix scheme for the classification of the extra knowledge required.

	Technical	Human	Organizational
Management Planning & Control	A	B	C
Data processing	D	E	F

In the next section we consider the content of each element of the metrix (identified by letter).

CLASSIFICATION OF REQUIREMENTS

A. Management planning and control techniques vary greatly according to the level of management and the type of organisation. For example consider the following four cases:-
  1. A company model for long range planning.
  2. A budgetary control and cost accounting system for middle level management planning and control in manufacturing industries.
  3. Project planning and control systems in the construction industry.
  4. Real-time display of aircrew scheduling information for an airline.

Important basic concepts are the distinction between operating and reporting (or directive) information -

(1) the distinction between programmed and non-programmed decisions and the relationship of decision making to information requirements.
(2) a good knowledge of the relevant techniques (e.g. budgetary planning and control methods)is also required, and consideration should be given to techniques for presenting information to managers, e.g. statistical and graphical techniques. There is no shortage of literature on the techniques of management planning and control - the problem is to make a good selection suitable for the purposes of the systems analyst.

B. The use of the above mentioned techniques may have a profound influence on the behaviour of people. For example, human problems in the use

of budgetary control have been well described(3),
and the author has himself discussed human
problems in project planning and control elsewhere (4). We are here dealing with socio-
technical problems (5) and a good basic
knowledge of the findings of industrial
sociologists, especially studies of motivation
and group behaviour, will be of untold value to
the analyst working with a group as sensitive
to human relations as manager.

C. There is a close connection between organisation
and information flows. It is thus important to
study organisation theory. The classic work is
March and Simon (6). The issue of centralisation or decentrlisation is worthy of study,
since many managers are afraid of the computer's
seeming influence for centralisation. A critical
review of the conepts involved (7) is perhaps a
good starting point.
Generally speaking, the more the systems
analyst can come to understand the problems
faced by managers, the more he is likely to be
able to contribute in the creation of a workable
MIS.

D. An MIS frequently rests upon a foundation of
integrated operational systems (e.g. payroll and
costing, sales ledger, stock control etc.). In
the creation of such systems, organizations are
increasingly making use of data bases with quite
complex file structures and associated data
management software. A good understanding of

the potential (and limitations!) of these
systems is desirable.

E. Human problems are always encountered in the
   introduction of computer systems. These
   problems are often particularly acute in the
   case of MIS, because the people involved are
   in many cases very much senior to the systems
   analysts working on the job.
   The usual problems of resistance to change
   will be met, and this subject will repay close
   study starting with the classic work of Coch
   and French (8). The analyst is also well
   advised to look at the work of psychologists
   on interpersonal behaviour (9), particularly
   as this relates to their own social skills
   such as interviewing.

F. Finally we come to the difficult set of
   problems related to the organisation required
   for the successful implementation of MIS.
   Top management support is usually listed as an
   essential prerequisite for success in any data
   processing project, though the precise nature
   of the support required is not usually stated.

   For MIS this problem is especially acute, since
   top management may be themselves closely
   involved. Some literature (10) contains
   useful discussions of this problem.

We have now reviewed the subject matter which we feel a system analyst about to embark on work on an MIS should study in addition to his basic knowledge. In the next section we describe some course material prepared by The National Computing Centre (NCC) in the U.K. relevant to these needs.

NCC COURSE MATERIAL

The rationale of the NCC Advanced Systems Training Programme has been described by the author elsewhere (11). Basically the scheme consists, at the moment, of five modules:-

Business Information Systems.
Operational Research.
Advanced Hardware and Software.
On-Line Systems.
Systems Evaluation.

These course modules are intended to be given as fully residential courses of duration two weeks in the case of Business Information Systems, one week each otherwise.

Of course, no one supposes that all the knowledge necessary to do excellent work on MIS can be collected in a few weeks, but the above courses contain at least a good introduction to all the topics we listed above. There is no one course devoted to MIS, but the following lecture titles, exercise and case study descriptions will give an indication of the parts of each course elevant to MIS work.

Business Information Systems

Principles of Management.
Organization Theory.

Decision Making.

Human Relations.

Accounting Information Systems: Financial.

Accounting Information Systems:
                    Management.

Statistics and the Presentation of
                    Information.

Approaches to Systems Work.

Interpersonal Behaviour.

Making Changes.

Management Information Systems.

General Systems Theory.

Management Game: Planning & Control.

Case Studies: MIS at Imperial Smelting Co.
          REME (British Army) MIS.

XYZ Co. Case Exercise: Design of
          integrated system with MIS
          component.

Operational Research

Model Building.

Simulation.

Advanced Hardware and Software

File Processing Techniques.

File Organization.

Date Management Systems.

Exercises: File design for information
          retrieval.
          File design for XYZ Co. System.

We have good reason, therefore, to assert that within the NCC Advanced Systems Training material there exists the nucleus of the knowledge needed by a systems anlayst to engage in work on MIS.

References

(1) A.M. McDonough and L.J. Garrett
> Management Systems Chap 3
>> Homewood, Ill. 1967.

   B Langefors
> Theoretical Analysis of Information Systems
>> Lund 1966

(2) H A Simon
> The New Science of Management Decision
>> New York 1960

(3) C Argyris
> Human Problems with Budgets
>> Harvard Business Review 1963, 31(1)

(4) P G Raymont
> Information Systems for Project Planning and Control
>> Procedings of symposium: MIS-A Challenge to Scientific Research
>>> Cologne 1970 (to be published)

(5) F E Emery and E L Trist
> Socio-technical Systems
> in Management Sciente, Models and Techniques
>> London 1960

(6) J G March and H A Simon
> Organisations
>> New York 1958

(7) Z S Zannetas
> On the Theory of Divisional Structures
>> Management Science 1965, 12(4)

(8) L Coch and J R P French Jr
         Overcoming Resistance to Change
         Human Relations 1948, I

(9) M Argyle
         The Psychology of Interpersonal Behaviour
         London 1969

(10) Philips
         Information Systems Handbook – ARDI
         Eindhoven 1968

(11) P G Raymont
         Some proposals for Systems Training
         IAG Journal 1969, 2(2)

THE REAL WORLD, THE REAL MANAGER
AND THE MIS PROJECT

Tore M. Danielsen
Kemikoncernens Data AB
Sweden

INTRODUCTION

Companies A and B decided after the usual set of preliminaries
to develop and implement computer based materials management
systems. The companies are of roughly the same size and operate
within the same industries.

Company A assigned a highly qualified executive as project manager. At his disposal were placed full-time personnel from the
EDP and production planning departments. A feasibility study was
carried out. It resulted in detailed specifications and plans,
based on objectives clearly stated by top management, who also
followed up the project via half-day sittings every month for
its entire duration. Great care was taken to change existing
policies in order to utilize fully the advantages of new methods
and equipment, whenever this was profitable.

Company B placed the manager of the planning department in
charge of the project. As he was pressed for time due to temporary difficulties in meeting deliveries, a qualified systems

analyst was made assistant project manager. It was the intention
to have personnel from the planning department work full time on
the project, but due to a just then heavy workload it was difficult for them to fullfill their engagement. The problem was solved
by assigning additional programmers to the project and of course
the line personnel was available to answer any question. It was
the intention of management to change policies and methods if
necessary, but for several reasons this proved difficult to
carry through. Top management had agreed to state overall objectives and to follow up the project carefully, but they were
busy with a merger and in addition the company experienced
problems with one of its major product lines that was threatened
by competition. Due to the many changes in the project framework, the network plans originally drawn up were impossible to
maintain.

Needless to say, company B ran into bad trouble when it finally
reached the implementation phase. Many important elements had
been left out of the system in spite of the fact that the
programs had become very comprehensive due to the many exep-
tions from rules. The system was not accepted well in the planning department, whose employees claimed that they had not expected it to function the way it did. The system broke down
after a couple of months and a costly restart had to be carried
out. Only after a few years did it work moderately well.

As for the implementation within company A, nothing can be said
about it because situations such as the one described only exist
in articles in professional and data processing journals. Most
of these articles solve the problem of implementation by saying,
that if we behave like company A, no major problems will occur
and that it is top management's job to see to it that we behave
that way.

This statement is true, easy to make and out of touch with the
real world towards wich this paper is oriented. It has the dubious merit of defining the problem away.

This paper concentrates on managerial behavior during design,
development and implementation of management information systems
and on how this behavior influences their success. It begins
with a brief review of the conditions under which a manager
operates. It continues with real, but disguised esamples of
observed behavior for improvement of management information
system installations. It also contains some remarks on the role
of the manager in the process of such installations, and concludes with some simple rules which have proved valuable in
actual practise.

2. M.I.S. AND THE OPERATING MANAGER

The middle manager is the center of this paper. The reason for
this is, that most M.I.S.-projects in the 1970´s will be concerned
with his work. The manager operates in an environment where many
different types of demands are placed upon him. He is expected to
concentrate on development of tomorrow´s production methods. He is
expected to take the broad view and have details at his command.
He is expected to give a high degree of service at a low cost to
those dependent on his work.

At the same time he is surrounded by severe limitations. He lives
in an environment which he can only partially influence. There
are company policies, there are customers and suppliers, there
are budgets and targets and there are other people within the
organisation.

He also has limitations within himself. He has a certain amount of practical experience which he has accumulated on his way to his present position. He has an education which he generally acquired before he started his career and this education is probably outdated. He has a certain social position to maintain, a tremendously important factor if his company is located in a small community.

The behavioral scientists have taught us that industrial man has a number of roles, that these roles often are in conflict with one another and that one given person generally performs better in some of these roles than in others. The classical example is the clash between the planner and the doer in us. If the demands and limitations mentioned are added to the role aspects, we find the manager as a center of conflict, and it is not strange that one of his omjectives is to keep these conflicts at a tolerable level.

One of the major conflict sources is the introduction of change. Whenever a change is imposed upon the manager or whenever he creates a change himself, his roles will be affected and his pattern of behavior must be adjusted. Changes also mean that his experience is no longer as relevant as it was and whenever a change is implemented he feels the inadequacy of his education. This means, that a manager will tend to oppose changes unless he is convinced that they will reduce the stress of conflict.

It may safely be said, that the introduction of major changes in the information systems within a corporation is perhaps the agent that influences an operating manager most of all. It is therefore not unnatural that the introduction of such changes constitutes one of the must difficult areas in the management of change and that

it is reasonable to expect a number of different and often
fairly violent reactions to occur among the managers in such
cases.

3. EXAMPLES OF MANAGERIAL BEHAVIOR

The following examples have been chosen to illustrate a number
of classes of reaction. The list may be considerably extended,
but some fairly common reactions are included.

The most frequent one observed is the "hurt feelings syndrome".

> The top management of a large corporation decided to
> install a corporate wide purchase control system to
> handle all routine work connected with purchasing and to
> enable the use of full corporate strength in negotia-
> tions with suppliers. One very able division purchasing
> manager regarded this decision as a personal injury to
> his ability. In the following detailed specification work
> he overemphasized the importance of programming into the
> computer the difficult decision problems that he had to
> face, accompanied by statements like "let´s see if you
> computer guys can handle this!" His data handling and
> materials management problems which by no means were small
> and which were exellently suited to the computer, were
> treated in a more superficial manner. This resulted in a
> system suffering from severe weaknesses in the input area
> whereas the decision algorithms became so complex that
> the buyers could not handle the system. Shortly after
> implementation the manager retired and his successor was
> able to make the system fully operational in a short time

by simply having the complicated decisions eliminated from the programs and by modifications of the data controls. Substantial savings were obtained.

The cases of hurt feelings are as a rule fairly simple to avoid. What is needed is an awareness of the situation in advance, together with simple communication to the manager of the real objectives. (Of course there will always be cases where feelings simply will have to be hurt).

The next example describes a much more difficult problem that might be called "the survival syndrome".

A manufacturing company decided to develop integrated systems for financial planning and control. The manager of the accounting department was very enthusiastic about the project. He participated in all meetings and always came up with suggestions for areas that ought to be looked into before the final specifications were frozen. After about one year most members of the task force were certain that he really did not want the system and that he was just trying to stall the project. A final meeting was called where all areas had been investigated and is was made clear in advance that the final decision was to be made by the accounting manager. On the day of the meeting he was absent due to illness.The manager in question had been with the company for ten years. He had a scant formal education, had learned to operate the existing system at his previous job where he had worked as an accountant for fifteen years and he had introduced that system into his present company. He strongly felt that his entire existence was seriously treatened by the new demands which in fact tore away his entire background.

Such cases can usually only be resolved by sidetracking the manager to another job where his knowledge is put to use.

Another group of observations reflects what might be called "the empire encroachment syndrome".

An assistant personnel manager in a company with several thousand employees violently opposed a proposal to computerize the personnel records. His arguments were that more people would probably be needed to operate the records, that it would be very unwieldy to get information from the records and that it was inhuman to change people into punched cards as he expressed it. This manager had developed his own set of manual records which in fact made him the only person in the corporation who could compile the data needed for the yearly negotiations with the unions. To him a computer system meant that his yearly walk in the halls of top management would be eliminated because of the fact that one of the proposed computer programs would produce just this information.

The empire building tendency can usually be handled by development of systems that strengthen the empire while at the same time making it accessible to other people. The following example shows this:

The manager of a production preparation department was considered to be difficult to cooperate with. He was thourough and careful but never could explain why delays occured in his department. The engineering and production departments often gave him the blame for things that were not his fault. In connection with the development of materials managements system he was given the task of designing

71

the necessary forms and procedures for a computer based
system of production preparation. This turned out to be
his strong side. He designed foolproof procedures, collected
all necessary data and built accurate files. When the systems later on were implemented they functioned very well.
This boosted his position with the corporation considerably, while at the same time providing his surroundings
with insight to his job.

Often encountered is the "exposure syndrome" which mirrors the
manager's reluctance to having his maneuverability reduced and
his anxiety that if other people see his systems they might be
able to spot errors in his conduct.

A feasibility study revealed that one company's system for
development, engineering and marketing of new products was
inadequate and that in fact no real decision points and no
clear responsibilities could be discerned. The managers of
market planning and engineering wanted a formalized system
to facilitate administration and improve effectiveness.
This met with violent opposition from the director of R
and D, who frankly declared that such a system would be
the end of all constructive development within the corporation. This man had a contemptous attitude towards sales
people and customers whom, he declared, did not know what
was best for themselves. He had been at liberty to develop
the products he thought were the right ones and he clearly
saw, that a market oriented information system would partly
divest him of this power, force him to document his plans,
and lay mistakes open to everybody. He won top management
for his points of view, yet the project was carried through
because the middle managers wanted it badly. They were the

people who were pushed back and forth in the absence of
clearcut dicisions and who were blamed for inefficiency.
The first product developed according to the new sets of
rules turned out to be a success. After this, top management endorsed the system fully which led to a markedly
increased effectiveness in the new product area.

Whenever the exposure syndrome is encountered, it pays to work
at the organizational levels above or below the person in question,
this is where you find those who pay the prize. An additional
example illustrates it:

A management information system usually entails a data
base of some sort. Managers react in different manners to
the creation of such a data base. Above all the data base
lays the manager open the surroundings so that in principle everybody can inspect what he is doing - it is a
means of exposure. One company introduced a central item-
file which contained most of the information on given
items. For years a struggle had gone on between sales
and production in that particular company, regarding the
transfer prices. In many cases the sales manager claimed
that he had never accepted the prices charged him by the
production manager. These conditions even existed for
standard items. Several people were employed full-time
on both sides of the fence to administrate and control
the transfer pricing process. After two of these agreed to
load the transfer prices into the item file, the quarrels
more or less disappeared and the staff could be reduced
by several persons. However, both the sales and production manager expressed theirs dissatisfaction with the
principle of centrally stored transfer prices, citing many

different reasons for this. In reality they experienced a reduced maneuverability.

Some managers use methods which show up in the "run-rabbit-run - syndrome".

A field sales manager had very high operational costs. After complaints from the sales director, he called in staff members and initiated a project on sales planning. He was very enthusiastic about this project and pushed it along until the date came near when the system was to be implemented. Then he suddenly called in a firm of consultants on the pretext that the conditions had changed in the sales area, and had them make a feasibility study. The consultants came out with a solution, that in reality was the same as the one proposed by the internal staff, but the sales manager hailed it as new and revolutionary. It was decided to let the consultants develop a new system. When work had progressed far enough, a new set of consultants were brought in and finally the job was turned back to the internal staff department. By this method the manager succeeded in kicking the ball out of reach for top management for a period of several years until he was removed.

This phenomenon is sharply curtailed if one conducts development in small steps. Such a mode of operations will make it much easier to plan and follow up programs for improvement.

One should not forget that even the systems management is a part of management. They are perceived by other managers as dangerous competitors for promotion and highly paid jobs. The most common reaction with systems management is the "Messiah´

complex" which means that they see mostly incompetence around them and that they must carry other people´s burdens in order that the company survive.

One company decided to develop order processing systems of a fairly complicated type. The need for such a system was clearly perceived throughout the company. However, the decision to make the new order processing system computer based was not popular with the employees, who feared that they would be out of work. As a consequence of this, they did not do their part of the development work as they should have done, thus delaying the project. The DP-manager was blamed for the extra costs and was told that the idea to computerize was a bad one, that everything would be more cumbersome than it had been before and that costs would soar. In reaction to this the DP-department increased their effort, pushed through development and put the system on stream at the date originally planned. At this time however, the data base was far from adequate, which finally led to a systems break-down and a very costly restart.

The DP-manager should have reviewed the situation with top management and asked their advice. If a management perceives conditions such as the one above, it probably has a Messiah complex on its hands and should take action.

The last example describes the "Long live the Bronx and to blazes with the US syndrome".

In one company production planning and product costing was carried out in the same department. As one phase of management information system development, a fairly advanced inventory control system was installed. The system proved very effective and cut inventories of finished products by 25%. In spite of this the planners did not think highly of the system, although they had participated in systems development. Complaints were frequent, usually concerning very small things such as lay-out of lists etc. The department suffered from hurt feelings, a fact that was not relieved by the excellent results produced by the system. Because of this attitude the data processing department regarded the planning department as a hopeless customer. Yet, when the DP-department on request developed a system for standard costing, utilizing product structure, operations and work center files, the planning department turned around completely. This was an area where they had all sorts of problems and they were being assailed by the controller's department for their lack of up-to-date costing of products. As soon as the costing system was in stream, the department was full of praise for the inventory control system as well.

This type of situation can only be met by helping people to solve what they regard as their problems. If top management had set an inventory budget for the department and demanded that it be met, no problems would have occurred.

What conclusions can be drawn from these examples? First of all, it can safely be stated, that the professional quality of the systems is only a part of the satisfaction perceived by the organisation as regards information systems. Secondly, by using information about the people in the organisation and by classifying possible reactions into different groups, not necessarily

the ones used here, it should be possible to predict at least
partially what is going to happen when a manager is subjected
to a change in systems. Finally, a number of practical rules
can be set up. A few are listed at the end of the paper. But
first a few words about the discrepancy between what people
say and what they do.

4. DO AS I SAY, DO NOT ACT LIKE I DO

The beginning of this paper describes an exellent way to keep
out of trouble when installing management information systems.
Just do as company A did and nothing will go wrong. Of course
it is impossible to object to such a claim. Everybody in this
room knows exactly how one should conduct an M.I.S.-project.
Reams of paper have been written on the subject and they all
suggest the same line of approach. Yet, nobody seems to know
a company where things are carried out in the manner described.
Why is it then, that what we say is so differentfrom what we do?

Of course, one aspect of our duties as professionals is to
point out the directions in which one should go to obtain better
results. Still, this fact alone can not account for the almost
total abscence in the literature of descriptions of what one can
do in a real company to make small improvements in the practices
that can be observed. Other possible explanations exist. For
instance, the people who write in professional journals want to
be on the frontier of development and when you consider that
most practical applications today are at least ten years behind
the theoretical possibilities, it is not strange that the real
world only occurs now and then in the literature. Furthermore,
most people are not too anxious to present their failures and
the history of implemantation is one of trying and trying again.
The literature of implementation is probably highly distorted.

The situation is reinforced by the fact, that the same kind of talk goes on within companies. There is a need for the individual to survive in the organisation. In order to do this he keeps up a certain facade, giving the impression, that he himself is in full control of the situation, but surrounded by incompetence in adjoining departments. If they only would do as he says, the company would soon show a much better profit. Really, he has no information system problems whatsoever, if only the other departments would feed him with the correct data shen they are supposed to do so. To prove what he says, he may cite the literature or repeat the sayings or consultants. Thus, there is a distortion of truth even at this level.

Another aspect is the need for room to maneuver in relation to the directives given by higher management. Managers at higher levels can not possibly have the full knowledge of the detailed operations and will therefore often give orders, that would be very costly if they carried out to the letter. An operating manager must therefore be able to pay lip-service to some of the ideas, that come down from above, while in reality he operates in a slightly different manner. There is nothing wrong with this - you can not operate effectively in an organisation where everybody is in head on conflict all the time due to different opinions over operating matters.

The search for the panacea - the final and total solution of a problem - plays a certain role. Consultants often enter a company giving the impression that they know exactly how to solve the problems and that they actually have solved such problems in many other organisations. This gives management hope for a solution on the grand scale, something which also tends to influence the official problem solving talk in the organisation.

However, the human factors mentioned do not account for the entire discrepancy. An additional professional factor of great importance exists. The people who really develop the management information systems are professionals. The operating managers seldom have the conceptual background nor the personality to be the people who break new land in this area. Until a few years ago, professionals as a rule concerned themselves with the elements of systems. Examples of this are the development of products, the conduct of market analysis, the development of better production methods. The emphasis of professional work tends to be one of technique - to develop better tools and better methods of analysis, and the systems analyst as a true professional concentrated on technique. Perhaps the real job of the systems analyst should be to investigate the process by which the elements of a system are kept together. This is in fact one of the important parts of the process of management. The manager can get by with fairly simple tools if he is good at combining them. The last ten years have yielded important improvements in the development of managements techniques but I feel that I seldom see systems analysts who make real contributions, however small, to the process of management itself which is infinitely more complex and vital. Of course, working with systems it is impossible to get away from the management process and therefore we often see real problems defined away, generally pushed into the arms of other types of scientists or the manager himself.

Even if the conditions mentioned above do not give any full explanation of the discrepancy of what we say and what we do, they at least should prevent us from being surprised over its existence.

5. SOME SUGGESTIONS

The last part of this paper contains some principles that have
proved useful during development and implementation of management information systems. The principles are based on the
reactions previously described and have been tested in actual
practice.

First of all, the most difficult part of the problem is not
information systems analysis or data processing, it is the
management of change. Therefore it is necessary to keep the
rate of change at a reasonable level. (Experience indicates
that one man year of development work per year and 50 employees affected, gives a high rate of change.) It is also
important to carry out the changes in a way the organisation
can accept. This means that one must accept the managerial
style of the organisation and not base the M.I.S.-project
on a managerial performance which can not be produced.
There is general agreement on the fact that managerial involvement is needed if the project is to experience any degree
of success. The difficulty is to obtain this involvement. One
way of securing it, is to use the despised priority rule,
stating that the manager who screams the loudest for assistance
should get the highest priority - provided of course, that the
applications considered have a reasonable profit potential.

Development should be carried out at the manager's own speed
and the systems ambition level should be set close to the managers own ambition level. It is often said, that by heavy use
of education, high quality systems may be introduced. This is
partially true, but a man can not be educated beyond his potential and it must be remembered, that a company on the average
consists of average people. Systems should be developed in

small steps and a new step should not be started until the previous one works. The larger a project becomes, the more difficult it is for the manager to see the end of it. What he does not see he generally does not believe and consequently probability of total failure will increase. This set of observations defines a very important role of the operating manager in the delopment of new information systems: The manager is the pace-setter.

If the development principles mentioned above are followed without any central coordination, a costly misuse of resources will be experienced. Therefore a qualified systems staff should be placed centrally in the corporation and should be given the task of drawing up a master plan for the management information system. This is not such an insurmountable task as one might think. If the systems staff carries on a continuous dialogue with other people in the organisation, they will get a fair amount of knowledge of the problems experienced. On the basis of this knowledge and on the basis of their own knowledge about systems, a framework may be constructed. Separate funds should be made available for creation of data bases and other central data processing aids. The remainder of the task is then to have all the small separate projects carried out within the central framework. It is a help if this central framework is made known to the managers although as a rule most of these are not particularly interested in the big picture - what they want to do is to make their own operations work. However, it is of material importance that top management understands this basic philosophy, something they can do without allocating enormous amounts of time to M.I.S.-development.

If people are told, honestly and in terms they can understand, what is to be obtained by the management information system project, many problems disappear. If they know that the objective is better profits and lower costs and if they are shown how these benefits are to be obtained, for instance, by not hiring new people or by cutting inventories, a surprisingly high level of acceptance can be established. Mealy-mouthed generalities such as that by implementingthe system in question they will have more time to concentrate on the important and interesting aspects of their job will scare them, because most people think, that the world is difficult enough as it is.

The operating manager can run the show in the area where he is strong. Staff resources can reinforce him in the areas where he is weak and of course function as professionals. Usually no more involvement is needed from line management. The line manager is usually strong in steady-state operations of a system and in implementation, often in problem spotting, but rarely in definitions of objectives or in analysis and synthesis of systems. He may or may not be good at evaluating whether his real problems are being solved by the systems developed, consequently great care must be taken to ascertain this. In the areas where the line manager is weak he usually wants to be told what to do by staff people. If nothing else he then has someone to share the blame with if things go wrong.

If the important laws of pace-setting are violated by pushing development faster than a manager can take it, several outcomes are possible. In some cases, when the manager is weak, he may have strong subordinates able to absorbe a higher rate of change, in which case he is pushed out. In most cases however, the manager is not that weak which means, that the system is pushed out. In every such case it will cost the company money and lots of morale.

These principles are not too difficult to follow. Professional systems analysts should not find it hard to control that the line manager is with the project all the time in those areas where he is not really running it himself.

There are plenty of practical tricks that can be utilized, for instance the well-known one of letting the manager himself explain the systems to his subordinates. The most difficult situation that can occur is when somebody in top management for one reason or another starts to think that progress is too slow and wants the systems staff to step up the pace of a development that is already running at maximum possible speed without wanting to change the management of the line. As of today there seems to be no general solutions to that problem.

6. CONCLUSIONS

The most important conclusions can be summarized as followa:

- The management of change is as important as systems analysis and data processing for the success of a management information system.

- Human reactions to a proposed change can usually be predicated better than they are in present projects where they are by and large observed in retrospect and used as a basis for bargaining and compromise.

- Work with the organisation instead of against it.

- Most managers are pace-setters of development and steady-state operators of systems and cannot be expected to act as analysts.

- Work with small projects within a large framework.

Whenever you feel like passing the buck upwards for objectives and definitions, or whenever you feel like defining the real problem away, or whenever you feel like delving into some esoteric protion of information systems techniques, ask yourself the following question: -"Will what I now intend to do, help real managers, operating in a real world to perform better within a reasonable period of time?" If the answer is not an unconditional "yes", then the time has come for reappraisal.

CORPORATE PLANNING FOR DATA PROCESSING
AND MANAGEMENT INFORMATION SYSTEMS

D.W. Moore
Peat, Marwick, Mitchell & Co.
England

REVIEW OF DEVELOPMENT OF COMMERCIAL D.P.

Commercial data processing using computers has now been
established for long enough to suppose that this method
will continue to be used for the foreseeable future, and
all the indications are that there will be expansion into
even more fields.

In absolute terms, the history is comparatively short, and
experience to date has shown that the success rate of users
varies significantly. A large proportion of companies have
expressed disappointment with the results achieved in terms
of original expectations, costs incurred, development effort
expended and the time required to bring projects to effective
fruition.

The reasons for this disillusionment can be summarised as
follows:-

i.   Inexperience and lack of knowledge on the part of
        both management responsible for acquiring the

computer, and technical staff responsible for
system development and implementation.

ii.   Poor communication and ineffective control
procedures between the technical staff and
line management.

iii.   The disposition of management to acquire a
computer to replace existing equipment and
failure to recognise the fundamental changes
in approach that are required if its
potential is to be exploited.

iv.   An understandable reluctance during their
computer initiation to recognise the
significant role that computers will play
in the following 5/10 years.   This leads to
the choice of hardware unsuitable for the
long term development plans of the company.

HISTORICAL METHODS OF IDENTIFYING PROJECTS

The decision to use computers in the past for any given
application, has usually been to identify areas of high
volume/ high staff, and to make the case for using the
computer on a very approximate cost-benefit analysis.
Alternatively, if the cost-benefit case was weak, the
system was sold on some new, or more speedy piece of
management information that could be produced.   In
addition, the systems were usually designed and agreed
by local and functional management, with very little
involvement by top management.

This type of "one-shot" approach to systems work caused
machines to be purchased, and systems to be developed
which had little regard to future development and

and concentrated on limited functional areas of the company controlled by the same management that had controlled the non-mechanised system.   This is illustrated by Fig. 1 :-

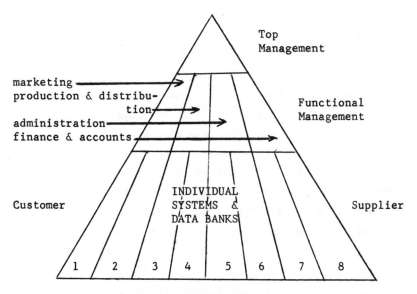

Fig. I - Historical Organisation for Control of Systems

THE NEED FOR A NEW APPROACH

Although the approach to systems development work described above has never been entirely satisfactory it did at least produce results of a kind, but for the future an entirely new approach is necessary. The reasons for this are given below.

i.   Business trends and computer potential
        The trend is for decisions to be made
        using up-to-date factual information

rather than "seat of the pants" hunches on
the information according to Mr. X. or
Mrs. Y.

Comparatively speaking the facts contained
in the individual data banks shown in
figure 1 are very limited compared with the
information that is derived from them and
stored.   Furthermore the data contained in
the individual banks is often common but the
"Information" it creates is often unrecognisable
as having been derived from the same base.

This has led to the recognition of the need
for centrally controlled banks of accurate
data which are available to all levels and
functions of management, for the data to be
kept up-to-date and for the information to be
derived as it is required.   It should also
be produced in the format appropriate to the
particular individual and the problem he is
trying to solve.

These data banks and the processing required
for the creation of information can only
readily and economically be maintained and
provided by computer systems.

ii.   Increasing level of investment
The continuing development of data processing
and management information systems are leading
to the need for larger, more complex and more
expensive computers.   The costs of the
associated software and system development
are becoming an increasing proportion of the

cost of the total computer operation.
Computer systems are already an expensive
investment and the trend is for them to
become even more so. It is essential that
they justify their cost.

iii. Compatibility

Companies that have had more than one
generation of computer have been faced with
hardware and programming compatibility
problems that have been very expensive to
solve. The same problems have arisen
on the change of manufacturers and to a
much lesser extent on replacements by a
larger machine in the same range.

Development of data banks and the increasing
number of application systems using the data,
will lead to a continuing need for upward
compatible equipment if this type of
recurring non-productive expense of time
and money is to be avoided.

To keep hardware investment to a practical
minimum the amount of unused capacity should
be limited to what will be required for
developments over the two years following
delivery. On the other hand, the capabilities
must be adequate for the systems being
developed. The design of the system that is
currently being developed for the long term
will decide the machine configurations.
Short period overloads or the need for

computers with particular capabilities for
limited periods can be met by the use of
contract facilities and this can help
contain development costs.

These hardware aspects indicate the need
for a manufacturer and hardware acquisition
plan which integrates with the systems
development plan.

iv.   Shortage of computer staff

Companies must take account of the overall
market shortage of trained computer staff
which is likely to continue for some time.
This makes it imperative to make the most
effective use of the available resources,
and to make provision for development
requirements and the replacement of losses
by a recruiting, training and development
programme.

v.   Management awareness

Enlightened management are now becoming aware
of the potential of the computer.   They are
beginning to criticise existing systems and
in some cases appreciate that the weaknesses
are due to their own failure to contribute
to the design.   They are now prepared to
become more involved on the grounds of self
interest rather than leave it to the
computer professionals who do not always
appreciate the management problems.

It is essential in both the company and

shareholders' interest to take advantage
of the situation and harness the
management contribution potential.

ESTABLISHMENT OF CORPORATE D.P. & M.I.S. OBJECTIVES

i.   ### General appraisal

The use of computers in the commercial field
has now reached the stage where it is desirable
to take stock of the current situation in each
company and to ask the following questions,

- where are we going?
- how are we going to get there?
- where are we now?
- what ought we to do about our
  current organisation and methods
  of operation if we are going to
  reach our objectives?

The first two questions cannot be answered in
isolation.   The computer is a tool designed
to serve a company in both its planning and
operating roles and these must therefore be
understood before any satisfactory development
plan can be formulated.

There is, therefore, a need to examine the
individual functions of the company, identify
the system and management information
requirements, and then to consider how the
computer might be used to obtain more
effective results than are now achieved.
This study will help to separate the data
processing operations from the provision of
information needed by different types

and levels of management within the functions.

The systems and management information requirements then need to be examined collectively and corporate systems and data banks designed.

These corporate systems will replace the isolated functional systems that now exist, and the objectives for the DP and MIS development plans will be established.

ii.   Current situation

Before embarking on a grandiose scheme to reach the objectives it is essential to review the current situation.

This will necessitate an appraisal of the existing organisation, its method of operation, the effectiveness of the existing systems and the capability of the staff to maintain current systems and develop and implement the concepts that will arise from the corporate planning mentioned above.

Particular attention to the staffing problem will be required.   Systems will be designed from quite a different aspect in the future. Systems analysts will need to align themselves with commercial operating problems and design systems that will provide information to all levels of management.   They will therefore need to become involved in the management problem areas.   They will need to have a clear understanding of the functions for which they

are designing systems and to associate
themselves with the staff that will
operate them.

The programmers will be faced with
designing data bases and machine systems
that will keep these bases up to date as
well as retaining historical data. The
application programs will need to be
designed to make use of the base without
necessarily disturbing it. Knowledge
of the manufacturers software and the
ability to design the necessary interfaces
will require a higher level of capability
than exists in many installations today.

General management and computer professionals
recognise the need for these appraisals but
the question arises as to who should undertake
them. Failure to answer this question and
the lack of disposition to expose the
organisation to a detailed scrutiny encourages
a laissez-faire attitude. As a result there
is no knowledge of how well the computer
organisation is operated or of its strengths
and weaknesses other than those expressed by
the man in charge.

Appraisals need to be undertaken by individuals
with a wide experience of computers, data
processing and of general management problems.
They need to be impartial but have sympathy
with the problems that have arisen in the past

and exist at present. Once started the
appraisal should continue as quickly as
possible until it is finished and it
should therefore be regarded as a full-
time commitment for the staff assigned.
This staff should, of course, be discreet
as the findings will be critical of people
and management, and these criticisms must
be treated with utmost discretion if goodwill
is to be maintained and corrective action taken
with the minimum amount of emotion.

The next problem is to find these people.
They may exist in the organisation, it may
be possible to make exchange arrangements with
other organisations with whom the user shares
a mutual trust and confidence, or experienced
outside consultants might be used.

Appraisals are an emotional problem and a
management responsibility. They are the only
effective way for management to know how
efficiently their data processing organisation
operates and its suitability for the developments
that will be undertaken in the next few years.

iii.   <u>Formulation of the development plan</u>

iii.1. <u>Functional level</u>

As already stated, the first requirement is to
identify the functional requirements. As the
recommendations from any study will in due course
affect the functional director's methods of
operation, responsibility for the study must rest

with him.

He will need to establish a study team whose
task will be to outline what methods of
operation should be in use in say five years'
time to identify the projects that will need
to be undertaken to achieve them.

Each project will need to be examined in
some depth for feasibility.   Any recommendations
should be supported by an outline of the proposed
revised system, the benefits it will provide, its
relationship with other projects and the resources
required to implement it.

It will then be for the responsible director
to formulate a priority list and to submit his
recommendations to the board for consideration.

iii.2.   Corporate level

A study team acting on behalf of corporate
management will be required to receive the
functional proposals, and from them design
corporate systems and identify the projects.
These projects will need to be compared with
the functional proposals and where these have
to be modified or adjusted the changes agreed
with the functional management.

The result of the corporate study will be a
model of the systems that management would
use if it were given an opportunity to
establish the business afresh.   The work
in designing the systems will have identified
redundancies in current operations and the

many inefficiencies that have accumulated through expediencies of the past.

Once agreed, this study team will create the corporate project list which will state the recommended priority for each project and the resources of staff, time, machine power and money required to implement and maintain it.

These priorities will need to be agreed by corporate management who will take into particular account the significance of the project to the company rather than the wishes of any particular functional director. It will include projects to improve systems in the short term, the need for which was recognised during the review.

Once the list is established with an assessment of the resources required to implement and maintain each project, corporate management will be in a position to formulate the plan, using the resources they consider that they can make available. The authorisation of expenditure is only one, and one of the less important factors, to be taken into account.

They need to consider the availability of trained staff, the time of management involved in systems design, development and implementation and the degree of disturbance that they are prepared to accept in the introduction of new systems.

They should be prepared to seriously consider the use of resources outside of their own

organisation.   If the benefits justify it,
they should be prepared to use computer
bureaux, software houses and consultants to
speed up the implementation of the total plan.
This method will help to limit the recruiting
and training problem and overcome the possible
worry of redundancy of staff when all systems
are operational.

Management must bear in mind the need to
ensure that the total organisation does not
become unbalanced during the development,
and that the business continues to earn
profits to meet its responsibilities to its
shareholders as well as meeting the cost of
the development.

IMPLEMENTATION OF THE DEVELOPMENT PLAN

i.   Control and responsibility

By the time the project list is complete the
appraisal of the current organisation should
have been completed and corrective action
started.   The corrective action will become
a project or a number of projects and these
should be included in the corporate list
and given the appropriate priority.   Although
frustrating to the management and staff who
are anxious to start something new, it will
probably be advisable to give priority to
establishing the existing organisation on
a sound footing.

Responsibility for each project should rest

with the main executive board. They will
authorise the project and its budget, and
they should expect to see a regular report
showing progress against the prescribed plan,
the reasons for the variance and the action
proposed to correct any adverse variances.
If the anticipated outcome of the variance
or its correction is significant they will
probably, and should, wish to become involved.

The content of individual systems projects and
their output, whether regular or on demand,
will be the responsibility of the functional
or 'customer' management. Some thought
should therefore be given to the project
leader coming from this source. If this
is not practicable then individuals vested
with the appropriate authority should be
nominated by the 'customer' and it will be
their responsibility to agree systems contents,
data flows and control systems and agree progress
reports with the technical staff.

ii.   <u>Organisational requirements</u>

The foregoing has demonstrated the need for,

-       a team either part time or full time
        for a limited period in the customer
        area to identify the long and short
        term system requirements. These
        projects will be sponsored by the
        customer management. When
        authorised, the same management will

be responsible either directly or indirectly,
for project management.

- a team at corporate level to formulate corporate
systems and to create a corporate projects list
from their own studies and the submissions from
functional management.   The result of their
work will be the corporate plan authorised by
corporate management,

- mixed teams made up from the customer organisation
and specialists from management services,

- a well defined control procedure for planning and
a firm discipline for controlling the implementation
of the authorised projects,

- some changes in the organisation of computer
departments.
There is likely to be a move to limit data
processing departments to managing the hardware
and programming and moving systems development
staff to a separate unit within the organisation.
This staff will include a wide range of
capabilities, and individuals will be formed
into teams for particular projects.   The
recruitment, training and allocation of staff
to projects will require to be managed by staff
with an understanding of the problems that the
staff are likely to face.   It will require to
have an understanding of the business and a
recognition of the need to maintain a degree
of flexibility to ensure that the continually
varying needs of the business are met and that
full use is made of the available resources.

CONCLUSION

Computers, data processing and management information
systems are no longer the novelty they were ten years ago.
They have now 'come of age' and are an integral part of
a business.

There is sufficient evidence to indicate that management
of successful companies will rely significantly on computer
based systems during the next decade.   As the hardware and
systems only exist to service and support a business and
have no justification whatever for an isolated or
independent existence the time has come for their development
to be incorporated into the plans of the business that
justifies their being.   This is the message for the staff
responsible for systems development and maintenance.

Functional management should by now have recognised that the
success of systems which they have authorised tends to be
directly related to their own involvement and the contribution
that is made by the "customer" staff.   Furthermore they will
have become aware that the fundamentals of the control
procedures used in the longer established professions and
industries can apply equally well to computer projects and
systems.   They have also become aware of the potential of
the machine and recognise that if used properly it is not
equipment for individual systems of functional management but
a potential reservoir for company data.   It has the capability
of displaying and manipulating this data in a way that is of
value to all levels of management.   This in turn has shown
that the selection of individual systems for particular
'customers' within the business is no longer viable or
acceptable.

With this awareness there is now the need for study, planning
and control to ensure that the very large investment of

resources that has been made should now justify itself.

This is not something that can be done quickly it it is
to be done well and as success in five to ten years' time
will be dependent on the initial work, it is worth doing
well.

Neither can it be done in isolation by computer specialists.
Computers have become part of the structure of corporate
systems and the trend will increase rapidly, particularly
in successful companies operating in competitive markets.

The planning for data processing and management information
systems is part of the corporate planning of the organisation
and it therefore needs to be undertaken in the formalised
manner necessary in any form of corporate planning.

There will be many computer professionals who will regret
and resist the passing of the halcyon days of informality,
perpetual panic and instant decision making, and will be
irritated by the involvement of customer management. They
must now recognise that the period of adolescence is over
and accept the responsibilities and disciplines of an
established profession and identify themselves with the
aims and objectives of their customers if the profession is
to fulfil its potential.

IMPLEMENTATION OF A MANAGEMENT INFORMATION
SYSTEM; ORGANIZATIONAL APPROACH

J.M.S. Bedet/A.J. Dieleman
N.V. Philips' Gloeilampenfabrieken
Holland

SUMMARY

This paper is to give the view of an organization expert,
who worked as a chief systems designer himself, on the
process taking place during implementation of a M. I. S.

1. The first part deals with what is going on in the various
   stages (system requirements, -design and -implementation)
   and pays attention to subjects as: relation between system
   and organisation, analysis of formal ánd informal
   procedures, change of skills and attitudes, occurring
   role conflicts and the like.

2. The second part is based on this experience and deals
   with the forms of cooperation during system build-up.
   The author pleads a formalized group structure:
   (steering group, design- and implementation groups)
   which yielded favourable results in practice.

INTRODUCTION

"Management Information Systems" have existed ever since
there have been organizations. The management has always
felt a need of systematic information; and also the existing
systems can always be improved. Just in the computer era
the attention for this matter has increased. But – at least
in our experience – the aims in view are often not attained.

Management Information Systems in our days are accompanied
by many technical problems, which are too frequently
underestimated by inexpert people. But still it is our opinion,
and maybe yours, that many failures are to be imputed to
organisational problems.

That is why we have deliberately traced, in Chapter 1,
what will happen within in organisation in case a   M. I. S.
is implemented. Management scientists will observe that in
this study organization, too, has been considered as a
system, and the implementation of a M. I. S. primarily as a
process of "planned change", inspired to a considerable
extent by recent American literature.

On the basis of this knowledge we have approached, in
European circumstances, the organisational problems of
a large project (over 200 men–year) more deliberately.
By trial and error we have come to an approach with
formalized groups:

> – steering group
> – design group(s)
> – implementation group(s)

the experiences with which have been favourable. (Chapter 2).

Chapter 1

IMPLEMENTATION OF M. I. S. – A PROCESS OF CHANGE

Implementation of a M. I. S. is a process of change, mostly planned change. Defining phases in a process like this is of course an arbitrary choice. Our presentation has been based on scheme A (see next page) with a distinction in three main phases:

- Preparation
- Design
- Implementation.

More important than the distinction, however, is the connection of the various phases in this process of change. In this study we intend to focus primarily on the problems of "implementation". It will be clear that this is often the moment when the symptoms of a faulty approach appear, but that evil may root in the previous phases, e. g.

- incomplete requirement specification;
(or not approved by all concerned .. ')
- insufficient analysis of the réal problems;
- lack of insight, or motivation;
etc. etc.

That is why we have paid broad attention to the previous phases too.

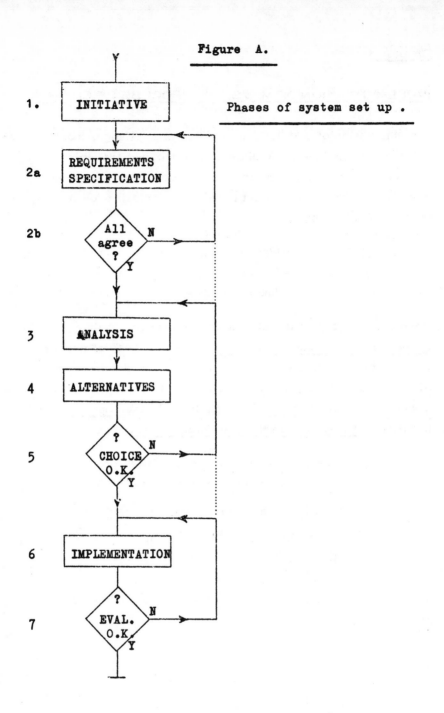

Figure A.

Phases of system set up .

Another aspect of this process is its _iterative_ character.

As we have seen in figure A, the three main phases are three "loops" which are performed more than one time. In problematic cases one even" jumps back" to a previous "loop".

It is clear that satisfactory standards may be attainable, but aiming for high quality (or "optimal criteria") may prolong the duration of the project and inflate its cost enormously. Implementing a M. I. S. therefore is a process which is difficult to control (which already many managers have found out . . . . . !) and hence makes high demands on the organisational approach.

_ _ _ _ _
_ _ _
_

We shall now discuss the various phases successively:

1. Initiative for system change;
2. Specification of requirements;
3. Analysis of existing situation;
4. Working out of alternatives;
5. Selection from alternatives;
6. Implementation;
7. Evaluation.

_ _ _ _ _
_ _ _
_

1.1 INITIATIVE FOR SYSTEM CHANGE

Initiative for a change of an existing system may arise
from various sources: subordinate workers themselves,
management or external body (e. g. organizational advisor).

Junior staff or subordinates may take initiatives themselves,
and certainly in case they are hampered in their work by a
badly operating system and know that it could be improved.
Their approach, however, will frequently result in problem
solving, ever correcting the existing approach, without
attaining drastic innovations.

The management, perhaps confronted with sub-normal behaviour
of the organisation (in their opinion) will most probably start
a research into the causes and might think to find a solution
in introduction or improvement of their M. I. S.

The advisor, who generally speaking has a wider experience,
will most often be the initiator; he can compare the present
situation with others he knows and he may have the opinion
that improvement is very well possible. It has to be hoped
that he is so experienced that he recognizes also problems
and solutions which have nothing to do with M. I. S. or
computers !

Any initiative for change means criticism

upon the existing system (and people) !

Any initiator should realize this beforehand, and can steer
clear of this rock by participation of all concerned,from the
very outset.

1.2 SPECIFICATION OF REQUIREMENTS

The programme of requirements for the new situation will
then be laid down. It is clear that it is a good thing not to
immediately rush into the requirements of the new information
system, but to make a step backwards and reflect upon the
basic objective of the organisation it self. Anyhow, the
programme of requirements will have to contain an operational
goal (although it may be derived from non-operational main
objectives). Vague goals, e.g. "increasing the flexibility",
"better customer service" etc., are out of place in these
specifications.

When designing an information system it will appear that
there is a difference between maximum and optimum information.
In the case of "maximum" one starts so to say from the
technical possibilities (quantity, quality or speed); whereas
in the case of "optimum" the aim is the total performance of
the organization.

As an example: the speed of the information system.

An activity in the organisation may suffer from the fact
that its information system (batch processing) is always
lagging behind. A technical solution (on line, real time) is
possible and will reduce the time lag to 0; it is quite costly,
however. Another approach could be: speeding up the
present (Batch) system, by increasing machine and personnel
capacity. When one systematically confronts the advantages
to the organization it self with the costs of the information
systems ... the optimum turns out.

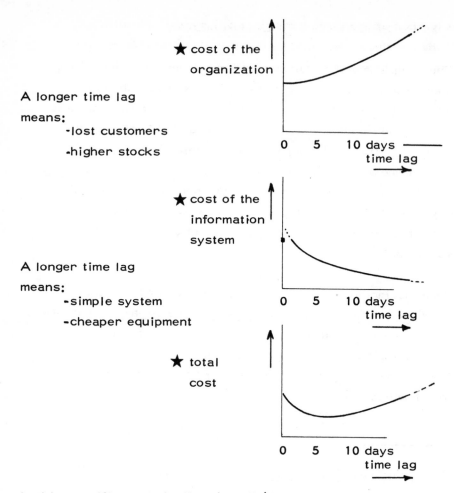

A longer time lag means:
- -lost customers
- -higher stocks

★ cost of the organization

0   5   10 days
time lag

A longer time lag means:
- -simple system
- -cheaper equipment

★ cost of the information system

0   5   10 days
time lag

★ total cost

0   5   10 days
time lag

In this specific case the "maximum" (the best real-time system a computer fiddler could invent) is definitely not the "optimum".

This – somewhat academic – argument can very easily be used in practice as a train of thought, also if quantification would not well be possible.

·A number of boundary conditions will have to be fulfilled,
if the organization would be benefitted by the information
system to be designed:

1. 2. 1 The system must fit in the already existing
        organization, e. g. ,
        – it must start from a reasonable degree of
          formalization as usual on the spot
        – it must fit in the climate of the business.

1. 2. 2 The <u>relation between the systems</u> (newly to be
        designed) and other subsystems should be outlined.
Time schedules may be geared into one another or there
may be interdependence regarding to information used by
more units of an integrated system.

        E. g. "Will store receipts from outside suppliers
              "be registered after technical approval
              "– or – after receipt of a booking document,
              "invoice, etc. ?

              Planning department and accounts department
              will most probably not agree !

1. 2. 3 No <u>fossilization</u> should occur in the new system.
        Since there is every chance of somebody (who is
concerned with the set up of a new system) identifying
himself considerably with it, there is also a risk that
later on no criticisms on the system ("HIS system") will
come home to him. With more extensive projects it may
therefore be a good thing to include the possibility of
<u>job rotation</u> in the programme of requirements.

1. 2. 4 <u>Information system and management</u> should fit

The new system will have to fit in with the nature
of the executives, the type of leadership and the positions
of authority and it has to be adapted to the specific
dexterities of the management.

> (E. g. an impulsive management, who thinks
> improvisation the most important, will
> not be benefit ted by the "integral planning"
> which the advisor dreamt of . . . . .)

1. 2. 5 <u>Information system and staff</u> should fit

In other words, the system must fit in what can be
reasonably expected of the staff members, who have to
deal with the system. We then think of:

- knowledge and skills
- extent of systematics and improvisation
- ambition level.

We will not only base ourselves on the present behaviour,
but also aim at that what can reasonably be expected of
these people after influencing (education, training, change
of attitudes).

In addition it would be realistic to find out which staff
changes will be necessary, in case other means might fail.

- - - - -
- - -
-

1.3 ANALYSIS OF THE EXISTING SITUATION

The analysis starts with the study of the main objective to
be attained and the sub-objectives derived from it.
In this stage one must go to rather a high level of
abstraction in order to avoid that one cannot see the wood
from the trees. The principal and participants, too, must
have this general view and that is why the advisors contacts
with the higher management are just here.

Example:

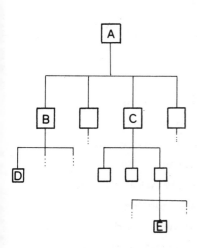

When the main goal of an
organization has been split up into
sub-goals, and the structure of
the organization has been adapted
to this split-up, the integration of
the sub-goals will also take place
at the level where the sub-systems
meet.

- with A the integration occurs;

- B and C will still be able to
  reasonably estimate their
  respective contribution to the
  whole process;

- for D and E the distinction
  between "main- and side-issues"
  (main goal and sub-goals) proves
  already very difficult.

113

The more so to the advisor, if he would have too little
opportunity also to exchange views with A (= management).
He will have to direct his attention to the main objective,
and not to sub-goals or sub-systems (which may even be
dysfunctional). Does not everybody know these problems
by his own experience:

- introducing "planning systems"
  while process control is missing;

- developing "control mechanisms"
  while basic data are completely
  unreliable, ...

- etc. etc.

Sofar for the goals and sub-goals.

- - - - -
- - -
-

1.3.1 After the research of the objectives, partly at
the policy-making level, it is the turn of the
examination of the present system. To get to know how it
is functioning, contacts now should be made with the
executive level. To be able to value the information obtained,
one should give oneself some time. Only a vague idea is got
about the rules, but many stories about incidents and
exceptions. Time-perspective also plays an important role:
a recent incident is likely to be exaggerated and to be
brought forward as a symptomatic case.

This risk of a distorted picture can be prevented in two ways:

- analysis from historical data;
  ("how often did it really happen ?")
  which is a laborious job, and often even
  impossible;

- repeated interviews after a few weeks;
  (many accidental incidents prove to have
  been of little or no importance).

The information on all sorts of incidents, problems and exceptions is still very valuable. It cannot be dispensed with in a later stage, for testing the system concepts.

Note: That in this phase, when a department is interviewed, extensive information is got on the functioning, or not-, of other departments, and the opposite, is quite clear. It is tempting to use this information as a cross-check, but it is a dangerous game !

1.3.2 A system research is incomplete without an analysis of the informal behaviour of the participants

We cannot too strongly emphasize this matter.
Each formal system needs an informal component, which is a literal condition of life. However, the inventory of it asks a good social skill and (preferably also) experience in analogous situations. Mutual trust will prove essential; it can be built up gradually during other joint activities.

<u>As a example:</u>

> At the present many computers projects
> are started with one main objective:
> acceleration of information.

In quite a number of these cases the truth is, that the
<u>formal</u> information has been accelerated for weeks.
But the truth often also is, that the most relevant information,
through <u>informal</u> channels, is often faster than the computer
.... as fast as it always had been !

In informal procedures there are often activities which
are not permissible in the formal system, but are deemed
necessary by those concerned. These are matters which
will visualize only after some time and should be handled
with care in reports and the like.

Anyhow: without paying attention to informal behaviour the
analysis is not complete.

$$- \ - \ - \ - \ -$$
$$- \ - \ -$$
$$-$$

1.4 WORKING OUT OF ALTERNATIVES

When man encounters certain problems in his executive
work, he will sooner be inclined to gradual adaptation than
structural innovation. The latter is more likely to be
expected of an outsider (advisor). This becomes manifest
immediately in the selection of alternatives. Each worker
is used to his work, attached to the system with which he

feels familiar. From his activity he sees the main goal.
The advisor, however, departs from the main goal and
so he looks at those activities; therefore diametrically.
If their advice (and their relation !) should not be
diametrical, a participative approach is a psychological
condition.

1.4.1 The way somebody is attached to his system may
be twofold:

1. He is attached to it for rational reasons (he is of the
opinion that this way he serves the organisation best)
In this case rational arguments may plead for
alternative systems.

2. If, however, he is attached to it on emotional grounds
(e. g. a system he feels safe with, or a system he has
designed himself with much trouble) rational discourses
will not work. Only an appeal to other emotions (his
daring to experiment, his career ambitions) can make
an alternative system still acceptable.

This distinction – and investigation of motives – is
certainly worth while.

1.4.2 <u>Model building</u> is an aspect of the research for
alternatives. In broad outline one may arrive at
the conception of an alternative approach. Not all details
of reality can be incorporated if the model would have to
remain easy to handle. Nor would it be possible to omit
too many relevant practical data, if the model would still
have to serve as a basis for conclusions with regard to
reality. This choice will remain a somewhat arbitrary one.
When the theorist is already of the opinion that too many
variables are included – due to which the model is difficult
to handle – the practical man will still hardly recognize
his reality in the same model.

Who does not know the practical cases in which the advisor
aims at "decision models", which the doubtful user rejects,
asking for "not more than a handy list" he can work with ......

Much can be reached by honestly trying to get an insight
into one anothers train of thought. It would be better still
to build it up – <u>together.</u>

– – – – –
– – –
–

1.5 SELECTION FROM ALTERNATIVES

Finally a choice should be made.

Any iterative process , if it should not last eternally , will have to be interrupted in case the result approximates the optimum reasonably. This also applies to the process in question (searching and evaluating alternatives) : searching longer and longer always yields better results . But it is a wise manager who finds the right moment to call it to a halt.

<u>Harmonization of the interests</u> of those concerned belongs to this selection process. The above emphasises once more that not everybody can be satisfied. The ways in which the interests are weighed may differ :

1. If everybody would only be concerned in the main goal to be reached , and would have the same information , and the same scale of values ...., well , then the solution would be easy to find .

2. The realistic situation , however , is that some interests are opposite each other . In other words : <u>a selection is preceded by negotiations.</u>

It would be useful not to obscure the fact that the choice is a situation of negotiations, but to make the respective aims explicit where possible.

Kindness should not supersede clearness !

It may be useful to open negotiations already in an early stage (during the evaluation of the alternatives), so that constructive and action-oriented work can be done.

It would be pleasant for all those concerned to know about what the different participants can make decisions, or not. But situations, in which people must act in the name of "their back-benchers" (under social control of their departments, etc.) should definitely be prevented.

- - - - -
- - -
-

In conclusion:

A choice is a definitive moment. If a choice is made in the end, it should be made quite explicitly, all advantages ánd disadvantages explained, so that there will be no misunderstandings or frustrations later on.

The time of choice is a moment for renewed enthousiasm (possibly roused by management): the last phase commences during which everything has to be realized.

- - - - -
- - -
-

1.6 IMPLEMENTATION

The implementation is the final stage. Here too, it is
a question of iteration (introduction and evaluation),
indicated in figure A, as the third "loop". If the previous
phases of preparation and design have been carried out
correctly, there will not be any more essential problems in
this stage. So we shall be brief in discussing it.

$$- - - - -$$
$$- - -$$
$$-$$

That we often meet with "difficulties on the implementation"
does not mean that the implementation itself is so difficult.
It does prove, as we stated in the preceding, that only in
this stage the consequences of a wrong approach in the
earlier stages become manifest. In case of really major
problems the solution will not be found in a "skiful and
ready introduction" either .... ! We should make a step back
to one of the previous "loop" of figure A (i.e. a renewed
preparation or design).

If, however, the preliminary stage has been set up properly
the implementation will be (logically ánd emotionally) a
natural continuation of the preparatory work.

During implementation changes occur with regard to
organization-structure, management and staff. They – in
their turn – presuppose changes in:

- rational behaviour (fresh knowledge, new skill)
- emotional   "   (expectations and attitudes).

1.6.1 <u>New skill</u> is required <u>of the management,</u> so that
    they are able to control the organization less
direct, but by manipulation of the system. This will only
be attained by exercise; the first few results yielded by
the new system being often inferior to the previously
reached results in the old system. Much of the exercise
can already be obtained in the design stage, during the
"trial exercises".

<u>New skill</u> also is required <u>of those who are going to work</u>
<u>with the system</u> (and perhaps discarding "former skills"!).
Working in more formalized system, handling decision rules,
working in a more integrated relation to others; all this has
to be learnt. Perhaps training courses may be a contribution
in this respect, but in our experience they are often too
abstract for the end in view. Intensive training in the work
itself, proper coaching can impart the relevant knowledge
much quicker.

1.6.2 <u>New attitudes</u> are expected <u>from management and</u>
    <u>staff.</u> The expectation is that the management will
take a less tactical, and more strategic, position, due to
which they may get the feeling that their "grip" on the day-
to-day routine is decreasing. The staff members are
expected to adapt themselves to more formal systematics which
leave no room anymore for each exception. Etc., etc.,
Moreover, there will be a temporary doubt whether or not
the system functions really as expected, especially if there
are still "growing pains".

In this stage the advisor should manifest a "firm belief";
At the same time it will be useful if – in the design stage –

all the pople concerned would be prepared to meet these temporary difficulties.

1.6.3 In most recent literature on organizations, the distinction between "control" and "break-through" can be found. (Juran). While control has to do with the "normal continuation of the business", breakthrough implies changes in policies, adaptation of new methods, and the like.

In our opinion, in this literature, the role-conflict (control versus breakthrough) for the members of the organization is not emphasized enough. Control and breakthrough are not always two types of approach that are separated by time or differ per activity. Sometimes, especially in periods of system changes they do interfere.

Example: the planning department, introducing a new planning and information system (= breakthrough) will simultaneously also have to take care that "the show goes on" (= control).

If one depends on limited means (time !) the real choice will have to be made between control and breakthrough. People's personal attitudes and the interpretation of their tasks will then determine whát will have priority.

This may even be the case when sufficient time is available. Man is inclined to think "perspectively in time": any important long-term issue is mostly superseded by short-term matter (maybe less important) that thrusts on people.

Employees, primarily being _selected_ to their fitness to work in a _control_ situation (so with their strongest capabilities for this kind of work) will need quite some extra backing in order to _spend their time on innovation._

Sometimes it will be necessary to overcome this role-conflict (control-breakthrough) by assigning just one role to some people. Discharging them fully from control (their day-to-day work) and assigning a piece of innovation to them, might be the only way. In this case they will become full-time members of e. g. a design or implementation group and concentrate on this single role.

— — — — —
— — —
—

1. 7 EVALUATION

On evaluation – the end of figure A – we can be brief. During and after the introduction of the new system, the results of the new way of working will be regularly checked against the requirement programme. In the course of time this confrontation will be carried out less intensively and less frequently; certainly if the end in view has been reasonably approximated. This evaluation is a management decision, as it is the final milestone of the whole.

With the described evaluation we have clearly meant the process of _confrontation with a fixed requirements programme._ This will succeed so much the better, when the requirements have been put black on white (see 1. 2).

Another evaluation process is : the comparison of the system with demands that vary with time; as this is a continous process. The demands set will depend on external circumstances , and vary with them. A system that has been satisfactory for years on end will no longer satisfy the gradually changed requirements. This again creates an initiative for a system change (see 1. 1).

It is necessary to draw a distinction between these two different evaluations. Evaluating a systems performance versus variable requirements is no good measure to define whether " the goal has been reached " . Especially in the case of implementing M. I. S. – which takes years and years – requirements will change during all this time.
Evaluation with the wrong yardstick gives the impression – at least to the layman – that this kind of work never gets finished. . . . . . !

- - - - -
- - -
-

In describing the seven phases of "implementation of a M. I. S. " we have mentioned some phenomena which presented themselves as important to us. Though we have mentioned in the text above some remedies already, we will now turn to the subject of the organizational approach of this process.

- - - - -
- - -
-

Chapter 2

FORMS OF ORGANIZATION IN THE PROCESS OF CHANGE

In this chapter we do not intend to pay attention to changes
in the main organisation, and the differences before ánd
after implementation of a M. I. S. We would like to focus on
those forms of organization, whose main purpose is to
contribute to the implementation (and the changes in other
parts, needed therefore) in the main organization.

For drastic system changes of long duration there are in
practice separate organizations, for which the system change
is the only objective. They are established at the start
(e. g. of the introduction of a M. I. S.) and they are abolished
when the project is over.
Below we shall indicate:

2. 1 which cooperative relations occur in the several
    stages of the process (e. g. analysis, design,
    etc.)
    (i. e. the 7 phases we mentioned in chapter 1)

2. 2 which formalized form of cooperation-in-groups
    has proved applicable in practice. (steering
    group, design group(s), implementation groups).

First we will demonstrate the cooperative relations in the
various phases – using a simple organization chart as a
stylized model (see fig. 2. 1. 0 – next page).

Figure 2. 1. 0

COMPONENTS OF THE SEVERAL ORGANIZATIONS

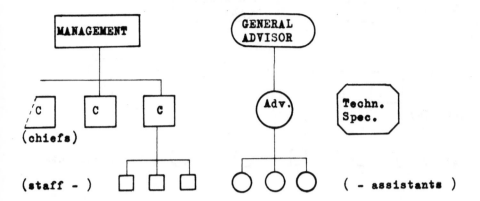

Before cooperation commences:

In this stylized model we distinguish:

1. A simplified line-organization:
   - the department of a chief with his staff, where a
     M. I. S. will be introduced in due course;
   - the management to which they all report.

2. An independent advisory body:
   - the advisor (with his system analysts and programmers),
     who will act as project leader;
   - general advisor, whom the former is subordinate to
     (e. g. partner of advisory bureau)

3. Expert help:
   - a "super-specialist" who can only deal with a
     technical speciality (e. g. software specialist or so)

Figure 2. 1. 1.

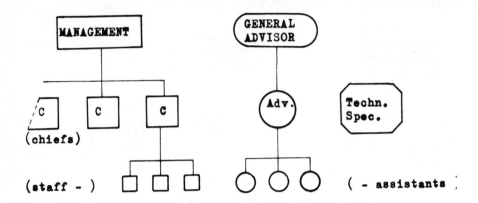

INITIATIVE

In this stage there is not yet any cooperative relation
with regard to innovation.

Figure 2. 1. 2

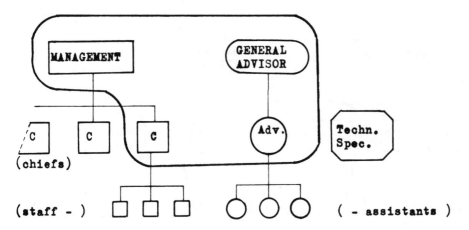

SPECIFICATION OF REQUIREMENTS

A phase in which the management plays a decisive role,
but the general advisor, too, commits himself to
a certain approach.

Goals are set, for which a realistic insight in the
existing organization and people, ánd the general
possibilities of a M. I. S. are both necessary.

Chief and advisor have to take care that it all comes
true in due course and therefore they are indispensable.

Figure 2.1.3

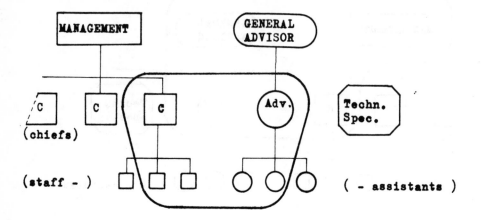

ANALYSIS OF THE EXISTING SITUATION

The inventory is conducted by the advisor, who knows
the methods of analysis, and by the chief who is familiar
with the main outline of the work.

The execution is put in the hands of the advisors
assistants (system analysts), who will have to do their
task in close cooperation with some of the staffmembers
of the department.

Figure 2. 1. 4

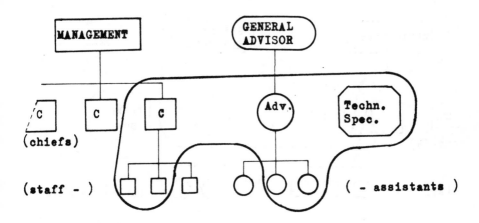

WORKING OUT OF ALTERNATIVES

Together with the advisor, who holds a central position,
the various (sometimes rather theoretical) alternatives
are worked out in detail. It is the advisor who maintains
the relations with the "technical expert", interpreting
between specialism and organizational needs.
The chief plays a critical and pragmatic role, while his
staff-members and the advisors assistents give help in
working out all these alternatives. (For a part they are
the same people as in the previous stage and partly
others, depending on their capacities).

Figure 2.1.5

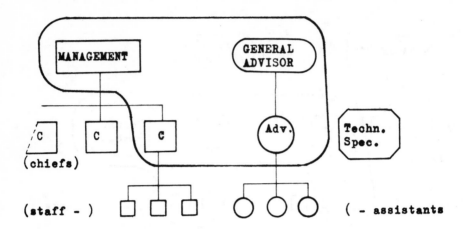

SELECTION FROM ALTERNATIVES

An important step, under the responsibility of management, who in this stage must also depend on the chief.

On the other hand this choosing process is so determining for the further proceedings that both the general advisor and the advisor himself will have to agree.

Figure 2. 1. 6

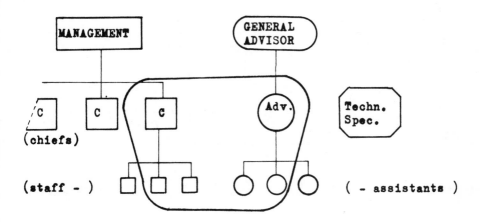

IMPLEMENTATION

The implementation takes place within the sphere of
responsibility of the chief, but with advisors support.
Staff will be indoctrinated and trained; they will get
backing from the advisor and his assistants.

Figure 2. 1. 7

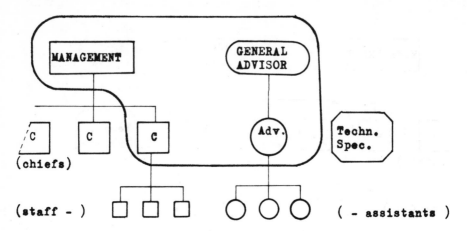

EVALUATION

The management, informed by chief and others will
check whether or not the new M. I. S. operates in
accordance with the original requirements.

From his professional experience the general advisor
will be able to help in the formation of a judgment;
the opinion (on the local situation) of the advisor himself
being indispensable.

Figure B.

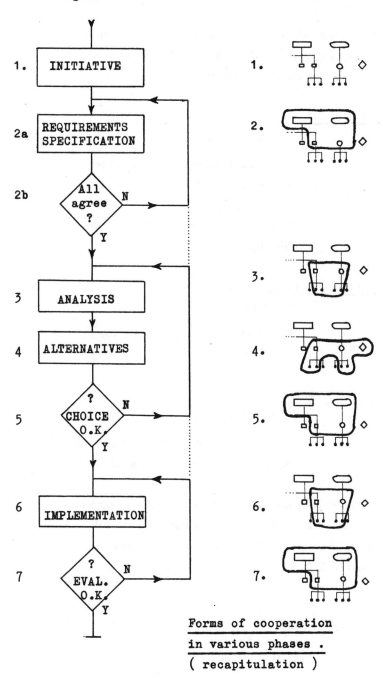

1. INITIATIVE

2a REQUIREMENTS
    SPECIFICATION

2b All
    agree
    ?   N

    Y

3   ANALYSIS

4   ALTERNATIVES

    ?   N
5   CHOICE
    O.K.

    Y

6   IMPLEMENTATION

    ?   N
7   EVAL.
    O.K.

    Y

1.

2.

3.

4.

5.

6.

7.

Forms of cooperation
in various phases .
(recapitulation)

2. 2 FORMALIZED ORGANIZATIONS FOR THE CHANGE

In the previous consideration of the relations in which cooperation takes place for the implementation of a M. I. S. three main forms are conspicuous (figure B):

- managerial decision

> in the phases:
>
> > **2.** Requirements specification
> > **5.** Selection from alternatives
> > **7.** Evaluation
> > (these are the ends of the loops
> > of fig. A !)

- diversity of alternatives

> in phase:
>
> > **4.** Working out of alternatives
> > (the main stage of creativity)

- details in performance

> in the phases:
>
> > **3.** Analysis of the existing situation
> > **6.** Introduction of new systems

The above may explain the fact that in practice, starting from these forms of cooperation, also the formalized groups have an analogous structure and appearance. (See fig. 2. 2. 1 – 2. 2. 3).

Figure 2. 2. 1

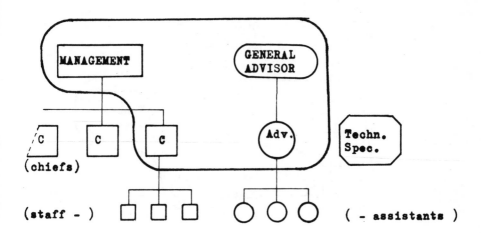

STEERING GROUP

Management as chairman – members of a high level.

Goal: control of this process of change, as to:

- system contents
- time
- cost

Tasks: supervision of design group and implementation
group(s);
conclusion of the vital phases.

Figure 2. 2. 2

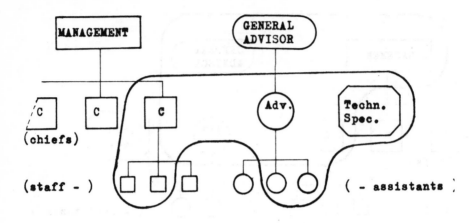

DESIGN GROUP

Advisor in central position; contributions from many directions.

Goal: Designing alternative solutions within boundary
conditions. Balancing of theory and practice.

Tasks: Evaluation of external experiences, working out
of alternatives, model building, etc.

Figure 2. 2. 3

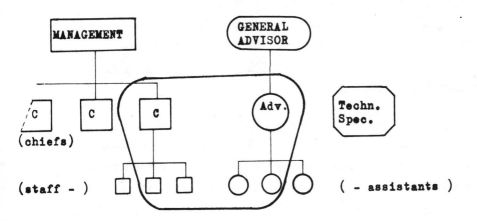

IMPLEMENTATION GROUP

Directed mainly towards execution and performance,
frequently in detail.

Goal: Mutual adaptation of organization and system by
analysis beforehand and coaching afterwards.

Tasks: Detailed analysis of the systematics serving
as a starting point for the change.
Reorganization (including training, etc.)
on the introduction of the new system.

The motives of the formalization

We have not the intention here to make a plea for sharp
task descriptions, rigid procedures or the like (which
do not fit to well in European business culture), but
we will advocate some formalization here for the sake
of organizational clearness.

Projects of implementing a M. I. S. are quite complex.
Quite a numer of people are involved, during many years.
Added to this the personal mobility of people (which seems
unavoidable in this profession ..... !) a reasonable
continuity sets great demands.

It is therefore that we are in favour of some delineation
of goals and tasks, especially in the cases where one
person plays various roles, with different partners.
He then has various rights and various duties, different
responsibilities he shares with different people.
That is why we make a plea for formalized groups in the
structure:

> – steering group
> > – design group(s)
> > – implementation group(s)

As for the steering group we have not experienced much
debate about the need for this structure. The task is
too complex for one man, and the decision–making calls
for a formalized approach.

About the distinction between " design " and " implementation "
not all do agree. Some argue that for the greater part it
concerns the same people, and that in the activities too
it is sometimes difficult to draw the line (which is right).

Our arguments , anyhow , are that there do exist essential
differences between design and implementation :

- From the designers quite a bit of creativity is
  expected; thinking in alternatives, experimenting with
  models - sometimes at an abstract level.
  In implementation , however , it is concrete business,
  no fictitious ideas are called for , it is reality what counts.

- In design , thinking in broad lines is appropriate,
  taking distance from the problems. But in implementation
  one goes into the smallest detail, 100% of the details ,
  both feet on the ground.

- Also the work differs ; in design there often occur unique
  activities which offer a chance for self-expression.
  In implementation it cannot be denied that much of the work
  has a repetitive character , and often explicit criteria
  (as to quantity , quality , documentation, etc.) have to
  be observed.

- This all reflects in the organization.
  In the design group one will come across a rather diffuse
  leadership and a great autonomy of the group (organic regime).
  In the implementation group leadership can be more
  centralized and - for the sake of efficiency - a more
  mechanistic regime will be found.

From a person who (as a linking pin) plays a role in
both activities, it is expected that he is well aware of
all these differences. To us – in most of the cases –
these arguments sufficed to support people in this aspect
by formalizing the groups , and making clear whát was
the task of each group respectively.

In some five years good experiences were gained with
these groups , especially in major projects , where a
clear allocation of tasks is most important.

But for minor projects too , one may draw from this
experience by structuring the organization in a
somewhat simpler form – on the same principles.
That is a choice we gladly leave to the reader.

ACKNOWLEDGEMENTS .

The author is grateful to N. V. Philips Gloeilampenfabrieken
for permission to publish this paper. He is also much
indebted to colleagues throughout the company ; especially
Drs. A. J. Dieleman (Information Systems and Automation)
has to be mentioned. With him the author shared a number
of experiences and his ideas have been of great value.

THE STRUCTURE OF MIS

P. A. Losty
Cranfield School of Management
England

1.0   INTRODUCTION

I shall deal with the structure of MIS under three headings:

architectural models will be discussed in some detail, the report

structure will provide an alternative way of regarding the archi-

tectural models, and viewing MIS as a process will briefly suggest

a further approach.

MIS is regarded as synonymous with computer based management

information systems or, more precisely, with attempts to extend

the use of computers from routine data processing into the pro-

vision of information for management, at the level of senior manage-

ment their role at present is negligible. By definition every

company has a management information system. The novelty in

MIS lies in attempts at formal design combined with the data

processing ability of a computer.

Forcing problems through the techniques of systems design does

not ensure an acceptable solution, neither do the letters MIS mean that managers will automatically look for guidance to a system carrying this label. One sometimes hears systems designers bewailing the fact that their MIS is not used by managers, an 'information system' which does not inform'.

This paper is written in the belief that the structure of MIS will repay study. The role of the computer in MIS can be seen in perspective, and the MIS can be made to evolve in the context of the management.

1.1 DEFINITIONS

MIS is defined as 'a system of information inputs to managers designed to assist them in the discharge of their managerial tasks'.

The definition does not demand computers, neither does it imply 'total' systems or integrated systems. It does not define the managerial task, which I have attempted elsewhere (1). It does refer to a <u>designed</u> system, which presupposes that some degree of integration will be involved.

Systems designer will be used to cover all categories of staff who are involved in the design of any element of an MIS, systems analysts, operational research staff and consultants would all be included. Differentiation between them has no importance to my theme.

Information analyst will refer specifically to a person who forms the interface between MIS and its environment.

2.0 ARCHITECTURAL MODELS

The concepts in this section form a useful, if simplified, way of viewing MIS. They seem to be of practical help when faced with the task of formally designing a system which will inform managers.

A basic structure will be proposed and discussed, and three variations on it with practical implications suggested.

2.1   BASIC STRUCTURE

Figure 1 presents an overall schematic for relating the essential elements in MIS. Each element will now be considered in some detail.

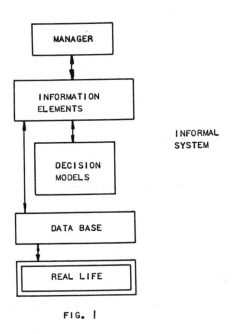

FIG. I

2.1.1   Real life

A vital function of all models is to represent real life.

When they cease to do so they become detached from real life and to that extent fail to represent anything meaningful. Systems designers with little experience of the real life situation must continually check for correspondence between their model and that which it is supposed to portray.

Models have other uses, planning, control and forecasting for example. Insofar as they are detached from reality their value is impaired.

2.1.2   Data base

The internal data base and the external data base, relating respectively to matters internal to the company to matters external
to it, have different characteristics. The term data base will include them both.

Three separate parts are distinguishable within the data base.

(i)   Written part.

Attention is usually focussed upon the written part, which includes
computer files. Organisation of the written part to ensure maximum
use of the data is important. Computer schemes for organisation
are occasionally represented as MIS in their own right, such
exaggeration does not help establish the name. Computer
organisational problems show scant prospects of solution by conceptual breakthrough. Sheer speed of disc devices and similar
backing store seems more likely to solve these problems where
several keys, or a complex of files, are involved.

Other major considerations are security, accuracy, frequency of
access and response time.

Security has two aspects.   Success in solving problems of
organisation may invite abuse of the new availability of data.
Ethical questions arise which demand solution. Accidental
damage caused by programs straying into the wrong files, or
incorrect manipulation of files, poses problems capable of
solution at a technical level.

Accuracy of the data base is necessary to avoid detachment in
a very fundamental sense. A key factor is the allocation of
responsibility for records to someone who has a vested interest
in their accuracy. Data preparation staff may not have an
appropriate feeling of responsibility.

Frequency of access to the data and desirable response time

are related questions. In the non-computer portion of the data base
they appear to pose little difficulty. However records may be out-
of-date thus making access to them unattractive so that investigation
of current access patterns may provide little help in designing an
improved system. In the computer portion frequency of access
must be assessed from first principles, management tending to
overstate their requirement. Response time need not necessarily
compete with that of the manual system - real-time response from
out-of-date records. The two factors combine to decide storage
media.

(ii)　　　Verbal part.

Part of the data base will be derived from verbal messages and
may never be recorded in writing. Examples include currency
rates of exchange or commodity prices which might be ascertained
on the telephone and used as the basis of important decisions.
Attempts to formalise such data may involve recording a shifting
pattern of rates or prices which can be prohibitively expensive
to capture and update.

(iii)　　　Knowledge part.

A more subtle part of the data base is that recorded in the minds
of people who process data. A 'feel' for the response of
customers to some change in marketing strategy, an ability to
deal intuitively with exceptional cases, or the allocation of work
to machines and operators may be difficult to program.
Systems designers should program as much of the knowledge
part as is justified, and thereby improve the system. They
must also avoid the temptation of trying to program knowledge
which is best left to humans. Whilst there is strong intellect-
ual challenge in putting difficult jobs onto a computer the
economic advantage may lay with leaving them to a human.

Conversely managers are reluctant to concede that any programming is possible.

It may be argued that knowledge is not really part of the data base. What is certain is that it is part of the structure of MIS.

Internal data and external data also merit a mention.

(i)   Internal data.

Manipulation of internal data poses problems concerned with the cost of data compared with its value; the physical problems of sufficiently accurate collection; which medium to store the data on; how best to retrieve the data.

The length of storage life may be a difficult decision. Once data has been processed there will be a loss of detail which cannot be recreated if the records are destroyed.

Internal data is under the control of the organisation and standards can be enforced.

(ii)   External data.

Internal data bases can extend to billions of characters, the external data base could be extended to infinite size. Information about the economy, government policy, competitors, substitute products and the market or consumers may be necessary to support decisions.   Collection of data to derive such information poses formidable problems. A significant difficulty is the lack of control over the data, even over such minor details as the length of a customer order number.

Apart from the formal data base attention should be directed to the scanning of the environment. Aguilar proposes a scheme (2) which progresses from undirected viewing to formal search by a series of responses to the material scanned, and to the decisions to be made.   Scanning is appropriate where data cannot be formally incorporated in the data base, the predominating characteristic in the external data base.

Before leaving the data base I would stress that the concept I have offered is much wider than that which most computer people seem to hold. Surely the data base must include all things which feed decision models or information elements.

2.1.3 Decision models

I do not propose to spend much time on decision models. Two distinct types can be distinguished although the distinction may be difficult in practice.

(i)   Algorithmic models.

An algorithm is a procedure for solving a problem in a finite number of steps. Following the algorithm leads to a best solution. Examples are mathematical programming, queueing theory and inventory control theory.

(ii)   Heuristic models.

Where no algorithm exists or computation is impossible a heuristic model may help. Either some empirical rules are set to cut down the size of computation (shop scheduling), or the problem is solved by a set of logical rules and variation is parameter values (e.g. Forrester (3)). Simulation is the principal heuristic tool.

Both types may be heavy users of data. They may also be dependent upon the accuracy of the data supplied, although sensitivity analysis may indicate which of the data are critical in terms of accuracy, and what error is acceptable. Two fundamentally different approaches to the building of models are available. At one extreme a model of the management process is constructed and data to support it are then assembled; at the other extreme data processing is con-

tinually refined until model building evolves quite naturally from
it. Both approaches are legitimate, but the computer based MIS
gives a new impetus to the latter.

2.1.4   Information elements

All other elements communicate with management through some
well defined information elements. Consideration of these in
specific cases points to a basic dilemma common to designers of
MIS and Operational Research models. Information elements
must be within the ability of management to comprehend. It is
not enough to express the answer in terms they understand (e.g.
profit), they must grasp the fundamentals of the system from
which information elements are derived.

It is surprising that the design of MIS so often proceeds from
manipulation of the data base, rather than from designing
information elements. If it proves impossible to design information elements there is no point in proceeding to design
the system. Failure to recognise this is one reason for MIS
which managers do not use.

Some thoughts follow from this line of argument. Problems
of acceptance of change are involved, education of the management may be prerequisite to comprehension. No manager
would refuse help, he is rightly reluctant to be guided by something he cannot understand. Acceptance is essential, you cannot inform a manager against his will.

Three types of information element predominate in present MIS,
accounting, statistical and performance indicators.

(i)   Accounting information.

Accounting information originated in the need to account for
shareholders assets. A central function of most business is
the need to raise funds and to earn a suitable return. Cost,
profit, standard costing and budgetary control, and management

accounting ratios are the main information concepts. Computers do not add to these concepts, they make possible faster processing and the summarising of greater quantities of data.

(ii)   Statistics.

Basic techniques include mean and dispersion. The use of dispersion in setting exception limits is relatively rare although it is often the best technique. Correlation and regression are examples of techniques made easier by the computer. Sampling and significance testing have a different implication, it may not be necessary to process all the data to obtain sufficient accuracy in the result, a point especially important in the external data base.

Unlike accounting information the use of statistical techniques have been advanced by the computer. Our ability to compute has partially outstripped our ability to interpret the results.

(iii)   Performance indicators.

These may be either crude or standardised. The former would exist when a decision to increase sales by 10% lead to an increase in target for all salesmen by this amount. The latter would involve adjusting each territory target with due regard to sales potential so as to reach the overall target of 10%. Standardised indicators are more satisfactory, and in the example more equitable, but they make greater demands on the management process. Performance indicators cover all aspects of the organisation, including facility utilisation, quality of the system and reliability.

In some instances computers make it possible to use performance indicators not otherwise feasible, one example is the measurement of facility loading some months ahead in a complex production control system.

Further treatment of information elements will be found under 3.0 where the report structure is examined, and 4.0 where a new approach to information elements is suggested.

2.1.5   Data/information streams

In Figure 1 a series of arrows represent the flow of information and data, they are two-directional to represent the flow between the elements. In practice each arrow represents a trunk carrying many individual streams.

What the streams are vary from system to system, but they can always be clearly identified. Examples include personnel data, cost data, material flow, machine availability and utilisation, interest rates, revenue and so on.

Each stream is brought into existence with some primary purpose in mind, the art of systems design is to co-ordinate the streams to improve the value of the information elements.

2.1.6   Informal system

Figure 1 shows the informal system enveloping the formal structure. The latter is the skeleton, whilst the former is the flesh which provides protection. Between them they give each MIS its distinctive shape.

A proper aim of the systems designer is to formalise systems as far as practicable, but he must recognise that some things are better left to the informal system.

Informal is a relative term. Production may be scheduled on a weekly basis by a formal system leaving difficulties within that period to be solved by an 'informal' human system. In fact the human system may have a programmed response to some difficulties, leaving less usual ones to be dealt with on an ad hoc or informal basis.

Casual conversations may pass information much faster than the formal system, so that when the formal information arrives corrective action has been taken.

ACTIVE AND PASSIVE SYSTEMS

Figure 2 represents a modified schematic.

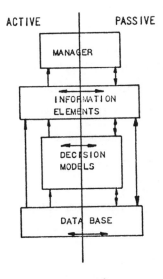

FIG. 2

A useful distinction can be drawn between the active and passive
roles of a system. Data streams in the latter are two-directional,
whilst in the former they are predominantly towards the manager.
Active systems process data and emit information without any
action on the part of the manager, hopefully directing his
attention to where it is needed. Passive systems wait for the
manager to interrogate them and then respond. Most of the software systems developed for MIS are essentially passive, they
may permit file processing but rarely emit information.
The active and passive roles have implications for each
element.

2.2.1   Data base

Active systems can often be adequately supported by batch
processing, passive systems tend to call for extension into
a real-time mode. Sometimes real-time interrogation can

153

be supported by batch processing, real-time can be expensive.
Rapid growth in file size poses difficulties for passive systems
using more than one key and more than one file. Some organisations use restricted size files for the passive system and accept
the double updating necessary.

2.2.2 Decision models

Similar problems are encountered to those of the data base. A
large model, e.g. linear programming or simulation, can be
run at intervals and information emitted. Asking 'what if'
questions of a large model may be expensive, and simplification
of the model may prove attractive.

2.2.3 Information elements

The active/passive dichotomy is dealt with under 3.0, Report
Structure.

2.2.4 Informal systems

Informal systems function in the active sense, but on an
irregular basis. An example is information that a strike is
likely in some external area which would threaten supplies.
They also function in the passive sense, in response to
questions. Because the informal system is not designed great
care is necessary in evaluating the outputs.

2.3 MANAGER - MIS INTERACTION

A popular view of the relationship of managers to MIS is
represented by Figure 3 (a).

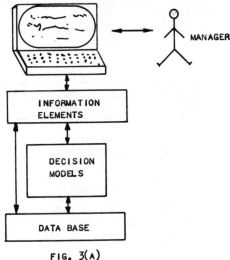

MANAGER

INFORMATION ELEMENTS

DECISION MODELS

DATA BASE

FIG. 3(A)

The manager operates through a visual display unit giving him unrestricted access to all elements in MIS, via information elements. At lower levels of management such systems certainly do operate, interrogation of the inventory control file to establish the position of individual items, or to establish aircraft booking positions in an airline seat reservation system. Information elements present no difficulties to systems designer or manager.

I can find no trace of a system of this type operating for senior managers. Figure 3 (b) represents the position which is likely to obtain for several years.

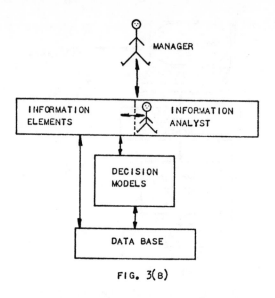

FIG. 3(B)

The senior manager will ask his questions of an information analyst who will advise him of the data available, and then produce information elements from the data base. The attributes which equip humans to be successful senior managers do not bestow an aptitude for learning some boolean based mumbo jumbo. Whether it is inability to learn the 'free-form' languages or, as Canning (4) suggests, a lack of familarity with file and data structure is immaterial. The task of information analyst is at present incompatible with the senior management role.

2.4   REAL LIFE - MIS INTERACTION

Where MIS interact with real life similar problems to those above exist. The forecast of sales for representatives is a simple exercise based on past experience. Scheduling production to individual machines rather than groups must be guided by simple principles. Yet a human intermediary is often used in both cases.

Figure 4 (b) may represent a more appropriate structure than Figure 4 (a).

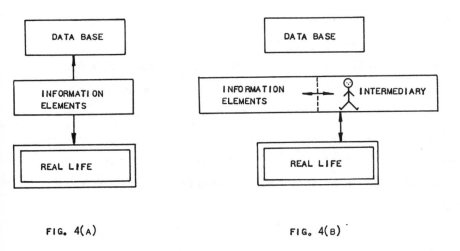

FIG. 4(A)   FIG. 4(B)

Information elements at this level may pose conceptual problems, or be incapable of viable solution by a computer system on the real life scale of operations. People may be indispensable in such cases.

3.0   **REPORT STRUCTURE**

The word report in this section will include any information element offered to managers. It therefore includes printed output, visual displays and graphical output. We are concerned only with formal reports.

The idea of considering the report structure is not new (Cloot (5)). It does provide a useful alternative way of regarding the

MIS from the viewpoint of the manager, rather than regarding the structure necessary to generate the reports. Under the headings active reports and passive reports seven types of report will be identified and their use discussed.

3.1 ACTIVE REPORTS

Three types will be identified, routine data reports, routine exception reports and triggered reports.

3.1.1 Routine data reports

At set intervals all the records on a file may be printed out, either in part or complete. Weekly print-out of all the items in a store giving part number, description, quantity on hand, quantity on order etc., is an example.

Such reports have little place in a proper structure of reports. Management may insist upon them, in which case the systems designer has no choice but to supply them. Alternatively the systems designer, frustrated by a failure to define exceptions, may produce routine data reports in the hope of informing managers.

It is this class of reports which is responsible for the stories of MIS output which arrives at the manager on a fork lift truck. Where such reports are called for exception reports should accompany them in preparation for their cancellation. Complete print outs should come within the category of detailed interrogation reports (3.2.1).

3.1.2 Routine exception reports

Although these are issued at regular intervals they deal only with exception items. Considerable computer time and paper may be saved, and more important a reduction in volume improves the information value to managers.

Whilst the implied principal of management by exception has

great attractions it can be infernally difficult to apply in practice.
The problem is to agree a definition of exceptions with management.
Elementary statistical techniques such as standard deviation are of
great value to screen out exceptions. Management has an understandable reluctance to leave the selection of material for their attention
to a technique they do not understand.

In inventory control exception reports might be printed where usage
is $\pm$ 2 standard deviations from the forecast, or an order is not met
after 1.5 s.d. from the lead time.

3.1.3 Triggered exception reports

Exception reports may be triggered by some exceptional condition
and only issued when that condition is encountered. They are of
special significance in real-time systems when they can be issued
at any time when the job is live. Large uncovered positions in
currency dealing or heavy demand for a booked aircraft would be
examples.

Reaction to the triggered report dealing with one item should not
be different from that with the whole position under review, a
possible weakness of management by exception.

3.2 PASSIVE REPORTS

Four separate categories will be identified, the first three in
response to predetermined procedures and the fourth one not.

3.2.1 Detailed interrogation reports

Access is required to one or more records, or in some cases to
an entire file. Most of the MIS packages available function in
this mode. Response time is a measure of the system, how long
is acceptable varies with each system.

File interrogation problems mentioned under 2.1.2 are important
in this connection.

3.2.2   Summary interrogation reports

The ability to interrogate a file and extract   statistical or accountancy information from it can be very important to the manager seeking a 'picture' of the situation represented by the file.

Many users have their own programs to perform this task, but the facility is only just beginning to appear in the packages (e.g. Informatics Mark IV and Find 2). Extension of such facilities would be a valuable enhancement of the packages.

3.2.3   Exception interrogation reports

Files can be examined against variable criteria and exceptions against these criteria requested. Routine exception reports operate against fixed criteria.

This facility is useful for establishing the parameters of a system which are of transient but important interest. Low limits tend to cause large volumes of print out, hopefully a mistake which will not be repeated.

3.2.4   Special reports

There will always be a demand for reports for which no procedure exists, or for which there are no data on file. The content and format of such reports cannot be predicted in advance.

File interrogation languages make it easier to compile the report where data are on file. Where they are not non-computer procedures must be considered. Cost, usefulness and the possibility of repetition of the request are factors to consider.

4.0   MIS AS A PROCESS

I shall conclude by taking another viewpoint. So far the conventional view of MIS as a hierarchical structure has been

followed, the system operates as a series of snapshots in time.
Information pyramids are constructed to correspond to the idea of
a management pyramid. MIS as a process supplements the conventional view, it does not replace it. I have argued that information elements have not changed to make more effective use of
computers, the concepts in this section indicate a necessary
direction of change.

Life is continuing process, and a major advance in MIS will take
place when managers regard the system they control as continuous. Some new concepts will have to become familiar to
managers, concepts which are well established in other spheres.
Three concepts will be briefly mentioned, they seem the most
important.

4.1   TIME PHASE PROBLEMS

The flow of data is unlikely to coincide exactly with the flow of
events, even in a real-time system. Real-time interrogation
based upon batch updating illustrates how great the time lag
can be. It is possible to buy off time constraints with a
computer, it is also true that exact coincidence in time is
rarely essential.

Managers consider their information problems will be solved
if only they can get information faster. In fact many cases can
be postulated where fast feedback is positively harmful.
Feedback must be divided into fast feedback and slow feedback,
considerable economy may be effected by using cheap slow
feedback loops where they are adequate.

Understanding of the process being controlled is more
important than fast information about its recent performance,
the two are not synonymous. If one can forecast accurately a
short time into the future slow feedback about present per-

formance may be acceptable.

4.2 PRESENTATION OF DATA

Presentation of information to represent the system as a process would help managers to envisage it as such. A CRT display trace as obtained from analogue computers would help, and whilst these can be simulated on a digital machine the representation is essentially static.

Graphical displays rather than tabular presentation assist the visualisation process. Some work is already being done in the U.S.A. on this topic.

4.3 SIMULATION OF MIS

I am strongly convinced that much more work must be done on the simulation of MIS to aid our understanding of it. Forrester (3) has shown how sub-systems, each logical in themselves, can combine to form an unstable system.

But perhaps I feel too strongly about this. It should be the subject of another paper!

REFERENCES

(1)   Designing a Management Information System.
        P.A. Losty. Computer Bulletin. May, 1969.

(2)   Scanning the Business Environment.
        F.J. Aguilar. Macmillan. 1967.

(3)   Industrial Dynamics. Jay W. Forrester.
        Wiley. 1961.

(4)   What's the Status of MIS. EDP Analyser.
        Canning Publications. October, 1969.

(5)   Management Information Systems - can computers
        help? P.L. Cloot. Computer Bulletin. March, 1968.

EVOLUTION OF A TOLL MIS - BELL CANADA

Robert F. Couch
Bell Canada
Canada

The information system described in this paper is
an evolving one to which must be added many other
facets before it can be regarded as approaching
an all-enveloping completeness. However, in evolving such a system every effort has been made to
avoid the "wedged bear" syndrome of Stafford
Beer. [1]

SECTION 1 - ROLE OF A MANAGEMENT INFORMATION SYSTEM

The role of a management information system is
simply to assist management in carrying out their
functions of planning, organizing and controlling.
The data streams that impinge on the manager are
of many types as they arise from actual interactions with other men or collections of men
(organizations).

[1] Stafford Beer, "Decision and Control" John
Wiley and Sons Ltd. 1966 p. 65

In the 19th century, the concept of "economic" man was widely accepted and planning that evolved about this concept centred largely on profit maximizing within a free enterprise economy. Simon identified the need to extend beyond the concept of economic man as we depart from slow-moving situations. "As the complexity of the environment increases or its speed of change, we need to know more and more about the mechanisms and processes that economic man uses to relate himself to that environment and achieve his goals."[2]

This has led to an increasing interweaving of economics with psychology as the decision maker is seen as exhibiting "adaptive and satisficing behaviour" - concepts drawn largely from psychology - concepts which "challenge sharply the classical picture of the maximizing entrepreneur".

There was a time during the early years of this century when affiliation with church sponsored organizations was considered to be important when they were conceived as being a meaningful focus of influence within the totality of community affairs. In one recent inventory of community affairs participation by management, it was specifically stated that church affiliated activities were not to be listed. Thus a management information system

[2] Theories of Decision-Making in Economics and Behavioural Sciences, H.A. Simon - Surveys of Economic Theory Vol. 3, MacMillan, New York, 1967 p. 125

established in say 1910 would have included information that dealt with religious man – by 1970 this
information was seen as being unnecessary. Thus a
system is not a "forever" institution – it must be
flexible and permit additions and deletions as the
environment shifts.

Beyond these levels of assessment there is an
"aesthetic" level[3] referred to by Doxiadis. The
concern for pollution that now envelopes Europe and
North America may well force a sharper interest on
the aesthetics of plant location, shape and association which in turn would cause a new set of information to take on enhanced values in the total
decision process.

By 1970 man is being seen in addition as a physiological being from the planning standpoint with on-
going needs for pure air and pure water. Decisions
then become more complex as the multi-dimensional
nature of their impacts is envisaged.

"Many of the most serious conflicts facing mankind
result from the interaction of social, economic,
technological, political and psychological forces
and can no longer be solved by factional approaches
from individual disciplines."

This statement from the Bellagio Declaration on
Planning is a reminder that planning impinges on
man in his many guises – that in any system there

[3] C.A. Doxiadis "Forces That Will Shape Ecumenopolis" Ekistics, Vol. 15 (1963) p. 250

is a need to plan that system "as a whole to understand the totality of factors involved and to in-
tervene in the structural design to achieve more
integrated operation".[4]

Man can be envisaged as a many-faceted character,
e.g., economic, social, political, religious,
physiological, psychological to name a few. He can
appear in any of these guises or combinations thereof
depending on the conditions surrounding an interaction.

The information system that must serve the manager
has a multi-dimensional task to   perform   within
a framework that has as many facets as there are
multiple characters of man. Portrayed as a matrix
this function would appear to have many cells, each
representing a sub-function being performed to meet
a particular need.

	PLAN	ORGANIZE	CONTROL
Economic			
Social			
Political			
Religious			
Physiological			
Psychological			

FIGURE 1

[4] Perspectives of Planning by Erich Jantsch
    Proceeding of the OECD Working Symposium on
    Long Range Forecasting & Planning Bellagio
    Italy 2 Nov 1969

A decision taken by a manager can involve one or more of these cells. The relative importance of a particular cell varies both with time and the type of decision.

It is for this reason that there does not seem to have emerged a clear cut concept of what is a "management information system". Such a system must be capable of serving the informational needs of each of the cells in the decision matrix. The level of refinement and structure of the information needed within each cell will depend on the relative importance of the cell at the time of the decision.

If a third dimension is added to the decision matrix showing this relative importance associated with a particular decision, the surface might appear as follows. The height suggests the relative depth of information required from each cell of the system.

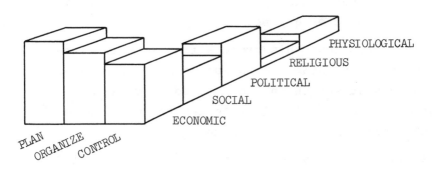

FIGURE 2

In this example the surface suggests that the economic consequences of a particular decision would loom largest and dictate the most highly regarded informational streams that would constitute a management information system that was seen as relevant. It will be noted that a political consequence is seen as being of some importance which would necessitate another stream of meaningful information being incorporated into the system.

The data behind the economic informational streams could be continuous while the political stream may be intermittent in nature. Thus, a management information system need not be thought of as a purely continuing flow of data from many sources and indeed may be of changing composition as the relative importance of the cells changes.

The management information system may be considered then to be that system operating continuously or intermittently that will provide information that is meaningful to the manager, as a man, in taking a decision that will impinge on other men in their numerous character guises.

It would seem that this broad a framework is without meaning in establishing such a system. However it focuses attention on the need for several sub-systems, each of which is relevant to one or more of the cells in the decision matrix.

In evolving a concept of what information is relevant to a particular decision cell the first step was to evolve a data base from which information could be extracted.

The process involved in extracting information from

a data base can range from simple visual inspection of the data, comparison within the observers brain to some standard expected and information evolving that suggests corrective action be taken or not.

However, as the amount of data - that has to be integrated in developing relevant information for decision making - increases, the human mind seems to boggle after some 5 to 7 variables are fed in simultaneously.

Thus it was in our toll (interurban) message business [5] that there were a host of variables at work both within the company and in the environment that needed to be integrated to move from the raw data flow state to the first stages of the evolution of a management information system.

In the following sections the evolution of the data base deemed essential for the subsequent management information system is described. Subsequently an abridged version of one of a family of computerized models is presented. This family of models translates the data streams into meaningful information flows as one segment of a continuously evolving management information system.

[5] the voice messages transmitted between two cities are called by various names e.g., toll, long distance, intercity, interurban

SECTION 2 - EVOLUTION OF THE DATA SYSTEM

The data base that has evolved thus far is directed solely toward the economic aspects of planning, organizing and controlling the toll message business. The content of this base was determined from the same conceptual framework that was used to develop the evaluative model.

This conceptual framework can be envisaged as starting with the output of the toll network in the real world. This network carries the toll messages from city to city within our territory. Output would be that portion of the toll message demand that is satisfied by the available supply of toll carrying capacity.

Toll message demand, which is customer-dependent, is influenced by the income of the customer, his value system and the relative price of the toll message. The company's response in terms of call carrying capacity is influenced by the state of technology, unit costs and growth rate in the environment to name a few. A conceptual framework reflecting these influences would appear as in Figure 3 below:

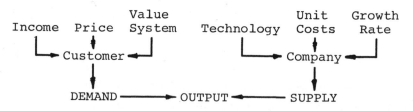

FIGURE 3

The data base that is evolved must satisfy the needs of both the DEMAND and SUPPLY side of this framework.

The development of a conceptual and theoretical framework covering the operations of the message toll business and a delineation of the various outputs of that business were carried out concurrently. This delineation of outputs was made in terms that were meaningful for operating and financial evaluations.

The first stage of this delineation process involved identifying broad classes or types of outputs e.g., station vs. person calling. Further subdivision was made on the basis of identity groupings and finally on the basis of the specific descriptive identities within each grouping. The ultimate objective was to establish a unique identification of each unit of output in terms that were meaningful for the purpose for which the information was to be used, whether it be operating or financial.

The unit of output was defined as the completed toll message. However to be meaningful in an evaluation system, the toll message had to be specified in the detail required to detect the effect of changes in demand on revenues, investment, expenses and facility requirements (trunks, switches, operators, etc.) Eight dimensions of a completed long distance message were identified as being needed.

a) Orig. geog. location
b) Term. geog. location
c) Time message orig.
d) Length of conversation

e) Cust. service class
f) Billing information
g) Type of service
h) Class of message

Geographic location, for example, had to be spelled out in terms of Numbering Plan Area, Central Office Number, Toll Switching Centre Code and Traffic Operator Unit. The Customer Service Class was specified as business, residence, coin. Some 25 words were employed to describe each message in sufficient detail that its revenue contribution and expense generating activities could be fully identified.

To achieve economies in the data base two forms of truncation were employed:

   i recording less than full data e.g., recording of
      the nearest minute rather than second

  ii sampling the continuous stream of output to ob-
      tain characteristics required

Further economies were realized by using different sampling fractions for different classes of traffic in different cities depending on the scarcity of the characteristics being sought. In larger centres samples could range as small as 1 in 200 while for smaller centres they could be as high as 100% of a particular class of traffic.

Decisions in this area were made after consultation with potential users of the data before truncation was undertaken to ensure their needs would be adequately met.

To obtain a continuous flow of data pertaining to the output, a Special Toll Analysis Sample (S.T.A.S.) was implemented. This was a continuous random sample of completed toll messages selected in the billing section of the accounting department.

This data provided the basic linkage between demand and supply and as such was fundamental to the development of other relationships. In addition, it provided the means of continuous evaluation through comparison of actual and predicted results. However, because of the detail required and the resulting necessity for truncation in the form of sampling, there were requirements inside and outside the business that it did not fulfil, e.g., accounting, collection etc. Thus other systems, often using much of the same detail, must be maintained in parallel. Ultimately there may be some advantage in attempting an integration of these separate systems.

A continuous sample of the output consists of approximately 800,000 message records each month from Bell Canada originated toll messages. It is used primarily to track changes in demand patterns over time and to validate and improve predictive capabilities of the evaluation system or model.

One of the necessary adjuncts to any data gathering system is an evaluation system that integrates the results of all analysis that has been carried out on the data. This evaluation system should be able to provide management with the intelligence which is contained in the data. Management then combines this intelligence with the social, political or other aspects of the problem and makes a final decision. The ultimate goal of the evaluation system is to relieve the decision maker of the necessity of quantitative analysis and to provide the intelligence (findings) from such analysis. It is this evaluation system that converts data flows, data banks, summaries, graphs, etc. into meaningful information.

The data base of the Management Information System provided the point of departure for planning, organizing and controlling a large segment of the toll business. Reports and summaries produced from the data on a regular basis indicate the impact of past decisions. They identify areas where prediction has been poor and improvements are needed. Usually special reports are issued to assist in this further evaluation.

Once the conceptual framework of the model was developed and a satisfactory definition of outputs achieved, the next step was to identify the various input factors affecting customer's demand and the company ability to provide supply. These fell into two groups - those over which the company had a degree of direct control and those over which it had none.

The first approach to determining relevant inputs was theoretical. In effect, no constraining assumptions re levels of resolution, availability of data etc. were made. This process identified input requirements not previously recognized or fully appreciated. Many analysts have attempted to avoid this step by merely accepting and mechanizing present data flows and as a result have overlooked significant variables affecting decision results.

After delineation of input requirements, there followed a review of available data. In our experience, there is usually substantially more and better detailed data available on factors over which the company exercises a degree of control. Data on factors beyond the control of the company, usually from government and some commercial sources, is sometimes sparse and when available is in highly aggregated terms.

This review of available data raised problems of levels of resolution and indeed with the question of feasibility regarding construction of a useful decision assisting model. The review became a process of recycling through the conceptual framework to determine the implications of data shortages and of assessing the time, effort and cost of supplementing data flows by intermittent survey or other appropriate methods. The objective here was to determine a practical approach to matching the level of resolution and the sensitivity of both the demand and supply sides of the conceptual framework.

This balancing process was of considerable significance as there was little use of producing an evaluation model in which the demand resolution was at a corporate level and the supply resolution was at a sub-corporate decision level.

In this process, there was concern with the extent of the impact of each factor. If the influence was found to be slight, based on evaluations, fairly broad measures were chosen and it was assumed that they applied relatively evenly over the spectrum of demand and supply functions. Where the influence of the factor was found to be great and the variation within the aggregates was found to be wide, greater

resolution of the input was essential if the predictive quality of the model was to be kept high.

In certain cases, the actual data obtained and used
represented a compromise and near-measures were
taken to represent the measure actually sought particularly for uncontrollable factors in the environment.

It would be remiss not to mention, however, that
tremendous strides have been made in many countries
in providing environmental data of relevance. We in
Canada are particularly fortunate in having both
Federal and Provincial governments, who, cognizant
of the data problems for industrial and corporate
planning and control, have been making an increasing
amount of useful and topical data available.

However, it was still only possible to use the best
input data that could be made available which
limited the predictive and tracking capability of
the model. This has necessitated an on-going effort
to improve these input data flows in terms of relevance and level of resolution. This search for
better data is as important to society as the continued search for better technology.

SECTION 3 - THE EVALUATION MODEL

Data can be thought of as a form of "intermediate output" in the sense that it becomes the input to a final output stage by which it is translated into information - the form of the final output. In this sense the information abstracted from the original data becomes the final product.

A vehicle is required to carry out this transformation of data into information that is relevant to the decision process being served. One such vehicle that will be described briefly in this section is in the form of computerized model of the toll message business of Bell Canada. Other models have been developed for other sectors of the business.

The toll message model was based on the same conceptual framework as the data system - ensuring consistency and relevance between these major parts of the total management information system viz data flow and model.

The Toll Message Evaluation System displayed in Figure 4 is an abridged version of the logic in the evaluation model that is used to assess alternatives open to the company.

The data concerning the real world is stored in two master files - the STAS file being the sampled output from the existing toll message network. The economic data file reflects the environment of the territory in which the company operates. A basic monthly forecast of completed messages, and conversation minutes is developed on a point-to-point

177

TOLL MESSAGE EVALUATION SYSTEM

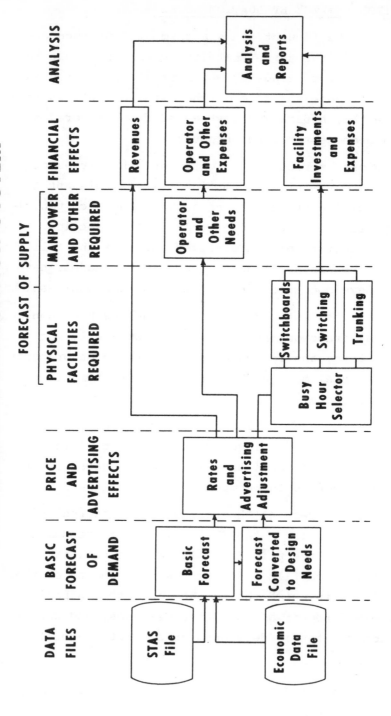

FIGURE 4

178

basis for the territory. This reflects the known exogeneous and endogeneous facts that influence growth e.g. telephones, seasonal effects, Labour Income, Industrial Production Index, Consumer Price Index.

With a change in the rate structure, new levels of demand and thus of output activities will be attained through stimulation, shift or change of message class. These new levels of messages and conversation minutes (outputs) are combined with the proposed rate structure to produce revenues.

In another set of sub-models the outputs are converted to estimates of physical facilities e.g. switchboards, switching and trunking depending on the peak-load period design requirements.

At the same time manpower and other requirements are evolved that are consistent with the physical facilities indicated. Combined with relevant unit costs the operating parameters of equipment and manpower are translated into financial parameters of investment and expenses.

Finally in the analysis stage cash flows, income statement and balance sheet impacts are assessed. Appropriate cash flows are used to develop Present Worth and Rate of Return statistics. Numerous print options are available to enable the user to select statistics on operating or financial impacts that may be of interest at several levels of detail.

The evaluation system reflected in this model is constantly being updated through numerous auxiliary data flows that reflect physical changes in the real world system e.g., additional telephones added to the network, new facility routing plans, revised expense figures from the operating departments.

As more complete data is gathered on the environment, improvements are made in the model to make its reactions more sensitive. Thus the model itself evolves and with it the data streams that are essential for the Management Information System most relevant to the toll message business of Bell Canada.

However, even in it's present stage of evolution it provides several benefits
- integrates the best available information at any time
- provides means to test sensitivity of parameters and indicates direction for further study
- identifies additional data flows to be established

SECTION 4 - LIMITATIONS OF A MANAGEMENT INFORMATION SYSTEM

A Management Information System can be thought of as a collection of channels carrying data, centres processing this data into information for decision and action.

The information carrying capacity of the channels connecting the various centres of the system as well as the information processing capacity of those centres are major limitations in its effectiveness.

The capacity of a channel will depend on the amount of interference present in the channel, the forms of messages it handles, the rate at which it can transmit and susceptibility to error.

The capacity of a centre will depend on the kinds of messages it processes, the actions or decisions required and the characteristics of the centre.

These limitations may be regarded as being a reflection of the structure of an organization. "An organization will not function smoothly if the amount of information to be sent on any channel or processed at any centre exceeds the capacity of that channel or centre."[6]

Failure to recognize the impact that an information system can have on an organization is not uncommon.

[6] Surveys of Economic Theory - Volume III
R. Dorfman - Operations Research p. 39
MacMillan, New York 1967

181

Fortunately there is a growing awareness of this impact and organizational restructuring is more frequently noted. [7]

It has been our experience that organizational restructuring is essential if the full value of the Management Information System is to be achieved. Perhaps the most common is a need to improve the capacity of the centre to receive and process the new streams of information made available.

It has not been found necessary to increase the physical channel capacity as this did not appear to be a limiting factor. Redundancy is suspected to be very high - as would be expected in a large organization. Whether it is too high - considering the large amount of noise or misleading signals that are also in the system - is difficult to assess at this time.

A second form of limitation emerges if the organization is envisaged as a group of centres connected by lines of communication or channels.

The separation of the centres means that no centre has all the information available to the organization. It also infers lags in transmitting information and distortions in transit.

How the organization will respond to changes in its environment or its condition will depend on the structure of the information flows and the decision

[7] Weyerhaeuser's Management Information System
R.A. Kronenberg - Datamation May 1967

rules employed by its various centres.

The fundamental assumption is that decision rules
may be envisaged as responses to discrepancies between - what is - and - what should be. Having identified these two ideal states all decisions are
intended to reduce these discrepancies.

On the technological side of the toll message business there are many such clearly defined decision
rules regarding network design, switching hierarchy,
and routing. The system described in this paper
identified where lags in data channels had resulted
in network design improvements being needed.

On the environmental side there are fewer rules,
less clearly defined and still being determined on
a somewhat empirical basis. The sufficiency of the
Management Information System on the environmental
side is not nearly as clear at this time as on the
technological side of the business.

It is certain that the sufficiency of that system
has been considerably enhanced by S.T.A.S. - and
will be further enhanced by a customer oriented information system now being tested. However the system will probably continue to evolve as the ability
to measure more of the relevant environmental
factors improves.

A further limitation on how well a Management
Information System may be conceived and executed
lies in the adequacy of the decision model available to the decision-maker.

Where the decisions are such that adequate models

can be constructed then such models will identify
what information is needed.[8] Where they are such
that adequate models cannot be constructed then
judgment must be used in setting up the data streams
and extracting the information deemed to be relevant.

The modules of the model of the toll message business - that describe the internal response of the
company (i.e. supply) in handling shifting demand -
are of the type that provide near-optimal solutions
in terms of a least-cost design. Here the information (design data) needs are quite specific.

The modules that describe the interface, between
the company, the customers and the environment are
not capable, at this time, of providing optimal
solutions. Here the information needs are less precise and are implied from economic theory as referred in Section 2.

[8] Analysis of Information Requirements
Russell L. Ackoff - Management Science
Vol. 14, No. 4 Dec. 1967 B-154

SECTION 5 - CONCLUSION

In evolving a Management Information System for
the toll message business in Canada it has proven
necessary to tap several sources of data simultaneously. These sources are portrayed in Figure 5.

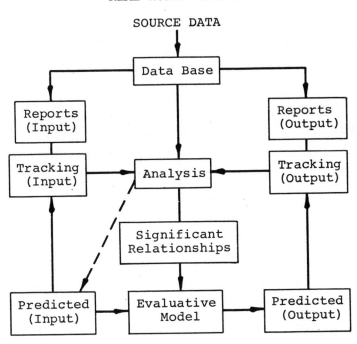

FIGURE 5

Some of these sources are continuous, such as the tap from OUTPUT, in the real world system. This continuous tap from the OUTPUT is known as the Special Toll Analysis Sample (STAS) and was described in Section 2 of this paper.

Intermittent data taps are employed via surveys of customers; studies of unit costs; studies of procedures for supplying the service, etc. Some of these are considered important enough that continuous surveillance systems are now being developed - particularly on customer usage and socio-economic characteristics.

From these multiple data sources have evolved specific reports on current status in the real world system and through analysis of the same data, relationships have been suggested between exogeneous real world variables and the observed demands on the toll message network.

Other relationships were also indicated and their predictive capability tested. Those relationships which appeared valid from the predictive test were reflected in an evaluative model that was described in Section 3. This sequence of events portrayed in Figure 5 merely suggests the scheme that was followed for abstracting the real world relationships from real world data streams for integration into an evaluative model.

Once the real world was abstracted into the model, various alternative proposals for repricing or for meeting demand could be evaluated. The PREDICTED

(OUTPUT) from the model is then compared, on an ongoing basis, with the TRACKING (OUTPUT) through a tracking mechanism. Thus the evaluative model becomes an integral part of the overall evolving Management Information System.

The present system reflects several classes of limitations and as these are identified corrective actions are taken. For example, one module of the evaluative model designs a switched hierarchial network for Bell Canada. This has led to structural changes in the real world network. Improvements, in information channels and in the information handling capability of various centres, are gradually being made.

At present this type of Management Information System (encompassing data flows, analysis and evaluative models) covers some 30% of Bell Canada's business. This concept is being applied gradually to other sectors of this business where it appears desirable to do so.

While the system described is limited, at present to the economic evaluative role, other systems are being evolved continuously to fulfil the other cells of the information matrix that are deemed relevant to the decision process. For example concern with environments in recent years has led Bell Canada to participate in future's studies of both a global and national nature. These studies will provide information for other cells of the information matrix that may prove to be as important as the economic cell in future decision processes.

BIBLIOGRAPHY

Ackoff, Russell L. *"Analysis of Information Requirements"* Management Science, Vol. 14, No. 4 December 1967.

Beer, Stafford. *Decision and Control.* New York: Wiley & Sons Ltd. 1966.

Dorfman, R. *Surveys of Economic Theory, Vol. 3.* New York: MacMillan 1967.

Doxiadis, C.A. *"Forces That Will Shape Ecumenopolis"* Ekistics, Vol. 15. 1963.

Jantsch, Erich. *"Perspectives of Planning"* O.E.C.D. Working Symposium. 1969.

Kronenberg, R.A. *"Weyerhaeuser's Management Information System"* Datamation. May 1967.

Simon, H.A. *Surveys of Economic Theory, Vol. 3.* New York: MacMillan 1967.

AN MIS FOR A COLLEGE OF TECHNOLOGY?

Bernard R.J. Staines
Enfield College of Technology
England

1. SUMMARY

This paper reviews one aspect of a preliminary systems study
carried out at Enfield College of Technology during 1969/1970.
Within this review four areas of study are discussed:

a) The decision making structures of the college

b) The information systems and flow

c) The data base elements to support a) and b) above

d) A further research program.

2. PURPOSE AND BACKGROUND

2.1 PURPOSE.

The purpose of this paper is to review some of the problems
encountered in the preliminary stages of analysis and design of
a Planning, Management and Operating system for a College of
Technology. In particular it is an attempt to clarify some of
the problems associated with the identification of a structure
within such a system.

2.2 BACKGROUND.

The findings of this paper are the result of a preliminary
study, which was conceived as the result of a number of informal
discussions which took place during the summer of 1969 within the

Enfield College Computing Centre concerning;

a) The scale of operations involved in Planning, Managing and Operating an organisation the size of this college

b) The problems inherent in the probable magnification of this scale occasioned by the formation of a Polytechnic

c) The possible mis-application of substantial resource if computerisation of isolated units within the college administration proceeded without an understanding of the interdependence of various sub-systems which constitute the 'College system'

At a meeting on 19th September 1969 attended by Mr. G.C. Blockley, Academic Registrar, Mr. D.J. Bush, Director of the Computing Centre, Mr. B.R. Staines, Senior Lecturer in Data Processing and Systems Analysis, it was agreed that;

"A study should be carried out by Mr. Staines to determine the possibility of developing and maintaining an integrated system for all Planning, Management and Operating functions of the College.

The study was born!

2.3 RESERVATIONS

Three features of this paper need emphasis,

a) This paper surveys only the preliminary study carried out in a very short space of time - it does little more than identify some of the problems.

b) At an early stage it became obvious that a substantial range of problems were associated with an identification of the type of decision making processes existent within an organisation unlike many commercial organisations.

c) The information sub-system associated with student activities, for use of students and their representatives is a vital area ommitted from this study. This is not a reflection on the magnitude and importance of the sub-system the inter action of this area is the subject of a seperate study.

2.4 STRUCTURE OF THE PAPER.

This paper is structured into four sections,

a) A discussion of the decision making structure of the College.

b) An attempt to fit the information flow to this decision
making structure.

c) A preliminary identification of the data elements necessary
to support the information flow.

d) Some indications of the further research program in this
study.

3. <u>COLLEGE DECISION MAKING STRUCTURE</u>

This section will identify the management systems operative in
the College and attempt a classification.

3.1 FORMAL STRUCTURE

At first sight there exists a clearly defined formal structure
within the College consisting of two parallel streams of activity
and authority. It would be reasonable to assume that the decision
making processes follow this significantly hierarchial structure.
Figure 3.1. is a schematic of the identified formal structure
of the College.

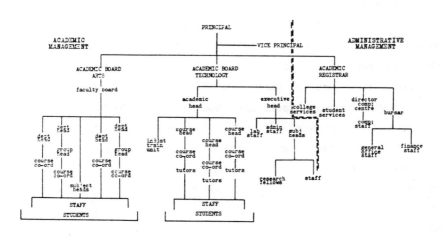

Figure 3.1   College formal structure (simplified)

The parallel streams indicated in Figure 3.1. which represent
the administration and academic functions of the College, each
have a range of unique responsibilities and a defined hierarchy.
It appears to be practical, even preferable, for each of the two
functions to operate independent of the other in the majority of
situations. The appearance however, is misleading; there is
virtually no decision made in one functional stream which does
not either require information which is common to the alternative
stream, or have repercussions in it. Therein lies one of the
significant operating problems of the College. The recognition
of this problem led to the second stage of the study, an attempt
to identify the management systems operative in each functional
stream.

3.2 MECHANISTIC OR ORGANIC?

In discussing management systems social scientists appear usually
to follow one of two paths. They have either accepted the
organisation chart as the 'formal organisation' - an imposed
system of controls, information and authority which seniors try
to get their subordinates to conform to - or have harked back to
Weber's ideal type of bureaucratic structure. Space and time
preclude a detailed study of these alternate approaches but an
exposition of the first can be found in 'Industrial Sociology'
(MILLER & FORM 1951), and a statement of the second view in
'Patterns of Industrial Bureaucracy' (GOULDNER A.W. 1956). In
this study Gouldner himself expresses some disatisfaction with
the "Ideal Bureaucracy" concept.

What all such kinds of view have in common is the assumption that
they are concerned with the same thing, that all working organisations are analysable in one or the other set of terms, the
choice depending not on the difference between organisations but
on the viewpoint of the writer.

In the last few years, however, there have emerged a number of
attempts at a synthetic appreciation of organisations which accept
more than one primary model for a concern. Early attempts at
such a synthesis are associated with H.A. Simon (SIMON. H.A. 1957)

and with Eisenstadt (EISENSTADT. S.N. 1958).

The most comprehensive study, however, and the one which formulated a dual classification seemingly very apposite to this present study was the work of Burns & Stalker in which they identified two distinct management systems as polar extremeties of the forms which management systems can take, and emphasised that 'different forms assumed by a working orgnaisation do exist objectively and are not merely interpretations offered by observers of different schools.' They attribute the polarity as being proportional to the scale of adaptation to a specific rate of technical and commercial change (BURNS. T. & STALKER. G.M. 1961). These two formally contrasted forms of management system were defined by Burns & Stalker as 'Mechanistic' and 'Organic'. The Mechanistic management system is appropriate to stable conditions and among its characteristics are:

a) the specialized differentiation of functional tasks into which the problems and tasks facing the concern as a whole are broken down;

b) the abstract nature of each individual task, which is pursued with techniques and purposes more or less distinct from those of the concern as a whole; i.e., the functionaries tend to pursue the technical improvement of means, rather than the accomplishment of the ends of the concern;

c) the reconciliation, for each level in the hierarchy, of these distinct performances by the immediate superiors, who are also, in turn, responsible for seeing that each is relevant in his own special part of the main task;

d) the precise definition of rights and obligations and technical methods attached to each functional role;

e) the translation of rights and obligations and methods into the responsiblities of a functional position;

f) hierarchic structure of control, authority and communication;

g) a reinforcement of the hierarchic structure by the location of knowledge of actualities exclusively at the top of the hierarchy, where the final reconciliation of distinct tasks and assessment of relevance is made.

h) a tendency for operations and working behaviour to be
governed by the instructions and decisions issued by superiors;

j) insistence on loyalty to the concern and obedience to
superiors as a condition of membership;

k) a greater importance and prestige attaching to internal
(local) than to general (cosmopolitan) knowledge, experience,
and skill.

The Organic form is more appropriate to changing conditions
which give rise constantly to fresh problems and unforseen
requirements for action which cannot be broken down or distributed
automatically. It includes among its characteristics:

a) the contributive nature of special knowledge and experience
to the common task of the concern;

b) the 'realistic' nature of the individual task, which is
seen as set by the total situation of the concern;

c) the adjustment and continual re-definition of individual
tasks through interaction with others;

d) the shedding of 'responsibility' as a limited field of rights,
obligations and methods.
(Problems may not be posted upwards, downwards or sideways as
being someone else's responsibility);

e) the spread of commitment to the concern beyond any technical
definition;

f) a network structure of control, authority, and communication.
The sanctions which apply to the individual's conduct in his
working role derive more from presumed community of interest
with the rest of the working organization in the survival and
growth of the firm, and less from a contractual relationship
between himself and a non-personal corporation, represented for
him by an immediate superior;

g) omniscience no longer imputed to the head of the concern;
knowledge about the technical or commercial nature of the here
and now task may be located anywhere in the network; this location
becoming the ad hoc centre of control authority and communication.

h) a lateral rather than a vertical direction of communication
through the organization, communication between people of different rank, also, resembling consultation rather than command;
i) a content of communication which consists of information
and advice rather than instructions and decisions;
j) commitment to the concern's tasks and to the 'technological
ethos' of material progress and expansion is more highly valued
than loyalty and obedience;
k) importance and prestige attach to affiliations and expertise
valid in the industrial and technical and commercial milieu
external to the firm.

It is important to realise that the two forms of system represent
a polarity not a dichotomy; there are intermediate stages
between the extremities expirically known. Also, the relation of
one form to the other is elastic, so that a concern may oscillate
between the two forms. Finally a concern may (and frequently
does) operate with a management system which includes both types.
3.3 THE DUAL SYSTEMS AT ENFIELD COLLEGE.
Using the above definitions in an attempt to classify the management system at Enfield College indicated that the two functional
streams identified in 3.1 each operated at a different point on
the scale between the two extremities. Whereas what we refer to
as the administrative (or non academic) function was biased towards
a 'mechanistic' system, the academic function showed a marked
tendency towards an 'organic' system. Whilst Burns & Stalker
accepted the existence of management systems including both
forms of control pattern, the existence of the two forms in
parallel but 'interacting streams as evidenced here appears
unusual and presents great problems when identifying the uses
to which each stream puts common information.
3.4 THE ADMINISTRATIVE STREAM.
In the administrative stream it is possible to put a hierarchial
value on composites of data which represent an informational
requirement at a particular level within the structure. These

informational requirements broadly follow two well established
concepts:

a) A filtering and refining process is applied to the information
required to serve decisions as one progresses upwards from an
operational base to the senior executive functions of planning
and control.

b) During the same progression the informational requirement
alters in content from a primarily deterministic (and internally
generated) data base to a largely probalistic (and externally
related) data content.

This identification is possible as a consequence of the mechanistic bias of the function stream, certain decision making
activities can be assigned with some confidence to particular
positions within the hierarchy, and consequently it is possible
to forsee, with reservations, the information structures which
would adequately serve the identifiable levels within the
structure.

3.5 THE ACADEMIC STREAM.

The alternate stream however, serving the academic functions of
the college, as a consequence of its bias towards the 'organic'
form poses an entirely different problem in respect of informational needs. It is difficult, even impossible, to construct
a durable model of the decision making structure within this
stream. The formal organisation chart shown in Figure 3.1 is a
valid representation of a hierarchial structure which does exist.
However, as emphasised by Burns & Stalker, the existence of a
formal hierarchy does not preclude the existence of an 'organic'
form of management system where decision making and control are
exercised by a totally different form of 'government' which does
not concur with the hierarchial formal structure. (BURNS. T.
& STALKER. G.M. 1961). This situation undoubtably exists within
the academic operating system of Enfield College, and it is a
possibility that many of the strength and the weaknesses of the
college operations stem from this situation.

3.6 THE PROBLEM OF DUALITY.

The important thing to bear in mind is the interactions and interdependance of the two streams identified. Neither one can function without the other and decisions in one have ramifications in the other. Furthermore both streams use as their base a common fund of data.

4. THE INFORMATION FLOW TO SUPPORT JOINT FUNCTIONS

An identification of the information flow to support the two functional forms of management at the college is made difficult by the different uses made of common data, and the difficulty is compounded by the imprecise model we have of the academic decision making structure. What is attempted here is an identification of the usable information form at the decision making points.

4.1 ADMINISTRATIVE MANAGEMENT

A first view of the information flow to support operations and decision making in the stream which I shall henceforth refer to as 'administrative management' as distinct from the alternate stream in future refered to as 'academic management', produced a model which is represented schematically in Figure 4.1. Certain features of this information flow and the zoning used deserve comment.

The lateral zoning into zones (a) to (d) represent an isolation of specific functions of the administrative processes - whilst these functions are recognisable as entities it is very important to realise that each of them uses information from others and passes restructured data into further zones.

The vertical zoning (1) to (5) represents both the basic processes applied to data to produce information and the levels within the hierarchial structure of decision making which the information serves. Zone (2) could be considered as one view of the data base required to support all academic management processes.

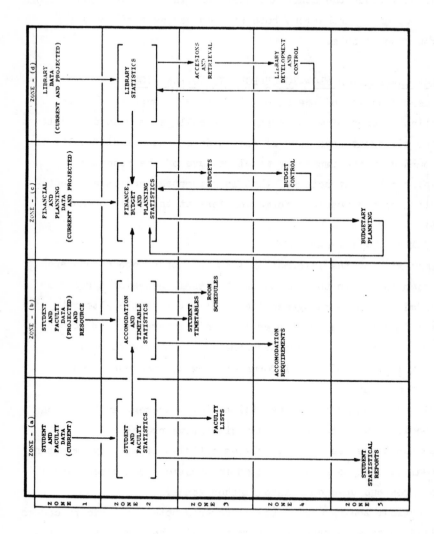

Figure 4.1   Administrative management information flow

Zones (3) to (5) equate roughly to a view of management levels
as noted by Perry Rosgrove in an earlier study of Management
Information systems (ROSGROVE. P.E. 1968). Figure 4.2 shows
these vertical levels and their integration.

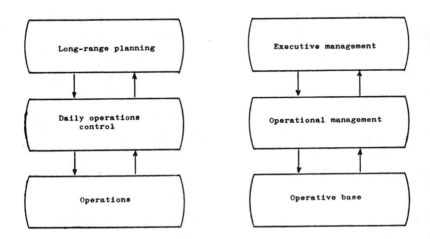

Figure 4.2   Vertical integration of functions
and management (Rosgrove.P.E 1968)

It is interesting to observe the same flow of information in
a vertical direction between Figure 4.1 and Figure 4.2.
The lateral information flow from zones (a) to (d) represent a
significant level of functional integration in which the Bursars
office and the Academic Registrar play key roles, almost all
decisions at level 4 are taken in these offices.
4.2 ACADEMIC MANAGEMENT.
It proved impossible during this brief study to construct a
realistic model of the decision making processes within the
stream of academic management. One of the major problems was

the lack of a clearly defined hierarchial pattern to the process.
I would emphasise that this should not be construed as a weakness.
As pointed out by Burns & Stalker this 'organic' structure of
management can be a source of great dynamism and professional
commitment. In the case of Enfield College many of the very
important academic strides made in the last five years, which
have resulted in some of the finest courses in the country, may be
directly attributable to this flexible 'organic' form of management. However, it has prevented the construction of a realistic
model. What has been possible is an identification of the
information elements which appear common to the majority of
decision processes, and it appears that with one notable exception is a current view of research and teaching being conducted
elsewhere on the national and international scene.

4.3 A COMMON INFORMATION BASE.

As a consequence of the study into the two management forms and
their informational requirements it appears possible to restruc-
ture the schematic of Figure 4.1 to represent a provisional
interpretation of an integrated information flow for the two
streams. This revised schematic is shown below in Figure 4.3.
This schematic indicates the interaction between the two streams
(here indicated as segments) but it has not yet proved possible
to stratify the 'academic' segment.

5. DATA ELEMENTS.

The common data base to support the diverse functions of the
two streams is not difficult to conceptualise, and a conceptual
schematic appears as Figure 5.1.

Zone 4: Resources.

Zone 4 is the very heart of the data structure because it
represents the three primary resources of higher education:
Students, faculty and facilities.

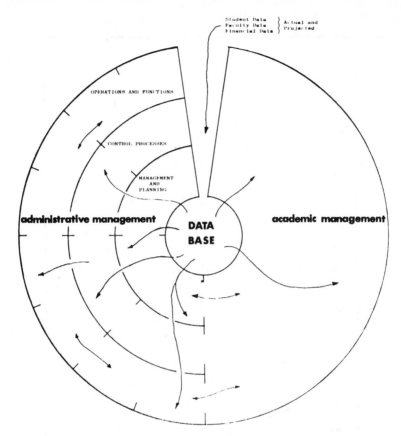

Figure 4.3   An integrated information base

Zone 3: Organization.

Some possible stratifications of data and data combinations
are represented in Zone 3.   Research in this area seems likely
to provide the linking mechanisms and coding structures for
the data base.

Zones 1 and 2: Population and Financial.

Zones 1 and 2 respresent the points of data collection, the
origins of the resources categorized in Zone 4.   It is envisaged
that these data would include both current and projected
statistics for student and manpower analysis, budgetary and
finance data would be both acutal and forecast.   It becomes
obvious that there are immediate and complex relationships
between Zones 1, 2 and 4.

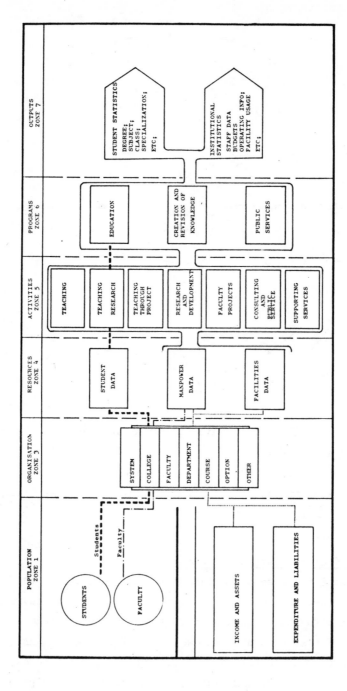

Figure 5.1 A suggested data organisation for a college data base – to support an MIS

Zone 5: Activities.

The College will inevitably seek better and more accurate methods of analysing resource allocation. Whilst the organizational data in Zone 3 will be an element in this analysis, an equally, if not more, important aspect of such analysis is a description of the uses to which its resources are put. To this end, the list of activities on Zone 5 is relevent.

Zone 6: College Programs.

This Zone sets forth the three basic programs of higher education. Theoretically all activities at the college should lend themselves to at least one of these programs, and these programs provide a further significant basis for a classification of resource utilization.

Zone 7: Outputs.

At the present time this zone is imprecisely defined. It recognises the fact that the prime object of all the other zones is to make information available to the environment, structured such as to make a maximum contribution to decision making activities at all levels of management within the college and its related bodies.

5.2 A CONCLUSION CONCERNING DATA UTILISATION.

The attempt to organise this data in a manner most applicable to the information needs of management has emphasised the importance of developing a more precise model of the decision making processes in the academic management stream. It appears that we are able to state with some degree of confidence the data required to service management, but are unable to determine at this stage how this needs to be made available to any one decision making situation.

6. FURTHER RESEARCH PROGRAM.

The study conducted this far has achieved certain limited ends, but primarily it has indicated further lines of study, some of which require a methodology which has not been available to this researcher. It has, for example, emphasised the need to construct a model incorporating a deeper understanding of the group behaviour within the stream of 'academic management'.

It is hoped to pursue this particular study in association with an experienced behavioural scientist.

A detailed study of methods for codification and classification of data elements within the general framework indicated in section 4 is now proceeding.

To date this study has proved of substantial value. It reflects the progressive views adopted by the College officers that they have supported this study in their belief that any attempt to design an M.I.S. for the college must be based on as full as possible an understanding of the information and decision making structures.

REFERENCES.

1. BURNS, T. and STALKER, G.M. 'The Management of Inevation'.
    London: Tavistock Publications Ltd., 1961.

2. EISENSTADT, S.N. 'Bureaucracy and Bureaucratisation'. In:
    'Current Sociology', 7, No 2 (Blackwell), 1958.

3. GOULDNER, A.W. 'Patterns of Industrial Bureaucracy'.
    London: Routledge, 1956.

4. MILLER, D.C. and FORM, W.A. 'Industrial Sociology'.
    New York: Harper, 1951.

5. ROSGROVE, P.E. 'Definition of an Information System'.
    In: Rosgrove, P.E. (ed) 'Developing Computer Based
    Information Systems', New York: Wiley, 1968.

6. SIMON, H.A. 'The Role of Expectation in an Adaptive or
    Behavioristic Model'. In: Bowman. (ed) 'Expectation,
    Uncertainty and Business Behavior'. New York: Social
    Science Research Council, 1958.

HUMAN FACTORS, ORGANIZATION CONTROL AND MIS

Rolf Høyer
Computing Centre, Technical University
Norway

Introduction

During the last years there has been an increasing interest in the present and future role and importance of computers in society, - in public
administration and in industry. It is emphasized that the computers will
have consequences undreamed of in most areas of our daily life, and
that the consequences will be far more difficult and unpredictable than
what we have been used to when observing introduction of new technological aids. A feature characteristic of discussions concerning these
questions is that the lay person has a feeling of fear and insecurity towards the new technology, - that the humanists regard the development
pessimistically and consider the computers potentially threatening to
vital human values, - whereas a third group, the computing personnel,
are uncomprehending of all scepticism and doggedly claim that modern
computing technique is a blessing to mankind and that all opposition is
based on ignorance.

Undoubtedly, people's general knowledge of modern computing technique
is random and incomplete, thus leading to a lot of biased discussion. However, this is probably a period of transition likely to change as computing

education is introduced in most schools. The matter to really worry about is the often extremely naive and primitive view displayed by system designers concerning the consequences of their work. In many ways, one may claim that their ignorance is much larger than that of the public as to computers, - an ignorance which might lead to dubious consequences.

It cannot be said that today there is any premeditated guidance of our progress into the computer society - we drift along in a process mainly determined from technical points of view, from what is realisable technically. One consequence of this is that the most pessimistic critics of society may turn out to be right when prophesising the situation of man in the future society. Another fact is that the system designers simply perform their work in organizations in an unqualified way, thus disqualifying themselves as experts and professionals by preserving an one-sided technical view on their work. This one-sided view is expressed in a naive conception that organizational efficiency is solely a matter of efficient and extensive computing, and that this goal can be pursued without reservations. This statement needs some further elaboration, and is below related to the concept of organizational effectiveness, a well-known topic in modern organizational theory.

Organizational effectiveness

The problems relating to work organizations taking up the use of new technological aids in their search for efficiency is one of the central aspects of modern organization theory. A topic receiving increasing interest in this connection is that in the planning process one must also consider that the technological change takes place in a human milieu, which is also heavily influenced. This milieu is functioning according to certain norms, rules, and assumptions far beyond the control areas of the planner. Accordingly, an action aimed towards improving efficiency in the shape of for instance an improved production process, a new production aid, or a computer, will have its contribution to the total organizational efficiency determined according to the degree in which the human milieu accepts the change and its consequences, and to which degree it is motivated for utilizing it according to the aims of the organization.

A large number of efficiency ventures in industrial organizations have been applied with an almost unconscious attitude towards the non-technical variables which are also being influenced. The technological optimization thereby becomes a suboptimization, which in view of the organization as a whole is far from optimal.

A very general model by Harold Leavitt will to an extent clarify this point. He states that of basic importance to the ability of the organization to fulfil its mission is the interaction of structural, technological and social systems. Due to the system properties a change in one point of the system will influence the functioning of other points, thus giving a compound effect on the total system.

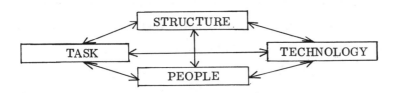

The aim of technical efficiency ventures must always be to improve the total organizational effectiveness. Since changing one variable will influence larger parts of the organizational structure, also including the social and human conditions, these factors must be evaluated as a whole. This is of importance to the organizations of today and tomorrow, since they will to an increasing degree have their viability determined by their ability of utilizing vital human qualities like creativity and responsibility of the members of the organization.

A consequence of this is that regard for, and insight into, the human conditions in connection with technological and administrative organizational changes must not necessarily be based on a solely humanistic interest, but is basically a very relevant means of furthering the interests of the organization. However, this implies a number of essential ethical questions. For example: how far may an organization permit itself to go in a deliberate attempt of eliciting self-sacrifice, cooperation, and motivation from the employees before it is rightly accused of manipulation of individuals and groups of individauls?

The computer and the organizational system

When organizations employ computers as an aid to their information- and management systems, this has consequences for the total organizational system due to the dominant influence of these systems. By extensive use of modern computing technology, a new set of system connection is thus established; i.e., between computer and the rest of the systems of the organization. These interactions influence existing systems and lead to structural changes of these. Some of these changes, mainly the most obvious ones, are planned and controlled by the system designer; however, some processes of change are often found to be neglected, in spite of the consequences thereof possibly being of vital importance to the contribution of the computing system to the total efficiency of the organization.

During the first and elementary applications of administrative computing, one aimed at automation of routine procedures in connection with bookkeeping, invoicing, etc. This heavily influenced the personnel in these departments. The new routines for work flow and new technical aids implied a change of tasks and also new working roles. Personnel unable to adjust to the new requirements dictated by the system designer had problems, and in difficult cases they were transferred to other departments. One may therefore say that in those cases the actual organizational system, also including the social systems, totally and definitely had to adjust to the computing system.

Business computing is no longer restricted to the accounting departments, but involves under more ambitious controlling systems more or less the whole technical/economic system of the organization. And while previously a small number of people were involved, consequences now arise for all employees. However, the system designer will discover that the social systems are quite able to neglect and even resist the requirements directly and indirectly formulated for adjustment, and he may also experience that his activity creates sub-effects spreading uncontrollably throughout the whole organizational system. It is dangerous that many system designers display an almost unconscious attitude towards these phenomena.

Very often system designers accuse people in the organization for lacking elementary will to collaborate under transition periods, for neglecting all rules for data discipline etc., - thus neglecting the elementary fact that maybe people generally do not share the same enthusiasm for computer systems as the systems people do. And, however, seldom the systems designers do much to improve this situation.

New technique and old-fashioned attitudes

A central feature of organization theory is a general agreement that
current organizations need to move from the traditional, hierarchic
power- and control oriented structure towards constructions oriented
towards self-realization for the employees as individuals and as members
or social groups within the organization.

For many of our organizations it is a long and difficult process to change
the mentality and motivations of the employees towards more involvement
in their working roles. One of the conditions for improvement in this area
touches some of the most well-founded conceptions of conventional administration; i.e., evaluation of the system for control and power. Motivation
cannot be forced into existence, just as one cannot hope to create enthusiasm
for a job if the employee feels distrusted and controlled in every detail of
the execution of his work.

Many investigations have proved that if the job itself seems too limited
and meaningless to the worker, his reaction will be to attempt to create
mening and challenge in the work situation by fooling and outwitting the
management and its control system, among other things by means of a
kind of "conspiration" with groups of his colleagues.

By means of a computer a control system can be designed aimed at the
single worker, able to outwit him almost completely in an instrumental
sense. Previously the worker could discover some of his activity by manipulating the extensive and often extremely confused system for reporting executed work. An automatized information system would discover
such attempts at an early stage and make management able to enforce
sanctions.

This manipulation may occur for example through production controlling systems in industry. Guidance of each production task within order-producing industries will within a few years generally be done directly (on-line) by the local computer; i.e., the single worker or worker group informs the computer via a terminal keyboard that a certain job has been executed. The computer will then search a new job suitable for the special abilities of the worker or the group, and at the same time being in accordance with the total planning system, dispatching it with orders and specifications concerning the new task. Simultaneously it controls elapsed time and resources on the previously executed job, and will inform the supervisory authority of any irregularities. All this may occur during a few seconds of computing time. This will most likely leave the employee with a feeling of powerlessness, thus leading to complete alienation to the corporate objectives and to the work situation.

Therefore, a modern computing system used in production control under a management philosophy which is old-fashioned and traditional, will in the long run do much harm to the entire organization system. This is the case in company milieus where the management gives priority to control rather than to cooperation. It is worth noting here that the management philosophy which is built into the computer system, often to a high degree stems from the personal opinions of the system designer. This because of communication problems between management and systems department.

Hence management philosophy will in a way be transformed through the design of the application programs.

A statement not quite unusual for current management philosophy is: "In principle, we agree to develop new patterns of management and develop more extensive form of cooperation based on delegation of responsibility and sound relations between management and employees. However, first we must of course secure order and complete control of the utilization of our resources, for instance of the efforts of the employees...."

Computers will definitely be efficient means of providing such control, but one must realize that they are also new and more efficient moves against the unsatisfied and frustrated employees. A move creating further resistance, which in its turn demands further control, and so on in a spiral destructive to both parts.

The problem of ACCEPTANCE: Interaction man - machine

Another factor important to efficient utilization of a computing system is to which degree it is accepted as a meaningful tool by the people who are going to use it.

Most people with a minimum of technical inclination will accept using aids which they feel will increase their capacity of solving meaningful tasks. An operator of a large, modern shovel-dozer appears to enjoy and take a greater interest in his work than his colleague still digging the earth with spade and wheel-barrow. Another example: In Norway, SAS ticket attendants use a computerized seat reservation system. By means of terminals they communicate with the central computer of the company in Copenhagen; exchanging information concerning reservations, etc. These attendants appear to the author not to have developed particularly negative attitudes towards the job and towards the clients compared to those working for the local airline company, Braathen, behind the neighbouring counter, who have to manage with manual routines. In fact, they appear rather to take a certain pride in being able to offer the customer extra service through the system.

Both of these examples deal with individuals who obviously have realized the meaningfulness and importance of their new technical devices as an integral part of the job. Although the SAS attendant only has a vague feeling of the ingenious program system serving him, this is insignificant to him, just as the shovel-dozer operator considers it quite natural that only a special service garage is authorized to check the complicated hydraulic systems of his machine. But if this feeling of meaningfulness is lacking, efficiency efforts will frequently meet passive resistance, simply because man may manifest himself through resistance. For instance, it would be naive to expect a lathe operator doing monotonous and boring work to show enthusiasm when his old machine with a 100 units per hour capacity is exchanged, solely because the new one has a capacity of 500.

The same effects may appear in a production control system and other management systems if the employees are unable to realize immediately that the computer offers them a new and efficient tool for increasing their competence when executing a task. And it would be really bad if they get a feeling of being subordinate to a machine system used for accomplishing a more efficient control of the individual and his output in the production context. An excessive control truly is perceived badly enough in a manual system, - but being controlled in detail by a machine will be unbearable in the long run.

Consequences for the formal and informal organization structure

When an organization starts using a computer in its management system, some significant changes in the formal organization are usually necessary. Changes in the formal structure imply changes in the informal one as well, both influencing the corresponding role structure of the individuals involved. If the changes are more than marginal, the individuals will perceive a situation of strain.

These strains are particularly heavy if the new situation is uncertain; i.e.,
it is not covered by previous experience, and the new role expectations
are indistinct. The strains, psycological in nature, are often felt very
unpleasantly and may, if the situation lasts for some time, also lead to
alienation of the situation and abandoning efforts to solve the problem.
This may be manifested by the individual either leaving the organization,
or he may be staying, but without desires of organizational integration.
Passive resistance and irrational behaviour are common effects.

The strain connected to a transition period is depending on many factors.
One may observe a rich variety of situations, ranging from smooth and
efficient change, to situations where new systems must be abandoned or
totally redesigned. Also within the same department some people experience serious problems, while others are motivated for the change and
quickly establish new and stable stuctures.

A general conclusion one may draw from the few research findings available, is that the implementation problems of a new system are more dependent on how the change is introduced, than on the system properties
themselves. In this connection factors like education, training, and support
are of central importance. Until now, most administrative computing has
taken place in limited parts of the organization, for instance accounting
departments, where the system designer has been authorized to redesign
the work routines completely. Great concern had to be given to train low
level employees to use new, expensive equipment correctly and to define
their jobs and responsibilities, this being an obvious necessity to make
the system operational at all. The work roles were then very clear to the
employees, this being a primary condition for developing a stable situation
with a new informal structure.

The cases where problems occur are frequently found among the first line supervisors of the accounting department. As a result of the complete change in procedures and work flow of the department, the professional roles of the medium level must also be changed. But these professional roles are difficult to determine immediately, both regarding duties and responsibilities. A common feature is that the professional duties change from being a control function distributing work, to work more characterized by problem solving, e.g., assistance in interpreting error listing from the computer (in connection with erroneously registered transactions) when the lower personnel is unable to find out themselves. The work will also include a larger degree of planning and system maintenance.

However, even when the professional role structure has been established, problems may arise. The medium level personnel conceive of their new role patterns in quite a different way than their subordinates, a conflict which may create considerable problems of cooperation.

So far the accounting departments. Today administrative data processing has grown out of the clerks' office, entering most essential company functions as production, sales, distribution, etc., thus creating the MIS-concept. The systems designers then find themselves operating on the total organization, involving 10-100 times the number of people they dealt with in the accounting department. People they no longer know, people they do not see. And they find themselves in a situation where the human interface to the organization system consists of higher management, and communicating with the rest of the organization mainly through their systems.

Presently, very little systematic experience is generally available on transition problems, in ambitious and comprehensive MIS projects. But experiences from more simple projects in the past decade, together with general knowledge from organization theory, may justify the following elaboration on formal and informal organization structure.

In departments employing the computer for planning and control, for instance production departments, the dilemma of the medium level also has relevance. This indicates that by implementing computerized production control in industry, it is essential that the supervisors have their professional roles defined as early as possible. One condition for solving this problem is that extensive and adequate education is given regarding the new system for production control. The best results are probably achieved when the personnel themselves take part in the planning of the new system.

For the individual worker in the production context another type of problem may arise. His professional duties are not necessarily changed as a result of the computer controlled production system. His direct professional role is constant, since in principle it makes no difference whether his orders come from (and he has to report to) a computer or a supervisor. In a computer aided production system it may well be imagined that due to the faster and more integrated scheduling, better utility of the abilities of each worker may be achieved by directly assigning him to the individual jobs. This is of particular interest when the production process is disturbed and revised assignment is urgently necessary. Existing work groups based on accepted and established task distribution and cooperation patterns are broken, thereby also breaking up established social relations between the employees. Large parts of the existing informal organization are demolished, and restructuring may be difficult to accomplish if the new production system is planned solely from the needs of technology, - in this case the computer. One may then easily run into a situation in principle equal to that of production departments which are completely based on ordinary assembly line technology. The typical aspect of the informal organization in this situation is that the technology renders it impossible to create groups, which is undoubtedly unfortunate as the personnel is unable to satisfy elementary social needs.

Information system and organization control

A steadily increasing part of systems development work is aimed at increasing the efficiency of the control or guidance systems of the organization. Much of the documented work, however, does not qualify for this ambitious goal. Merely putting together more or less arbitrary summary tables from operating computing systems for ordinary administrative routines will hardly improve radically the organizational control. The system work for a control system must instead be based on an extensive survey of the relevant goals or objectives for the various functions of the organization. The relevant need for information can only be derived from the decisions influencing the attainment of these goals.

Both theoretical analysis and practical experience show that a final clarification of the goal structure of an organization will never be reached. But the quality of the objectives on different levels may be constantly improved, thus offering a basis for a more systematic organizational control.

Two of the vital requirements of the goal structure are consistency and acceptability. By consistency we mean that the objectives on one level are formulated in order to contribute to the objectives on higher levels. Acceptability means that those persons whose activities influence the satisfaction of the objectives agree with them, that they realize their meaning, and are motived for pursuing them. Or, as formulated by B. Langefors

[1968]: "We have even found it necessary to take into consideration the possibility of the decision makers deciding according to their personal objectives, so that the control of decisions made on the top level, will depend on the possibility of either making them find out that if they make decisions according to assigned objectives, their own are favoured; or making them consider the objectives of the organization their own."

Current industrial organization research also indicates that acceptance of, and knowledge of, the goals of the organization is a condition of employee commitment. Thorsrud [1969] states: "The major part of available research results indicates that the more each individual is able to control his own duties and to see his contribution in connection with that of his co-workers, the more apt he will be to adapt a positive attitude. This positive attitude will manifest itself in various ways, which are of fundamental importance to a democratic milieu." [p.13]; and more explicitly about the goal of his cooperation research project: "Under which concrete conditions of work is it possible to diminish the feeling among the employees that they are not part of, or not engaged in, the objectives and activity of the organization?" [p.16]. Some people claim that this problem may be solved through efficient information on all levels, but practical experience always has shown that this alone by no means provides for a successful result. On the contrary, the inefficiency of the internal information system in organizations is often astonishing.

A radical improvement can hardly be expected before employees on all levels are offered, and experience, a possibility of themselves being able to influence upon the actual objectives. Only that way can the corporate objectives be realistic, which means that they are compatible with the individual goals and even influence upon them. Taking part in determination of goals is also a factor contributing to true engagement among employees for the organization and its problems. It is then the duty of the management to create consistency between goals of groups of people and of departments to the benefit of the whole organization, - in the extreme sense to create an organized anarchy, as expressed by some organization researchers. This effort of coordination, one of the prime duties of management (which was previously effectuated through absolute directives, compulsion and sanctions) must occur to a large degree through the information system of the organization. New elements here are distribution of information of the goals concerning objectives which are agreed upon, and information offering each employee and groups of employees possibilities of seeing their work as a meningful contribution to the total activity of the organization. This implies among other things that they are also given information about conditions in interfacing units of the organizational system, particularly where strong technological connections and dependencies exist. This is of paramount importance when workers are urged to maintain critical quality standards along a production line or in a continuous process, where the work of different groups interfere. The vital importance of information systems is also stressed by motivation researchers. Thorsrud [1969] claims in principle that: ".. Experience indicates that a technology characterized by automation and computers will imply that traditional technological differences tend to disappear. The problem will then be to achieve larger personal participation in systems dealing with information handling" [p.13].

Accordingly, one must conclude that organizational researchers (Thorsrud), management scholars (Langefors), as well as progressive organization leaders stress the central importance of the information system in modern organizational development. But one common aspect is that most of them are not particularly explicit when formulating how the information systems should be designed in detail. Then the system designers, the computing personnel, are left with a tremendous responsibility, because the way they construct and implement their systems, will be the key factor in realizing the modern principles of management. The system designers are thus faced with extremely challenging problems, the results of which are vital to the future existence of the organizations.

The image of the system designer as solely a technical expert is out of date

This expanded description of the duties of the system designer is important for his perspective and his role in the organizational milieu. Above all, his formerly established role as solely technical expert is no longer adequate. Obviously, an extensive change of mentality and new competence will presently be required. A large part of the system work done today has evidently only one limitation, namely, what is technically feasible. Already in 1960 I.R. Hoos criticized the system designers for their square and unrealistic attitude to factors not explicitly of a technical character. On basis of studies of automation in office work in 19 large American companies, she summed up some of her experiences in Harvard Business Review: "This failure to recognize the worker's point of view typifies most EDP executives in firms I have studied. Their replies to questions about personnel problems generally reveal great ambivalence. On the one hand, they are extremely sensitive about such matters as displacement, and are quick to say that EDP causes no job losses... Usually, they try to uphold the untenable and selfcontradictory proposition that EDP affects systems, but not jobs."

10 years of development in computing is a long time. Today we operate subject to a technology quite different from the one prevalent at the time of Hoos' research. The question is whether we, in attitude and knowledge,

222

are particularly different from the computing personnel of the late 50's in this field. A factor intensifying the situation is that the current problems are no longer solved only by being intuitively sensitive towards the requirements of the social systems - the system designer of today is faced with the most vital problems within modern organizational development and management, and this requires systematic knowledge and competence. The era of intuition is over in management.

It is doubted whether any radical improvement can be expected in this field until the educational system becomes more formalized and extensive, and, above all, may be based on scientific theory and research. Even today the academic activity is mainly aimed at the purely computer related problems. Generally, the problem areas of administrative computing may be divided into three groups, all of which ought to be covered in education systems for computing:

1) The purely computer oriented problem area. The internal organization of programs and files in the computer system.

2) The incorporation of the computer in the technical/economic systems of the organization. - Design of computerized information systems integrated in an analytically specified and systematized control process.

3) The adjustment of the computer in the social systems of the organization. - Problems in connection with interaction between the automatized information system and the human being and groups of human beings.

Not until this third problem area has been recognized and investigated will it be possible to design information systems which can support the organizational development movements currently under way.

References

Elizeur, D.   : A Structural Analysis of Behaviour in Organiza-
                       tions towards the Computer. Avanti-Zaltbommel,
                       The Netherlands, 1969.

Hoos, I.R.   : When the Computer Takes Over the Office.
                       Harvard Business Review, 4., 38, 1960.

Høyer, R.   : Organisasjonen, Datamaskinen og Individet.
                       (Organization, Computers, and the Individual.)
                       IB-ABD-rapp. Inst. för Informationsbehandl.
                       KTH, Stockholm, 1969

Langefors, B.   : System för Företagsstyrning. (Systems for
                       Corporate Control.) Studentlitteratur, Stockholm,
                       1968.

Thorsrud, E.   : Mot en ny bedriftsorganisasjon. Eksperimenter
                       i industrielt demokrati fra Samarbeidsprosjektet
                       LO/NAF. (Towards a new Corporate Organization.
                       Experiments in Industrial Democracy.) Tanum,
                       Oslo, 1969.

Part 2 – System Design

THE EVALUATION OF MANAGEMENT INFORMATION SYSTEMS

Charles H. Kriebel
Carnegie-Mellon University
USA

1. Introduction and Overview

In the spring of 1968 Professor Herbert A. Simon delivered the Karl
Taylor Compton lectures at the Massachusetts Institute of Technology
on "the sciences of the artificial" -- cf. Simon (1969). At the risk of
oversimplification, Simon's thesis in these lectures was that certain
phenomena are artificial in a very specific sense: they are as they are
only because a system has been molded, by goals or purposes, to the
environment in which it lives. By way of contrast, the scientific disciplines have traditionally concerned natural phenomena: how they are
and how they work. Today, one also observes studies of artificial phenomena: how to make artifacts that have desired properties and how to
design.

What is the process called "design"? Is it art or science? In simple terms:
design is decision making. It involves finding alternatives to change existing situations into preferred situations. For the engineer's analogy of the
black box, it concerns re-configuring the interval environment of the box,
so that given inputs yield desired outputs. The problem focus in design is
the interface between the natural laws within a system and the natural laws

without it. A designer is concerned with attaining goals by adapting characteristics of the former to the latter, and the process by which the
adaptation of means to environments is brought about. If this process is
unique to an individual and cannot be promulgated, the design is art. If
through research and understanding, however, we establish normative
principles to guide the process and can teach these rudiments to practi-
tioners, then we may speak of a "science of design." (To quote a French
scholar: "Art is I. Science is we.") Today, the discipline of design has
emerged as an "artificial science" in common with such professions as
engineering, architecture, medicine, law and management.

During the past decade, the phrase "management information systems" or
the acronym "MIS" has become increasingly popular for discussions of information processing support for management activities. The phrase in
one sense is more descriptive of the end-user's goals for the information
system (computer-based and otherwise) than the earlier terminology of
"business data processing". For convenience here, I forgot a discussion
of the etymology and semantics of MIS, and will assume the phrase is
synonymous with the several near equivalents appearing in the literature.

Much has been written on the subject of MIS, particularly on the process
of system design, development and implementation. Indeed, most introductory textbooks provide flowcharts in an early chapter of each stage in
systems development -- often including "cookbook" recipes and checklists
of "do's and don'ts", occasionally documented by the author's personal
experiences. Since these flowcharts are commonplace and reasonably consistent, there is no need to reproduce them. Rather in the space of this
essay, I wish to consider one aspect of the design and development process, namely: the milestone called evaluation. In particular, given a conceptual model of the design process that involves goal-directed search:

What does the literature propose on MIS evaluation? What is being done in practice? What is the state-of-the art today?

2. The problem: Information Economics

The issue of evaluation is conceptually straightforward. That is, one seeks to observe and measure output (results) within the framework of some "model" which describes the system environment (and interface) in terms of available resources, their capacities, given inputs, and cri- teria of performance on stated goals. As a technical matter one would optimize the performance criteria, or at least for any pairwise compa- rison of alternatives prefer the one which was more efficient under the stipulated measure of performance. Such a decision paradigm may be relatively easy, say, for the engineering consideration of a piece of ca- pital equipment; e.g., most accountants would employ a net-present-value criterion for the discounted "cash flow" of dollars associated with the investment. The decision becomes more difficult, however, when the investment involves a configuration of general purpose resources and the end-use alternatives of the resources must be included within the evalua- tion.

Information theory in communications engineering provides a formal frame- work for measuring the quantity of information and communications effi- ciency, cf Hartley (1928) or Shannon and Weaver (1948). In simple terms information theory is concerned with the activities of a "source" who en- codes a message, a "communications channel" which transmits the coded message, and a "receiver" who decodes the message upon receipt. As such the theory says nothing about the activities of either the "source" or the "receiver" outside the stated symbol processing system and, more specifically, it tells nothing of the value of the message communicated to the end user. (For example, was it "Mary had a little lamb" or "We are at war"?)

Decision theory in economics and statistics provides a formal framework for measuring the value of information to a decison maker, cf Wald (1950) or Raiffa (1968). In its simplest form, the decision theory model postulates an individual who must select a terminal action on the basis of either current information of additional information he can purchase, the outcome payoff being a function of the action selected and an uncertain event outside his control. This single-person model has been generalized under certain restrictive assumptions on behaviour to multi-person organizations through a framework called "the theory of team" cf Marschak (1955) and Radner (1962). More recently, Marschak has attempted to link the team decision model with the communications model of information theory, in effect, by preceding the "source" with an "observer" and following the "receiver" with a "decision-maker", cf Marschak (1968) and Chapter 3 in Kriebel, et al (1970). Other variations of the classical decision theory model are also beginning to appear in the literature of contemporary economics.[1]

The important aspect of this literature, irrespective of modeling details, is that decision theory provides the relevant theorem on information economics for system evaluation. Specifically, the expected value of information to a manager (i.e., decision maker), is computed from the expected net gain (benefits less cost) of his decision rule (strategy) including the information less the rule excluding that information, where mathematical expectations are calculated on a rational basis according to a priori pro-

---

1) For example, see the Program and Abstracts of Papers: Second World Congress of the Econometric Society (8-14 September 1970; Cambridge, England), particularly pages 47, 60, 95, 104, 120, 166, 187, and 215.

babilities. That is, information has value if its expected net gain is positive when computed according to the algorithm. To implement the theorem management must structure the decision problem such that the decision mechanism or rule for choosing terminal actions is made explicit, the space of outcomes is specified and ranked in order of preference (payoff), and information opportunities on uncertainties are encoded in terms of probability distributions. Do these requirements effectively preclude application of the procedure in any complex real world environment?

In general, I think the answer to this question is: no. Certainly, the broad principle of positive expected value is rational and consistent with our ex ante intuition. Furthermore, for many non-trivial situations -- if not at the "total MIS" level, perhaps -- the computations and analysis can be performed exactly. More broadly, however, it is important to recognize that the comparative gains of technology in information processing have been realized only by formal information systems in organizations. That is, the orders of magnitude increase in data processing efficiencies have been realized over the past decade through capital-intensive technology applied to formalized systems. In contrast, informal information systems which tend to be labor-intensive have not been affected by the economies and leverage of computers. For the foreseeable future, the demand for information processing capacity by managers and organizations appears ever increasing. To expand the supply and ability to service these demands will require increasing reliance on formal information systems and capital-based technology. Thus, the management information systems that we seek to design and evaluate will require specificity and explicit statements of decision mechanisms, uncertainty encoding, and the like, to the degree that they become formalized. To this degree, I think the decision theory construct for information value serves as a useful criteria in design.

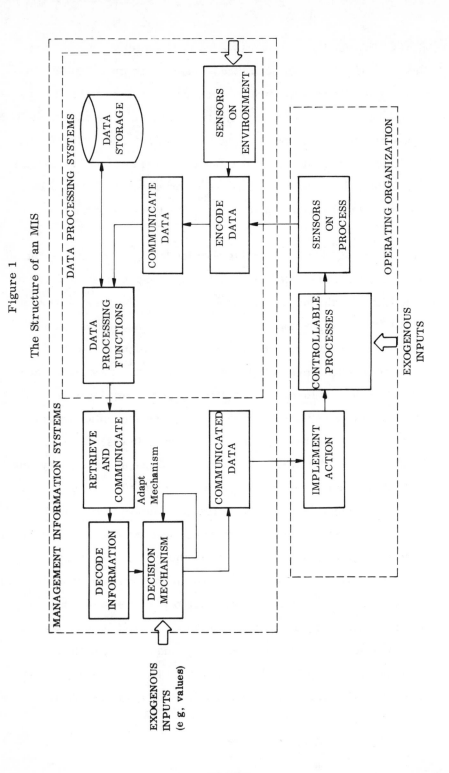

Figure 1

The Structure of an MIS

Maybe, I have overstated the case for theory in making the point for economic relevance. Certainly, the task of incorporating a representative characterization of the technology into a formal model is a major hurdle in evaluation, and many non-economic factors will influence the final design. For example, Figure 1 might be considered as one macro-flowchart which diagrams the "bare bones" structure of an MIS. Without dwelling on the details of the illustration, it is apparent that people are prominently involved as symbol processors in many stages of the cycle, and behavioral considerations will often dominate given situations. Figure 1 also highlights the sub-system role of data processing technology within the broader designation of a formal MIS. At this juncture it may be constructive to briefly consider the problem of evaluating the technological component of an MIS before returning to the broader issue.

3. The Evaluation of Information Processing Technology

Progress in building information processing hardware has far outdistanced progress in evaluating the performance of this technology in systems. As Sharpe (1969) recently remarked in his excellent book, it is one thing to write out a series of equations which purport to functionally describe a computer configuration, its another matter to obtain the true parameters and functions which pertain to an actual configuration.

For example, Henderson (1960) proposed an integer linear programming formulation of the problem of data processing design for an organization. In Henderson's model data requirements, report content and interrelations, data flows, processing capacities and technological constraints, etc were to be specified in the form of constraints and the linear criterion function of net benefits was to be maximized. Perhaps not too surprisingly, Henderson's model was not empirically-based and included the additional caveat that as presented the model was too large for existing (1960) computers and known linear-integer programming algorithms -- the latter qualification is still true today. [1] Similar linear programming models for computer selection have also appeared in the literature, e.g., Schneidewind (1966), where the criterion is cost minimization subject to given performance constraints. To date, the prospects for a completely objective model, such as LP, as a solution procedure do not appear particularly promising. Beyond the computational problem, the biggest obstacle appears to be the likelihood that the user (designer) can capture all of the interrelations and empirical measurements needed for a "statement" of performance requirements. For example, consider the difficulty of specifying the requisite detail for the factors listed in Table 1. A survey of other formalized models for design and evaluation is provided in Kriebel (1967) -- se also Sharpe (1969), Chapters 8-11.

At the opposite extreme of the completely "objective" mathematical model of the total system is the subjective approach, perhaps exemplified by "Competitive bidding". As commonly practiced today, the user effectively delegates the computer configuration design to the manufacturer by first preparing a "statement" of system requirements and then soliciting competitive bids from vendors on various system alternatives. In this regard the user may attempt to employ one of several informal decision models for the cost/value evaluation of proposals. For example, (1) the user specifies minimum performance and selects the minimum cost system proposed;

---

1) Note the reference here is not a criticism of Henderson's model, per se; to the contrary his research was an early and immaginative delination of the design problem.

Tabel 1

DIMENSIONS OF SYSTEM REQUIREMENTS STATEMENT AND
CONSTRAINTS

WORKLOAD: Applications
      Processing Functions
        Inputs, Compilation, Computation, Control Data
        Acquisition, File Maintenance, Media Conversion,
        Sorting, Storage and Retrieval, Outputs, Proces-
        sing Frequencies, Security/Privacy, Relative
        Priorities
      Development/Implementation Schedules
      Working Programs
      Production Operations Constraints
        Data Volumes, Thruput, Turn-around Times,
        Response Times, User Priorities, Physical
        Space
      Etc.

HARDWARE: Units
        Channels, Control Units, Direct-access Devices,
        Storage, Tape/Disk/Drum Drives, Processors,
        Terminals, Unit Record Devices
      Interfaces
        External Communication Networks, Man/Machine
        Interface, Other Computers, Recording Media

SOFTWARE: Source Language, Object Language
      System Functions, Supervisory Programs, Data
      Management, File Design, Task Control

SYSTEM ORGANIZATION:
      Conventional batch processing, Multiprocessing (Direct
      coupled Many Processors), Multiprogramming (Multi-
      tasking, Telecommunications, Multiple-access)
      Compatibility

DATA REPRESENTATION
PERSONNEL
OPERATIONS ORGANIZATION AND ADMINISTRATION
EDUCATION AND TRAINING
POLICY AND PROCEDURES
MANAGEMENT INTERFACE
ETC.

(2) the user specifies maximum cost and selects the maximum performance system proposed; or (3) the user specifies minimum performance and maximum cost, and selects the system having the maximum value/cost ratio, employing tie-breaking rules if necessary. A completely subjective procedure for the "competitive bid" approach suffers from all the obvious weaknesses of human judgment and error, conflict of interest with other goals, bias, inefficiencies, and so on. The "statement" of requirements in this case, if not as rigorous as implied by the total system model, must nevertheless attend to many of the same issues listed in Table 1. Furthermore, the imposition of any single rigid measure of performance and/or requirement for performance as a short-cut to the complete specification is almost assured to lead to a sub-optimal (and perhaps grossly inferior) result. For example, consider the relative uselessness of a single performance index for a computer, say "cycle time", as a basis for system evaluation. One concludes from experience that some middle ground between the complete model and a subjective procedure is more likely to lead to preferred and realistic results.

Pursuing the middle ground to technology evaluation the most common objective methods employed to guide a subjective decision process include: figures of merit, scoring systems, or instruction mixes; kernel timing estimates; (so-called) benchmark programs; and simulations. The first method may range from a fairly simple expression (such as: maximize the log {memory size/cycle time}) for performance of alternative hardware, to more lengthy formulas which subjectively weight non-hardware characteristics (such as, adaptability, supplier support, and so on) --
cf, Solomon (1966), Bromley (1965), Arbuckle (1966) and Knight (1963). Although relatively simple to use the difficulty with these methods lies in their highly subjective specification and myopic view of the larger problem. For example, through such a formula, one can obtain the result

that doubling the capacity of high speed core will double the thruput of a system -- which is absurd.

Kernel timing estimates are often employed for cost comparison among computers to perform a given task. Calingaert (1967) defines a program kernel as "the central processor coding required to execute a task of the order of magnitude of calculating a social security tax, inverting a matrix, or evaluating a polynomial". In comparing estimates one assumes equal efficiency and sophistication of the coding in assembly language for the various machine alternatives, cf IBM (1965). Benchmark programs differ from kernels in that they typically represent programs (or problems) which exist on a current system and for which execution times are desired on a proposed system. Alternatively, the Auerbach Corporation considers six benchmark problems for evaluation purposes: updating sequential files; updating files on random-access storage, sorting, matrix inversion, evaluation of complex equations, and statistical computations, cf Hillegass (1966). The final extension of replicating "representative" data processing workloads or requirements is to employ simulation. In addition to in-house or proprietary simulators several commercially packaged simulations have appeared on the market. A summary of the characteristics of three such packages is shown in Table 2; see Bairstow (1970), While simulation packages represent advance stage models they still suffer from the subjectivity of requirements specifications by the user (customer), they may present biased results, and, as indicated by Table 2, the commercial packages are relatively expensive.

Evaluating hardware technology -- the central processor, peripherals, and configuration alternatives -- is complex, but the inclusion of software performance considerably adds to the scope of the problem, cf Calingaert (1967). Even though the "unbundling decision" by the key manufacturers last year

Table 2

REPRESENTATIVE COMMERCIAL PACKAGES OF SIMULATORS FOR COMPUTER SYSTEM EVALUATION

PROGRAM	CASE	SAM	SCERT
NAME:	Computer-Aided System Evaluation	System Analysis Machine	System and Computer Evaluation and Review Technique
COMPANY:	Computer Learning and Systems Corp 5530 Wisconsin Ave.	Applied Data Research Route 206 Center Princeton, N.J. 08540	Comress 2 Research Court Rockville, Md. 20850
COSTS:			
Purchase	$ 50,000	Not for sale	Not for sale
Lease (Monthly)	$ 3,000 (1 yr. min.)	$ 3,500 (3 mo. min.)	$ 1,000–3,000 (1 yr. min.)
Single Study	$ 4,000 and up	$ 5,000 and up	$ 5,000 and up
Analyst support	$ 250/day	$ 250/day (after 10 days)	$ 250/day
EDUCATION:	$ 1,000 for 10 man-days (includes 10 man-days of analyst support)	5 man-days free	$ 500 for 10 man-days
SYSTEM:			
Available on	360/50, GE 600, CDC 6000	360/50	360/40 (and up), Univac 1108
Core needed	200K	225K	110K
Written in	Fortran	Fortran	Assembler
DATE AVAILABLE:	1969	To be released	1964

to price hardware and software separately appeared at first glance to simplify some of these issues, the software marketplace is still a morass of confusion. For example, during the past few years a major consideration in software design and development for MIS has been the appearance of "data (file) management systems" or "generalized data base management systems"; e.g. Byrnes and Steig (1969), and Fry and Gosden (1969). In broad terms, data management software is intended to de-couple the user from the technical details of the hardware in interfacing with a data bank; as such, it may be characterized as an extension of programming language capability for data manipulation. Today, however, there are more than fifty such software systems commercially available (cf, CODASYL, May 1969) to the bewildered customer, each offering a variety of features and approaches to data management, with relatively little hope (cf CODASYL, October 1969) for commonality or standards in the foreseeable future.

Beyond specific software technology, trends over the past decade strongly indicate that the largest cost element of systems is "people." Figure 2 summarizes the proportionate cost distribution since 1957 and projects the likely ratio for 1972. While relative costs are fairly easy to extrapolate is is clear from industrial experience that cost estimates for application projects, particularly personnel cost estimates, are usually poor and biased downwards. (e.g., see Laska (1970) for some unfortunate case histories). Thus, one concludes that the state-of-the-art in evaluating system technology today is still very subjective and to some degree the dark art of "magic". As a science there is much need for empirical research -- for those interested in more extensive bibliographies see Buchholz (1969) and the Metametrics Corporation (1969), as well as earlier citations. Rather than despair the issue entirely, it might be argued with caution that technological evaluation is not the crux of the problem in MIS. Indeed the management potential of a particular system application may provide benefits of a magnitude that overwhelm the need for a detailed appraisal of tech-

Figure 2

TREND COMPARISON OF COMPUTER SYSTEM COST DISTRIBUTION
IN TYPICAL COMPANY

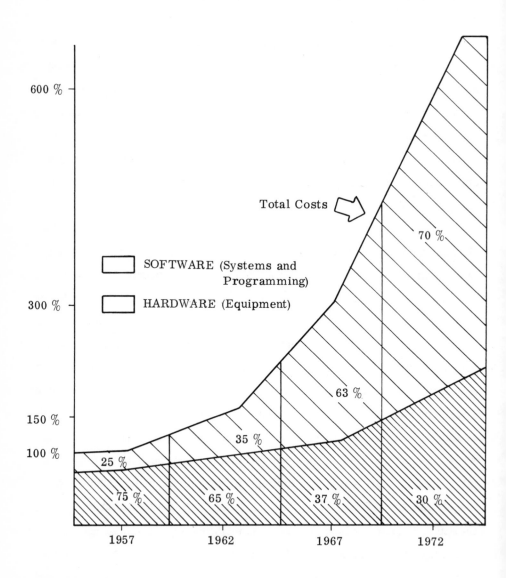

nological costs. Why sub-optimize the technological design when the primary considerations in MIS are <u>management</u> opportunities?

4. MIS Evaluation: The State-of-the Art

Perhaps the most important lesson of the past decade in the field of MIS has been the maxim that the relative success of a system application is a direct function of the participation by management in its design and development. McKinsey (1968) recently summarized this fact in an international survey of industrial corporations, by noting three dimensions of management system performance: technical feasibility, economic feasibility and operational feasibility. The third dimension, conspicuously absent in system failures, roughly translates into the requirement that the developed system be understood and used by managers. Given that a system (application) has successfully met the tests of technical and economic feasibility, "will managers adapt to the system, or will they resist or ignore it?" By analogy with Professor Churchman's (1968) perspective on "systems analysis," the principals involved in design and development, technicians and managers, must be sensitive to each other's value system -- they should try to see the world through one another's eyes. Having acquired this "sensitivity," they should put their relative expertise in perspective.

Within a large organization computer and data processing staff can be expected to possess a reasonable degree of technical competence, given educational and experience credentials. Staff technicians, however, rarely possess the broad guage focus of line management in understanding the economic and environmental factors critical for the particular organization's successful enterprise.

241

One approach to the goals and criterion problem is to seek a general
strategy statement from management for information systems design
and development, e.g., Kribel (1968). Another technique, that has received
acceptance in a variety of forms, is illustrated by the so-called "Study
Organization Plan (SOP)" of IBM (1963). In brief SOP approaches a systems
study in three phases: (1) understanding the present business, (2) determining system requirements, and (3) designing the new system. The first
phase of the study seeks a detailed description of the "present business"
through an economic analysis which includes: history and framework, industry background, firm goals and objectives, firm policies and practices,
government regulations, products and markets, materials and suppliers,
and resources (facilities, personnel, inventory, and financial). This description is then summarized into a list of "activities" which are costed.
Phase 2 of SOP analyzes the goals and objectives, economics, and procedure of execution for each activity in terms of input-output requirements
in operational detail . The final phase of SOP develops specific recommendations and plans for introducing a new business system. IBM gives five
criteria for choosing activities as automatic data processing candidates,
viz.: (1) Dominant performance criteria (e.g., response time to customer
inquiry). (2) High affectable dollar savings. (3) Large data processing size
(e.g., volumes). (4) Inefficiencies. (5) Management preference. The "technique" includes some welldesigned forms to assist conduct of the study at
each phase, and although the ideas are not "new" the logic is well-founded
and useful in practice.

In the absence of a direct policy statement by management or an extensive
economic analysis of "the business", perhaps the most important index of
the relative worth of a system application is the criticality of the activity
to the organization. Sometimes the index can be measured directly, e.g.,
cost savings or profitability; however, often it is a function of surrogate

measures. The role of surrogates as proximate criteria of performance may often be the only alternative available to the designer, particularly, if the system application is not <u>directly</u> tied to a management activity -- e.g., file maintenance. Surrogate criteria can also serve in performing a "dominance analysis" of the attributes or properties of design alternatives, in lieu of a uni-dimensional objective function. For example, the development of proximate criteria can serve to establish bounds and constraints on the search for design alternatives in much the same manner as a consumer product testing organization's report of "best buys" for household items. In this regard the decision theory criterion may provide a useful guideline for directing search.

It is clear today that the magnitude of the problem of MIS evaluation is going to grow during the nex decade and beyond. In the late 1950's and early 1960's clerical displacement, cost reduction and control of administrative expense were the primary criteria applied to management data processing system proposals. The direction and scope of MIS has long since left the domain of administrative and accounting applications. Last year Diebold (1969) projected a time frame for applications and evaluation criteria over the next 15 years. These forecasts are summarized in Table 3. Referring to the criteria column in the table, it is clear that during the next decade management and policy makers are going to face some serious questions if these projections are to materialize by applications area.

5. Conclusions

The development of management information systems has come a long way in the last ten years, heralded much by advances in technology. The computer, however, has been an expensive "fad" in companies where manage-

Table 3

PROJECTION OF CRITERIA USED IN EVALUATION OF MIS (Diebold, 1969)

DATE	SYSTEM GENERATION	MANAGEMENT APPLICATION	EVALUATION CRITERIA
1964	Second	Administration and Accounting	Clerical Displacement; cost reduction; control
1968	Third	Supervisory Information	Reduction in inventories; reduction in cash balance; personnel stability; customer relations; vendor/buyer relations; cost control
1975	Third + and Fourth	Middle Management and Tactical Planning	Optimum marketing budget; return on short-term portfolios; improved negotiating position; improved vendor performance; optimum use of plant; improved shipping schedules; more realism in forecasting
1985	Fifth	Top management and Strategic Planning	Product planning; capital requirements; labor and materials planning; resource planning; transportation and inventory planning.

ment has not taken the time to become involved in the process of MIS design. The milestone called "evaluation" is the most conspicuous and weakest stage in this process today. The techniques available and those employed for evaluation need much improvement. Perhaps as responses to this need for the short run are two industry trends. The first trend in evidence is the emergence within large corporations of the computer/information systems department as a "profit center" -- in some cases incorporated as a subsidiary, selling services to outside customers, as well. The second development is the appearance of software companies with the facilities to sell an MIS package (not limited to data management software) to a customer organization. The vendor in this case contracts a fixed-price-plus-maintenance agreement for design, development, implementation, and in some cases continuing operation (i.e., on the vendor's equipment or under an installation management arrangement). I think both trends are in the right direction, but represent only an interim solution to the evaluation issue. The time when a large computer installation is "justified" on the basis on intangibles alone is passed. There will be increasing pressure to evaluate MIS proposals on their economic potential -- though not on administrative cost reduction, as in the past. However, the economics of upper management decision processes, are not straight-forward or well understood, and many questions need to be answered. For example, what economic and behavioral issues should be detailed for an MIS in support of strategic planning? It is clear to me that many of the answers must come from the executives involved.

As a professional I am concerned about this major gap in the state-of-the-art of MIS, particularly when I see and feel the push of technology which says: Move! I suggest we all have much in common with the Red Queen's observation to Alice:

"Now, here, you see, it takes all the running you can do, to keep in the same place. If you want to get somewhere else, you must run twice as fast as that"

-(Through the Looking Glass).

I urge that we try to run twice as fast as we have, not in developing the brute force technology, but in deciding what we want the technology to do.

References

R.A. Arbuckle, "Computer Analysis and Thruput Evaluation," Computers and Automation (January 1966), p. 13.

J.N. Bairstow, "A Review of Systems Evaluation Packages," Computer Decisions (June 1970), p. 20.

J. Becker and R.M. Hayes, Information Storage and Retrieval: Tools, Elements, Theories (John Wiley and Sons, 1963).

B.F. Boyd and H.S. Krasnow, "Economic Evaluation of Management Information Systems," IBM Systems Journal (March 1963), p. 2-23.

A.C. Bromley, "Choosing a Set of Computers," Datamation (August 1965) p. 37-40.

W. Buchholz, "A Selected Bibliography on Computer System Performance Evaluation," Computer Group News I.E.E.E. (March 1969), p. 21-22.

C.J. Byrnes and D.B. Steig, "File Management Systems: A Current Summary." Datamation (November 1969), p. 138-142.

P. Calingaert, "System Performance Evaluation: Survey and Appraisal," Communications of the ACM (January 1967), p. 12-18.

C. West Churchman, The Systems Approach (Delacorte Press, 1968).

CODASYL Systems Committee, "A Survey of Generalized Data Base Management Systems" (May 1969), Association for Computing Machinery, New York City.

CODASYL Data Base Task Group, "October 1969 Report", Association for Computing Machinery, New York City.

John Diebold, "Bad Decisions on Computer Use," Harvard Business Review (January-February 1969), p 14-16 ff.

J. Fry and J. Gosden, "Survey of Management Information Systems and Their Languages, " p. 41-56 in F. Gruenberger (ed.), Critical Factors in Data Management (Prentice-Hall, 1969).

R.V.L. Hartley, "Transmission of Information," Bell System Technical Journal, Vol 7 (1928), p. 535-563.

P.B. Henderson, Jr., "A Theory of Data Systems for Economic Decisions," unpublished Ph. D. Thesis, Economics Department, M.I.T., Cambridge, Mass. (June 1960).

D.J. Herman and F.C. Ihrer, "The Use of a Computer to Evaluate Computers," Proceedings AFIPS 1964 Spring Joint Computer Conference, Vol. 25, (April 1964), p. 383-395.

John R. Hillegass, "Standardized Benchmark Problems Measure Computer Performance," Computers and Automation (January 1966), p. 16-19.

IBM Corp. (1963). Publications on "Study Organization Plan" (SOP): The Approach, F 20-8135; Documentation Techniques, C20-8075-0;

The Method Phase I, F20-8036-0; The Method Phase II, F20-8137;
The Method Phase III, F20-8138-0.

IBM: "Systems 360 Model 67 Time-Sharing System Technical Summary"
(August 18, 1965)

K.E. Knight, "A Study of Technological Innovation -- The Evolution of
Digital Computers," unpublished Ph. D. Thesis, Graduate
School of Industrial Admonistration, Carnegie-Mellon Univer-
sity (November 1963).

C.H. Kriebel, "Operations Research in the Design of Management Information Systems," Chapter 22, 375-390 in J.F. Pierce (ed.),
Operations Research and the Design of Management Information
Systems (Technical Association of the Pulp and Paper Industry
1967).

C.H. Kriebel, "The Strategic Dimension of Computer Systems Planning,"
Long Range Planning (September 1968), p. 7-12.

C.H. Kriebel, J.T. Heames, and R.L. Van Horn (ed.), Management Information Systems: Progress and Perspectives (Carnegie-Mellon
University, 1970).

R.M. Laska, "Keeping Your Computer Out of the Till", Computer Decisions
(May 1970), p.19-23.

Jacob Marschak, "Elements for a Theory of Teams, "Management Science
(January 1955), p. 127-137.

J. Marschak, "Economics of Inquiring, Communicating, Deciding,"
American Economic Review (May 1968), p. 1-18.

McKinsey and Company, Inc., Unlocking the Computer's Profit Potential
(New York City, 1968); reprinted in Computers and Automation
(April 1969), p.24-33.

"Computer Evaluation and Selection: A Bibliography," prepared for the
Association for Computing Machinery by Metametrics Corporation (1969); ACM Professional Developmen s Seminar. (61 entries).

H. Raiffa, Decision Analysis (Addison-Wesley, 1968).

Roy Radner, "Team Decision Problems," Annals of Mathematical Statistics (September 1962), p. 857-881.

N.F. Schneidewind, "Analytical Model for the Design and Selection of
Electronic Digital Computers," Unpublished D.B.A. Thesis,
Graduate School of Business, University of Southern Californ
(January 1966).

C.E. Shannon and W.Weaver, The Mathematical Theory of Communication
(University of Illinois Press, 1948).

William F. Sharpe, The Economics of Computers (Columbia University
Press, 1969).

H.A. Simon, The Sciences of the Artificial (MIT Press, 1969).

M.B. Solomon, Jr., "Economies of Scale and the IBM System/360,"
Communications of the ACM (June 1966), p. 435-440.

MIS THEORY AND MIS PRACTICE

Poul Sveistrup
A/S Regnecentralen
Denmark

Abstract

The lecture will be structured into three parts treating the
following three questions:

1. What should be understood by MIS, in theory and in practise?

2. What does practise expect or require from MIS, and what can
    theory offer to meet or fulfil these expectations and re-
    quirements?

3. What are the theoretical problems of designing and using
    MIS, and what can we do - or have to do - in practise?

The presentation is not a scientific note on the most relevant
answers to these questions but rather an attempt to present for
further discussion on this conference some practical answers
based on theoretical reasoning and arguing.

1. What is MIS?

To answer this question we will first make a short theoretical
analysis of the three concepts which are put together in these
popular symbols.

The word management is usually used for some part of a control
system - or rather steering system to prefer the european
terminology - of an enterprise. To give a more precise
definition we have to make a model of the steering system
showing the relevant parts, and then discuss which parts should
be included in the management concept.

The model applied partitions the steering system into five
subsystems performing the following main functions, cf. fig. 1:
- data collection (measurement and registration)
- data manipulation and storing (accounting and statistics)
- analysis, synthesis and evaluation (planning and budgetting)
- decision making (argumentation and choice)
- direction and instruction (ordergiving, motivation and
  initiating).

These functions are all based on data in a data system
consisting of the following datafiles, cf. fig. 1:
- original data (actual situations and events)
- recorded data (describing data)
- data base (accounts, statistics)
- proposals and consequences (alternative plans and budgets)
- decisions (orders, instructions, plans, budgets)
- result data (controlling data).

If the subsystems of the steering system considered are not
completely autonomous, we must further include the necessary
steering system as the sixth function in the model. The
structure of this system may itself be described by the model
(the principle of resursiveness).

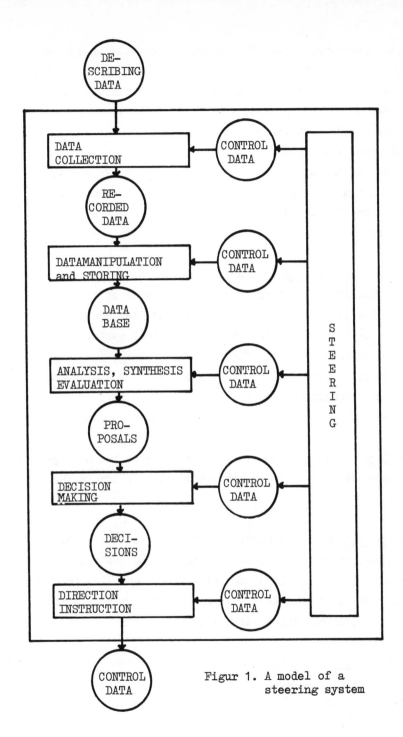

Figur 1. A model of a steering system

In the steering system all functions are based on data and produce data in the datasystem, and all are highly relevant for the accomplishment of the steering process. As the crucial point in the discussions of information systems is the relation between data and information, as we shall see below, all functions must be included in the management concept in the discussions of MIS. Therefore, in this context, management includes all functions, and the terms steering system and management system are taken as synonyms.

The word _information_ is usually used in many different ways. The following definition is based on a model of the one-way communication of a message. In this model the communication system is partitioned into three subsystems performing the following functions, cf. fig. 2:
- sender: formulating, generating and sending a message;
- channel: encoding, transmitting and decoding;
- receiver: receiving, perceiving and conceiving the message.

The _form_ of the message is the data in which the message is represented, which may be distorted due to noise in the channel.

The _content_ of the message, however, has to be distinguished into two concepts, the original content and the resulting content. As the result of the receiving process is the form perceived and conceived - i.e. what is informed - we will call this content information and the original one the meaning. Thus,
- _information_ is defined as the content of data seen relatively to a receiver, and
- _meaning_ is defined as the content of data seen relatively to a sender.

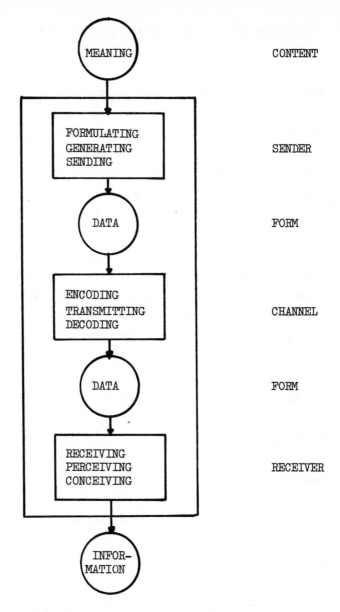

Fig 2. A model of a one-way communication system

- A <u>system</u> is a whole consisting of inter-related parts,
  i.e. a structured whole.

The words <u>Management Information Systems</u> may now be discussed
in this special context. A semantic analysis of the combination
of the terms gives at least the two following meanings:
- Informations Systems <u>for</u> Management in the sense that
  information systems should cover the first two (or three)
  of the above mentioned functions of the steering process,
  and the word management should only indicate the last two
  (or three) of these functions.
- Information Systems <u>in</u> Management in the sense that information
  systems are the reference structures of the managers. Thus
  the information system indicates how the data system must
  be structured if the data communicated shall be able to
  cover the needs of information of the managers, or eventually
  an automatic system performing a management function.

The first meaning is often used but in an irrelevant way from
the point of view that information is not treated as relative
to a receiving function but to a sending function, the data
processing system, - i.e. the term information is used for
meaning without taking the communication problems into acccunt.

The second meaning stresses the importance of the relativity
of information and is therefore preferred for the following
discussion.

From this theoretical analysis it may be concluded that every
management system in practise contains an information system
but that the communication in the management system depends
primarily on
- the structure of the information systems of the managers
- the structure of the data systems and
- the correspondence between these structures.

The importance of the conceiving function in the receiving process as part of the definition of information is emphasized, because it must be more relevant to talk about information as what is actually conceived than as what should be conceived by the receiver - i.e. what is meant - as this is the basic problem of communication.

As information is only defined relatively to a receiving process and this process depends on the receiver's reference system, information must be defined as a relation between two phenomena in a specific reference system.

Hence, the reference system must be structured in such a way that the relevant relations can be achieved, i.e. the reference system must include receiving algorithms as well as stored information. If we consider two-way communication processes or activities derived from the message the reference system must include algorithms also for them.

It follows from this definition of the concept of information that the process of receiving a message can be considered as a process of structuring a reference system.

In the most simple case this structuring process is just copying the structure of the data without making any further relations to the reference system, i.e. the perceiving function. Such information may only be used for later recognition or as simple impulses to well-defined actions. In the more complex cases relations are created to different parts of the reference system, i.e. the conceiving function.

The word system is often used in contexts where its special meaning is not needed. Nevertheless, the following definition should be generally accepted to-day:

In practise it often happens that the managers or the data
systems or both are ill-structured, but the crucial question
for this conference should rather be:

How do we ensure the correspondence between the data structures
and the reference structures of the managers as it is this
correspondence which makes the word information relevant in
this context. This requirement holds even when we use edp for
some of the functions of the managers.

My answer to this question is that the data structures always
have to be adjusted to the reference structures, rather than
vice versa; but of course there should be an interaction
between the structures. To perform this interactive structuring
process we need a special function in the steering of the
management process, which I will call MIS.

2. What should be required from MIS?

In practise it is often expected that theory can provide simple
solutions to simple problems - or even to complex problems
as it is often not conceived that most practical problems in
fact are very complex.

However, theory seldom offer such simple hocus-pocus-solutions
to practical problems, but only simple solutions to theoretical
problems, which means problems formulated so that they are
solvable by known theoretical methods. Nevertheless, it is
often said by salesmen that new ideas like MIS have such
hocus-pocus-facilities, which are offered as the solution of
the practical problems.

This situation is due to the fact that the complexity of the
real world is too great to overcome unless a procedure for

simplification of the problems is made as part of the solving process. In other words, theory cannot give the solutions but contribute to the design of problem solving systems in which the problem formulation process is interactive with the problem solving process. The idea is, that MIS should ensure this interaction in dealing with complex problems.

Formulating tasks and purposes, long range planning and budgetting and other modern ideas like these are very often discussed or even demanded, but very seldom used because they are too difficult to perform in practise unless a special system for these functions is designed and implemented as permanent functions of the management system. Again, the idea is that MIS should contribute to or perform these functions.

It is often said in practise, that it is only the results that counts, but this is equally true for the bad results.

The principle of <u>management by exception</u> is too primitive if it is taken in a too strict sense referring only to exceptional results, because it will often be too late to do anything which could prevent or utilize the exceptional results or rather the possible consequences of an exceptional situation. Further, the principle of management by exception says nothing about what to do when the exceptions are known if the problem is complex, and nothing about which situations should be treated as exceptional.

What we need is management systems which are more adequate for producing good results. This sounds evident but the crucial point is that such systems have to be steerable themselves, which means that the topmanagement must take a very active part in the design of such systems. The basic idea of MIS is that it should take part in the design process to ensure that the structuring problems are solved in a relevant way.

The most essential function in management should be that of <u>argumentation</u>. In practise, however, the argumentation is usually made after the decision or the preferred solution is chosen, but it must be emphasized, that the best decision is the well-argued decision.

Thus, we need two really advanced principles of management:

The first, <u>management by relevance</u>, says that it is necessary that all relevant messages are communicated in the system. The problem is that we do not know in beforehand which relations will be the relevant ones. Consequently, the data system has to be interactive with the receiving or data consuming system, i.e. a dialogue form must be applied, and the data system must be flexible and adaptive.

The second, <u>management by relativity</u>, stresses the fact that there is not enough information in a message which only tells that there is an exceptional difference between two data, e.g. the planned and actual figures. The data have to be related in a more complex picture of a situation which demands actions or reactions to the message.

The conclusion of these considerations is that practise needs no finished solutions but <u>tools</u> for the problem formulation and problem solving process and a creative milieu for the application of such tools. On the other hand, theory cannot deliver the ready tools but only models, methods, heuristics, and approaches for the development of the specific tools for the actual applications. Hence, MIS cannot be a solution to the practical problems, but a function which is able to develop the tools for solving the current problems.

The requirement of interaction between different functions indicates that the communication problem is one of the most urgent problems in MIS.

3. The problems of designing and using MIS.

The basic problem of designing MIS is the communication problem, i.e. to structure the data system so that it reflects the structure of the reference system of the users.

Due to the flexibility of management and changes in the environment we cannot define a priori which relations will be the relevant ones. Further, it is impossible just to describe all possible relations in a structure because of the exorbitant number of them (N! binary relations between N elements). Consequently, MIS has to be an adaptive subsystem in the management system which develops structures and methods (models, rules, heuristics and so on) both on the reference system and in the data systems.

This idea requires that the resources applied have the relevant abilities. This assumption is however very difficult to fulfil as the usual situation is that the specialists in designing data systems generally know too little about data application in management, and the users know too little about the special design and modern management techniques. Consequently, as it is impossible to give the managers of more than say 40 years old a sufficient post-graduate education to give them the necessary abilities in designing

and using modern management systems, and the specialists
younger than say 40 years old mostly have too little practical
experiences in the management field, we must try to utilize
in an efficient way the very scarce resources around the age
of 40, which indeed exist in this field.

As the qualifications discussed are needed especially on top
level of an organization it will not be enough to introduce
these scarce resources as consultants or staff members to the
top executives. The needed abilities should be found inside
the topmanagement group, in which the different abilities may
be represented in different persons, but the entire steering
function must be performed of the group as a whole. The usual
subdivision of a topmanagement group according to the
traditional functions like sales, production, etc. does not
serve this idea; if a subdivision is necessary it is MIS
which may be partitioned from the executive functions.

If it is not possible to create such a topmanagement group,
the abilities must be introduced on the level of the board of
directors independently of the executive level.

In the seventies we shall need a new category of people in the
private sector - the professional members of the board. I
imagine that each man can serve say 3 - 5 enterprises and
he may partly rely on consultants and staffmembers, but
his independence of the single firm should be secured.

The abilities of a PMB, i.e. a Professional Member of the
Board, must be general rather than special knowledge and
experiences, but concentrated on the field of management and
steering systems or cybernetics. The old term operations
research is too special in this context unless we redefine
OR in the direction of MIS in the sense discussed here.

The functions of a PMB should be in the heart of MIS, i.e.
initializing the long range planning functions, formulating
the tasks and purposes, and ensuring the adequecy of the data
systems.

Hence, the primary functions of the PMB are to formulate in
the necessary formalized way the vague and intuitive ideas
of the other members of the board and the top executives of
the elder generation, and to evaluate the relevance of the
special ideas of the younger generation for the other members
of the board to secure a high quality of the decisions and
the principal initiative of the board. He has to take an
active part in the major decisions of the board, and ensure
that these decisions really are made by the board. Regardless
he is not representing any group of stockholders or employees
he should be a fully responsible member of the board.

Conclusion.

The term MIS is - like many other slang expressions in the
computer field such as real time, ... etc. - so vague and
generally undefined that the user of the term may put the
meaning he wants into the symbols. And so did I.

Of course I know that the special meaning I have put into
the three letters in this lecture will not be generally
accepted as the definition of MIS, but I hope I have focused
on the real important problems in management information
systems.

These problems may be seen in the light of the great
revolutions:

The <u>agricultural revolution</u> turned the original democracy of the group work of hunters into a mono- or oligarchy of the landowners based on the principle of the right of property.

The <u>industrial revolution</u> was followed by political revolutions against the political rights based on the right of property, and later against this right itself, and established a political democracy based on economic and political organizations.

The <u>information revolution</u> will be followed by human revolutions against the establishment and the organizations to create a human democracy based on individuals in a direct groupwork or cooperation as in the original democracy. The primary reason for this is that the individuals cannot any more keep up with the rate of growth in knowledge, techniques, and economics which is generating a permanent and growing gap between the generations.

What we need is a way to bridge this gap.

To do this, i.e. to avoid a threatening technocracy and to give the human revolution the form of an evolution, it is necessary to introduce a flexibility in management systems (private or governmental) never seen in the traditional authoritative system. The idea of the PMB may be a catalyst for introducing the evolution from top level and downwards to prevent the technocracy and the revolution from the lower levels against the established top of the society.

The essential weakness of the idea of human democracy is that people in general are not skilled in the process of making group-decisions because of the lack of abilities in communicating and arguing. Indeed the PMB has to be only the catalyst and not the strong man in these groups to prevent the technocracy.

MIS CORPORATE PLANNING

Robert F. Williams
Parsons & Williams
Denmark

A B S T R A C T

Corporate Planning has been done until now in most cases with
minimal computer assistance.   That computer help, which is
available to Corporate Planners, is usually in the form of forecasting algorithms and statistical analysis routines which require
specialists to run and require that the data be prepared in a
special way for a one time analysis.   Some work has been done
with Corporate Models.

This paper describes a system which provides a set of integrated
programs which the Corporate Planner can use himself - either
from his own terminal in real-time or in batch mode.   The major
functional modules are described.

The Corporate Planners job is to shape the future of the firm.
Specifically he is not concerned with daily problems.   His planning
horizon may stretch many years into the future.   There are many
excellent tools for the Corporate Planner.   Among them are the
following:

Corporate Models
Interaction Analysis
Present Worth Algorithm
Forecasting Modules
Price/Volume Analysis
Product Life Cycle Analysis
Capital Budgeting Algorithm
Operational Budgeting Algorithm
Organization Planning Algorithm
Liquidity Planning Algorithm

The files which are required to support the various system modules are discussed.

The MIS for Corporate Planning is an integrated system for using the computer and the various program modules as a laboratory to test the hypotheses of the Corporate Planner and other members of the management team in arriving at means for achieving the future corporate goals and as a tool in arriving at significant management decisions.

SYSTEM STRUCTURE

The system structure for Corporate Planning is shown in
EXHIBIT I.   Corporate Planning is strategic in nature but on
the other hand much of the data for Corporate Planning may
be extracted from operational files.

Analytical Routines are needed to analyze the data flowing
through the operational files to determine important relationships.

Algorithms and calculation routines for forecasting and other
special needs are essential.

A special set of routines for the budgeting function are needed.

The most important parts of the MIS for Corporate Planning
are the Corporate Models.

A report generator presents the output to the Corporate Planner
at his terminal and/or by line printer.

A system monitor controls the operation of the total system.

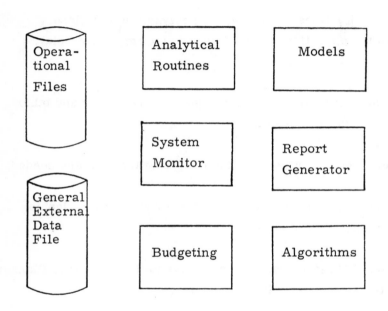

EXHIBIT I. SYSTEM STRUCTURE

CORPORATE MODELS

The most valuable tool in the hands of today's Corporate Planner
is the Corporate Model. These models are either static or
dynamic in nature. Modelling of the firm developed slowly during
the first half of this century mainly as a result of the work of
Liontief and Ragnar Frisch. Modellings received a tremendous
impulse with the advent of the computer in the last decade. The
work of Forrester (2) and Dantzig added to this impulse and
modelling improved becoming more widely used during the "sixties"
(1, 3, 5).

Model use has been largely limited by the difficulty of developing
an adequate data bank and its maintenance. Mattessich (6) has
shown, however, that the budgeting function is analogous to model
building. The development of computerized budgeting systems
and econometric models is largely a question of having available
the proper files organized in a suitable way, see Lynes, "A Manufacturing Information System" (4) and Williams, "Developing an
Integrated Data Bank" (8).

In most cases, if the firm engages in Budgeting and Production
Planning activities, the data is available; although it may not have
been placed in a suitably organized data bank.

Simulation has become widely used as a dynamic modelling technique.
The outstanding example is Industrial Dynamics, see Nord,
"Grouth of a New Product" (7) and EXHIBIT II.

The development of a Corporate Model has value in itself due to
the learning process involved - learning about the characteristics
of the firm and their interactions. It improves the communication

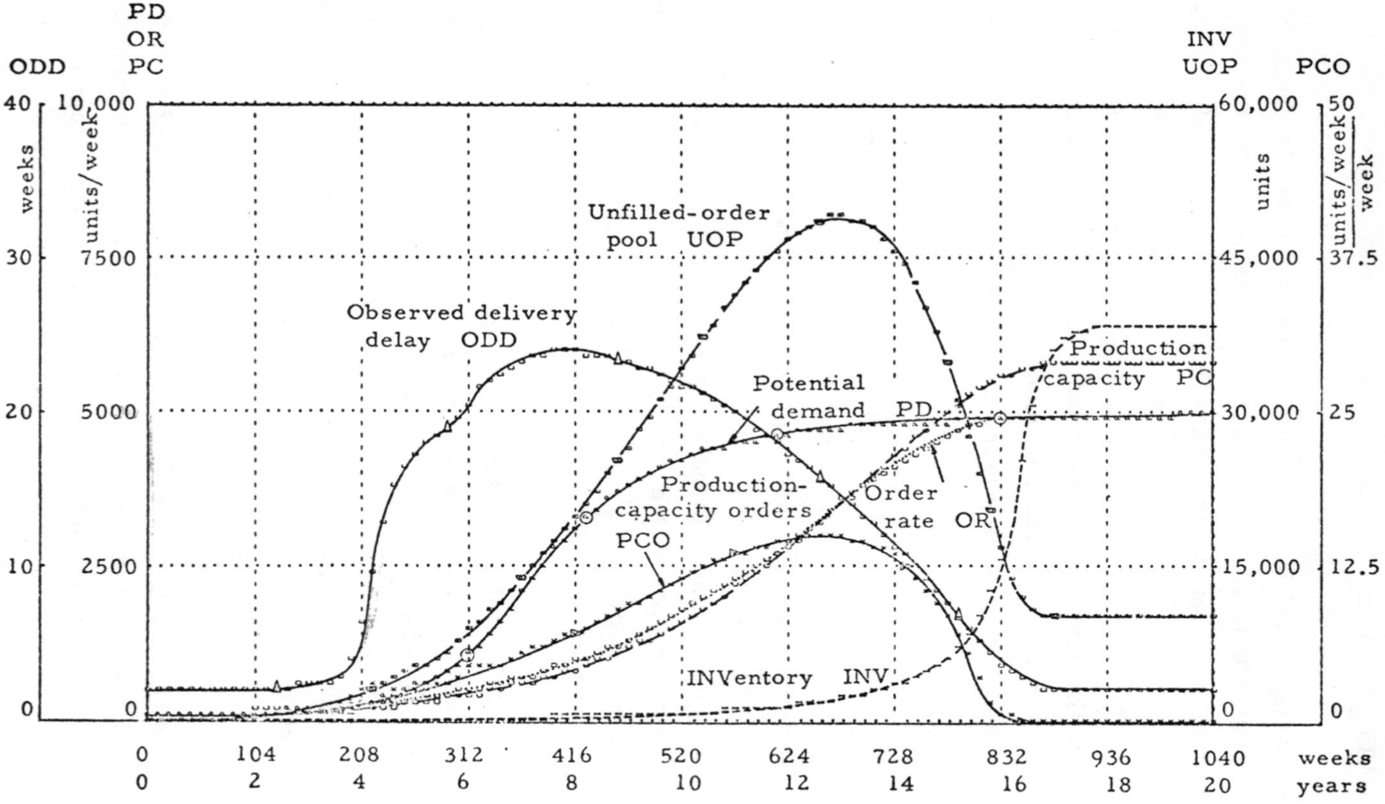

"Growth of a New Product", Ole C. Nord

EXHIBIT II

process within the firm.   It makes clear the data requirements and structure of the data bank for the Corporate MIS.   It is the contention of this paper that the proper strategy in developing a Corporate MIS should be an exercise in Corporate Modelling and that the major use of the Corporate MIS shall be Corporate Planning.

The remainder of this paper is devoted to specific sub-modules of a Corporate Planning System which are valuable elements of the Corporate MIS.

ANALYSIS

Corporate Models and Corporate Planning require not only raw data but extracted data: - that is analyzed data.   A set of routines which determine statistical, correlative and regression relations from the data passing and/or remaining in the operational files are needed for Corporate Planning.

For this type of analysis the manager has in the past been insulated from the computer by technical staff groups that perform the operation by batch manipulation.   Delays and communication problems inherent in this prodecure have dampened the interest of the manager. Further, many traditional analytical techniques suffer in that they are restricted to linear relationships whereas the true relationships are often non-linear.   Much interesting work has been done recently at the University of Michigan and by others to eliminate these objections.

The Corporate Planner is most often in search of a cause and effect relations.   The answer to one question often inspires a new question. To satisfy the manager, response time must be short.   It is desirable for the manager to prepare his own input in simple form or by time sharing terminal, the latter more than satisfying his desire for fast response.

ALGORITHMS

Some of the problems of the Corporate Planner require special algorithms. These must include algorithms for forecasting.

In support of the forecasting operation it is useful to have a General External file on-line containing information on such factors as GNP, Business Activity, Disposable Income, etc., which are used in more sophisticated forecasting techniques.

Life Cycle Analysis is another algorithm which is valuable in planning new product development and marketing.

For making analysis of capital investments today's managers are making extensive use of "Present Worth" and "Discounted Cash Flow" techniques. Algorithms for such analysis are excellent additions to a MIS for Corporate Planning.

Some Corporate Planners will be vitally interested in Price/Volume relations. Many would be interested in a simulation package which they could operate themselves.

Organization Planning is a function which falls under the broad category of Corporate Planning. An algorithm for this requires a Personnel File, on-line, containing information about people in the organization such as their skills, education, personality, experience, etc.

BUDGETING

Computerized budgeting can remove the drudgery and heavy work required for producing budgets. Managers often desire to ask the "What if" type of question. This is especially true of budgets.

The work required to produce a new budget manually under a
"What if" hypothesis is usually impractical. Computerized
budgeting procedures, constracted so that the manager can
easily pose such questions, are vital to any Corporate Planning
MIS.

Capital Budgeting, Operational Budgeting and Liquidity Planning
algorithms designed for user interaction are recommended.

Output should include Operating Statements and Balance Sheets
for the end of the budgeting period.

Budget Simulation where costs, prices, wages and sales volumes
are simulated to represent the unknown external climate can
give the manager valuable insights for stratetic planning and
budget preparation.

SYSTEM MONITOR

The System Monitor consists of a set of programs which make
it possible for the manager to easily and quickly communicate
with the Corporate Planning MIS to answer his questions, test
his hypotheses and provide him with a laboratory wherein he
can experimentally study his theories before putting them into
practice. The decision process must always be under the
control of the manager - not of the computer. The manager
should be able to change the logic, alter assumptions and modify
conditions without requiring reprogramming.

REPORT GENERATOR

An essential feature of the MIS is a report generator which presents
the output of the manager's use of the system. Some of the
output formats are inherent in the type of task but it should be

easy for the user to change the format to suit his own desires
without the assistance of a programmer.

CONCLUSION

A MIS for Corporate Planning will gain faster and wider use
if it is interactive with a reasonably fast response time. The
logical structure presented here is suitable for either batch
or real-time processing.

To develop an MIS for Corporate Planning one builds a model
of the system, determines the functions desired, the algorithms
and files needed and then produces a monitor to retrieve the
data needed for each algorithm and initialize the tasks required
to answer the manager's questions.

REFERENCES

1) Boulden, James B. and Buffa, Elwoods., "Corporate
   Models: On-Line, Real-Time Systems",
   Harvard Business Review, July-August 1970

2) Forrester, Jay W., "Industrial Dynamics", The MIT
   Press, 1961

3) Gershefski, George W., "Building A Corporate Financial Model", Harvard Business Review, July-August 1969

4) Lynes, Stewart.,"A Manufacturing Information System,"
   MIS Copenhagen 70

5) Kotler, Philip, "Corporate Models: Better Marketing Plans",
   Harvard Business Review, July-August 1970

6) Mattessich, Richard, "Accounting and Analytical Methods",
   Irwin, 1964

7) Nord, Ole C., "Grouth of a New Product" MIT Press, 1963

8) Williams, Robert F., "Developing an Integrated Data Bank",
   NordDATA 68, Helsinki.

PRACTICAL MANAGEMENT INFORMATION SYSTEM
FOR PLANNING AND CONTROL

M.H. Calvert-Evers
G.J. McCaul (PTY.) Ltd.
South Africa

A great deal has been written about Management Information Systems which has created the impression that
these concepts are somewhat nebulous or very complicated in their application. The following definition
is a contribution made toward the prevailing confusion
and mysticism:-

"A Management Information System should be a totally
integrated synergistic analog control system, with
digital input and output characteristics, which
categorically differentiates the data sets in alternate
axes and provides random and sequential axes to all
planning, operating, financial and other quantifiable
non-quantitative transactions in past, present and
future data planes. In conjunction with selective
interrogation of the stratified data metrix contained within the computerised data bank in combination with discriminate differentiation of the magnitude of variance limits of the multiple control
variables, providing accurately time-phased exception
reports for management decision and executive action!!!"

So much for the "buzz word" game which surrounds MIS.

As far as management are concerned, we believe that
they will not accept that they can "selectively interrogate a computerised data bank" but not be able
to determine until months after the end of an accounting period whether the company is earning a
profit or if production backlogs are causing des-
patches to fall behind schedule.

Management's task is basically to ensure that the
economic activity with which they are concerned is
not merely a collection of fixed assets, but a
dynamic organisation which has a single goal,
namely that of survival through making a profit.
This is done in two ways:-

1.   Developing a Plan of Action; which covers
1.1 The determining of the objectives to be
     achieved
1.2 Deciding on the best means to be employed
1.3 Establishing standards, criteria and
     targets by means of which progress and
     performance will be measured.

These processes can and are often carried out in
isolation.   The result is a "Blue print" which can
be filed away for future reference or can be used in
the second group of responsibilities below (2).

2.   Implementation and Control of the Plan.
2.1 Provision and preparation of the resources
     required
2.2 Analysing actual performance and progress

2.3 Comparing this with the Plan and taking
     appropriate action to deal with actual
     or threatened deviations (variances).

Such appropriate action may call for nothing more than
bringing the activity (back) into line while adhering
to the details of the Plan or, it may require some
modifications to be made to the Plan such as performance,
criteria targets, or means employed i.e. Control.

What exactly do we mean by the word "control"? Control
means to guide, steer or regulate; its synonym is
"manage". Control is required to maintain stability,
that is to say that when a system is dynamic and
controlled by negative feedback it attempts to balance
continuously the random influences causing it to deviate
from the prescribed goal (Plan) in such a way that the
output is maintained at the planned level.

It is clear, therefore, that for management to set the
Plan of Action and Control the Plan it is essential to
have an adequate system to enable it to sense immediately changes in conditions, both in its internal environment and the external environment e.g. rate or tempo at
which people work, machine breakdowns, failure of
material supplies to arrive on time, and so on, all
leading to a deviation from the goal set. Changes in
prices paid for factor inputs or prices obtained for
outputs also affect the stability. These changes must
also be brought to the management's attention for the
necessary executive action.

Management involved in the carrying on of an economic
activity are required to plan to a large extent for
the future. It is also necessary to forecast the
activity which can take place in the immediate future
without necessarily thinking of expansion. The basis
of a practical MIS is therefore the Budget which is
used to develop a Plan and to forecast the whole of
the activity of the organisation before it takes
place. The Budgets cover both the Cost aspect as well
as the Sales aspect. In each case the money values
are calculated by determining quantities and prices
for all the elements. Subsequently the accounting
system controls the actual results against the Budgets
and Standard Costs. These Budgets are set in a great
deal of detail by quantity. These quantities are then
subjected to a computer programme which calculates the
money values. The details forming all these budgets,
as will be seen as we go along, then form the data base
from which a great deal of information is extracted.

Basis of Budget.
The Basis of the Budget is the Cost Budget and NOT
the Sales Budget. This approach is used because an
organisation consists of a technical set-up with a
specific scale or size of operation. The combination
of the various factors makes this scale dependent
upon the number of the units of plant, machinery,
equipment, etc. which have been installed or are
available. It is therefore evident that the cost
structure and the product unit costs will be at a
minimum for a particular size of manufacturing unit
if that unit is fully utilised. The emphasis, there-

fore, falls on the cost structure and output obtainable if the installed production facilities are used efficiently and to full capacity, and not on the Sales forecast.

A complete register of the Fixed Assets including all plant and equipment installed is the starting point for our Budget concept. The Budget must express clearly the cost of operating the organisation at the full scale, and the unit product costs for different kinds of articles which may be made by the particular kinds of plant, machinery and equipment installed.

In practise these concepts express themselves in the form of an accounting control system which has a dual task. The accounting control system controls the actual results against the Budgets and calculated Standard Costs which have been set thus giving us a full system of Budgetary control. Secondly, Standard Cost calculations are made to give the various operating rates for the plant and machinery as well as the Standard Costs of the different products, which can be produced by the plant. In this system, therefore, the financial and industrial accounting, including all cost accounting controls, are combined in a single integrated system of accounting.

The pre-calculated costs form the standards which are subsequently used throughout the system for exercising the necessary control over the various aspects of both production and marketing. Day-to

day production control can be exercised by using the
standards set. Price policies and marketing strategies are also worked out, making use of the standard
costs and the budgetted capacities. This does not
imply, however, that the selling prices are set in
relation to the standard costs. The basic intention
of the whole concept, is that the standard costs
must represent the cost of making products in relation to the scale of operation, represented by the
installed plant capacity. This cost is a function
of the prices which must be paid for all the input
factors to the process. On the other hand, the price
which can be realised for any of the products which
can be made by these production processes is a matter
which is related completely and wholly to the kind of
market in which the economic activity operates. Known
marketing techniques can help towards improving the
prices which can be obtained for products. A standard
cost price when compared with the selling price which
can be realised is thus an indication as to whether the
manufacture and marketing of a particular product is
"economically rational". This comparison of Standard
Cost calculated in the manner described below, with
the realiseable selling prices, becomes the motivation
for a great many different kinds of managerial action.
It is thus of extreme importance that the Standard Cost
Price should be a clear expression of the technical
capabilities of the installed capacity in relation to
the prices which must be paid for the various input
factors such as labour, outside services, and raw
materials. This Standard Cost must be in no way influenced by the prices which can be obtained as selling

prices or the volume of sales which can currently be achieved. In other words, we are initially concerned with the quantity we can make using our plant capacity to the full, rather than the quantity we can sell. The setting up of procedures to establish the relationship between Standard Costs, utilisation of capacity, and selling prices thus becomes one of the important objectives of the Management Information System. It is necessary to set out the various aspects in relation to setting up the Budget and the calculation of Standard Costs below to enable one to appreciate the controls that are available to management in the form of variances from the standards set. It will also become clear that these controls are exercised not only on the financial aspects but also on the day-to-day operating aspects.

Register of Fixed Assets.
This Register shows the cost of acquiring the various kinds of fixed assets which form the basis of the installed capacity of the organisation. <u>This installed capacity represents the potential output of the organisation.</u> At the same time the various items of production machinery and equipment reflected as fixed assets give us a clear indication of what costs will arise when we operate installed capacity. Building accommodation, labour requirements and the various outside services are derived from this Register of Fixed Assets which can be expanded to represent a plant model.

Operating Cost Budget.

It is then possible to derive from a study of the whole of the fixed assets of the organisation the various kinds of costs which will be incurred in order to operate the business for the budget period. These costs are dervived from the single concept of establishing the quantities of the various kinds of input factors which are required to make production processes function. These quantities, when determined, are then multiplied by the prices which must be paid for the various factors using a budget computer programme developed by us. This then gives us the cost of operating the processes for the period of the budget. E.g. Number of persons employed in a department x the wage rate for the occupation + the social charges = personnel cost.

The determination of the quantities of the different factors which are acquired is a technical study which must be undertaken in close collaboration with the operating personnel. This means that the departmental head, supervisor or foreman will actually assist in determining the number of people required in the various occupations under his control as well as the consumable stores and spares and anticipated cost of repair and maintenance. In this way the procedure integrates the whole of the production function and its management into the process of budget setting. It will be found that the production personnel concerned in assisting with setting up the budget then take a very active interest in comparing the budget against the actual quantities used during the budget

period. The advantage is obvious. The determination
of prices on the other hand is one which necessitates
an enquiry into the market in which the various production input factors are to be obtained. It is clear,
therefore, that the production personnel continue to
be involved only in the quantities of items used and
are not so concerned with the money values. The
Operating Cost Budget is, therefore, far more
meaningful to them than the normal type of budget
which is set by money value only based on an estimate,
generally of an historical figure plus a percentage for
the anticipated increase. It is a well-known fact
that in the case of certain Public bodies where budgets
are set in terms of round money values, that towards the
end of the budget period the department goes on a
spending spree if they have not spent the money allocated under the budget for fear of receiving a cut
in their budget for the following period.

The operating cost budget will establish as two
distinct functions the cost of operating the manufacturing process on one hand, and the marketing and
distribution process on the other hand. These
operating cost budgets do not include the cost of
the raw material input needed for the different
products. These are taken up in the calculation of
the Standard Costs.

These operating cost budgets provide us finally
with process time rates for the various processes
needed to make the products. In the system used

and here described, it has been found practical to distribute the various service centres to the actual production activity centres, e.g. the service of the personnel department will be distributed to the production activity centres based on the number of people within those centres. In this way there is no need for a figure or a percentage to be added to the cost to represent the overheads. By doing this, we achieve a complete cost for each process. In much the same manner Temple Priests in earlier times received wool in an unworked form and then gave it to women to spin on a piece-work basis. These women took the wool home, spun it and returned it to the Priests. The payment made to them represented the total cost, that is to say labour, accommodation and plant usage, in processing the wool. This spun yarn could now be sent out on the same piece-work basis for weaving. When the cost of the wool was added to the piece-work rate for the spinning and weaving one arrived at the total cost to the Temple. The process time rates calculated are, as it were, integrals of the costs of all the various factor service inputs needed to make the processes ready and available to operate expressed as a unit of time. The rates may refer on the one hand to processes used for the manufacture of the articles and on the other hand to rates which are incurred in order to market and distribute products. An interesting aspect which arises out of these calculations concern those industries which operate a workshop. Arising out of our system of setting a budget and the redistribu-

tion of certain service centres it is a simple matter
to set-up an internal workshop control using an in-
clusive time rate. These rates would cover the cost
of the personnel working in the workshop plus consumable stores such as welding rods, oils and greases
and so on as well as the cost of operating the workshop
plant and machinery, accommodation costs, etc. By
charging out the workshop time to the other activity
centres, the utilisation of the workshop and its facilities can be checked. Secondly, the departments or
activity centres receiving the debits from the workshops
will have to set the costs incurred against their own
budget and in this way excessive charge-outs will be
checked and queried. Thus control is achieved of both
utilisation and output of the workshop.

Calculation of Standard Costs for Different Products.
The Standard Costs of products are made up of two basic
inputs, the material input and the process input. The
process input can be further divided into the production
processes, and the marketing and distribution process.

It is, of course, necessary to determine the quantities
of process input required before we can determine the
cost. We, therefore, calculate the material input
quantity and the process time input. The material
input at the prices which must be paid for the raw
materials will then give the Standard Cost of the
raw material. The process time at the standard process
time rate for the various processes needed to produce
the article, will give the process time cost. The two

together give us the total standard costs of a particular product being manufactured. To this must be
added the cost of marketing and distribution based
upon predetermined rates which reflect the nature
of these particular activities. With the determination of Standard Product Costs we have reached the
point where we can consider these costs in relation
to the market potential. It should be made clear
at this point that all the foregoing calculations
are done using computer programmes and the various
process time rates form part of our data base. The
details of the product requirements, i.e. the
quality of materials, and the quantity of each
process (time) now also form part of this base.
Provided the coding has been correctly structured
the Standard Cost Calculations are a simple matter.

Sales Forecast and Production Budget.
The Sales Forecasts set out the expected sales of
products for the budget period. This information
is derived in various ways such as statistical information, market investigation, and forecasts from
the marketing department. The information that is
needed is, once again, the quantities of the different products which, it is anticipated, will be
sold, as well as the prices which can be obtained.
It is possible that different prices can be obtained
in different sectors of the market for the same
product. The Sales Forecasts in quantities and
prices can be compared with the Standard Costs
which have been previously calculated. This

comparison, using our data base, can be made to reveal some interesting managerial aspects.

- The potential profit is shown based on the prices and quantities as forecast being realised.
- The extent to which these forecasts of sales would use the installed capacity of the processes; revealing in some detail which section or departments in the organisation are over- or under-utilised in relation to Sales Forecast.
- Various adjustments can then be made until an equilibrium position is reached in relation to the utilisation of the installed capacity; the volume of sales and the prices at which these sales are intended to take place. This also focuses attention on those products on which the maximum or minimum profit can be made in relation to the selling price obtainable.
- The final budget in this respect would then form what could be called the production budget or production plan for the budget period.
- It must, of course, be emphasized that this final equilibrium position is not an inflexible goal which cannot be altered in relation to changing circumstances. It only presents a possible

equilibrium position, which, because
an economic activity is dynamic, is
subject to random influences, both
external and internal. This equilibrium position represents the difference between the costs or prices
paid for the input factors as against
the prices we can realise when we sell
the products made by the processes.
This difference is the profit. There
is, obviously, more than one combination of products which can bring
about such an equilibrium position.
This equilibrium position is represented, in turn, by the clear-cut
concept that a satisfactory return
must be obtained on the capital employed in a business. It is, therefore, necessary to determine the
amount of capital employed in the
business.

Financial Budgets.
Based upon the foregoing budgets, a Financial Budget is
made out. This Financial Budget will reflect the level
of activity contemplated by the Sales Forecast and the
resulting production budgets. The various items such
as value of the inventory of raw materials, work in
progress and finished goods, as well as the outstanding
debtors and creditors, form some of the major aspects
of such a budget. In addition, any capital expenditure

will have to be included together with other
payments or receipts such as those coming from
loans made to the company or repayment of loans
by the company. As a by-product of this Financial
Budget, the programme produces a Source and Application of Funds statement as well as the Cash Flow
Statements. This budget and the subsidiary statements can be reviewed monthly especially if regression
analysis is applied to determine the sales pattern in
comparing the Sales Budget with the actual sales or
orders placed.

Accounting Control.
These Budgets and all the necessary information which
has been compiled in order to obtain them are used to
control the actual operation of the organisation
during the Budget period. The accounting control
system will produce accounts at monthly periods which
will show all the variances or deviations from the
budgets which have been set. The actual expenditure
for each period, as revealed by the financial accounting system, is compared with the budget of expenditure
set up in the Operating Cost Budget. The various production standards which have been set and used in the
calculation of Standard Product Costs, are also compared so that the production processes are kept up to
the standards set. The actual expenditure on marketing
and distribution costs is compared with the standards
which have been used in calculating these costs in setting up the Standard Product Costs. The accounts show
all this information for each month as well as the

cumulated position for each item from the beginning
of the period. The nett profit shown at the end of
each month is also cumulated and the total cumulative
nett profit at the end of a financial year is exactly
the same as the profit revealed by the final audited
accounts for that year. This results naturally from
the fact that this system is a fully integrated one
which does not require any form of reconciliation.

Cost Control.
Cost Control is exercised at short-term intervals
within the manufacturing operation to ensure that
the production standards which have been set and
used in the calculation of Standard Costs, are being
achieved. The following points are particularly
carefully reviewed:-

- Utilisation Factors.
  These are standards set for the degree of
  of utilisation of the plant and machinery
  installed. The only allowances made are
  for the unavoidable stoppages relating to
  breakdown, repair and maintenance, and
  the change of set-ups of machines for new
  products. All other lost time is treated
  as an avoidable loss including lack of
  orders, or absenteeism of operators.

  Utilisation is one of the most important
  aspects of any manufacturing activity.
  Low utilisation turns all the costs in-

curred to run the processes, into losses.
In the concept of cost as outlined the
losses due to non-utilisation of installed
capacity cannot be taken up in the cost of
the products which are made when the plant
is utilised. It therefore reveals clearly
that a number of problems confront management in ensuring that utilisation of the
installed capacity does, in fact, take
place. This means that a delicate balance
must be sought between the price at which
products are sold in order to utilise the
installed capacity as against the standard
cost of these products so that an eventual
profit is made to a sufficient degree to
yield the necessary return on the capital
employed. It also brings out very clearly
the fact that the installed capacity and
the production processes used can be
applied to a variety of products. Too
often the mistake is made regarding the
products which are made as being the only
ones possible. In an attempt to utilise
full capacity with existing products,
prices are often cut below economic levels.
The alternative of seeking other products
which can be made with the same processes
is not sufficiently explored. This particular aspect is brought forcibly to the
attention of management by revealing the
losses incurred through low utilisation.

An example with which everyone is
familiar, is the utilisation of a
large computer installation. If the
costs had been calculated on the basis
that the computer will be used for
twenty hours a day, and in actual fact
the computer is only being used for
ten hours a day, there is a loss of
50% on utilisation. On the other hand,
if the cost per hour was based on ten
hours, and one indulged in a bureau
type operation one would probably price
oneself out of the market.

- Rate of Output Factor.
  The standards which have been set for
  the product costs are based upon assumed
  efficiencies in using the production facilities when they are under control of
  the operating staff. This, of course,
  excludes the concept of the utilisation
  factor. If an operator is unable to make
  full use of the machine capabilities the
  rate of output will drop. This is also a
  very important aspect in realising the
  standards which have been set in determining
  the standard cost. Any deviation from the
  standards set indicates an error in either
  the setting of the machine or the inability
  on the part of the operator to maintain
  the tempo of work. This information can

lead management to a variety of aspects
and schemes to improve the position thus
revealed. This information would be produced by an internal control system on a
daily basis so that corrective measures
can immediately be undertaken by management who receive a prompt indication
of the variance from the standard set.
This emphasizes once more the motivation
of management towards action by the information resulting from this form of
control.

- Quality Control Standards.
  Any rejects which may arise in the
  manufacturing processes due to faults
  in operation or in setting of machines
  will also increase the cost because the
  rate of output is reduced. In setting
  standard product costs, the extent of
  rejects will be set as a standard percentage. The failure to achieve these
  would be shown up by the accounting control system. This also leads to motivation of management to find ways and means
  of improving this aspect.

- Material Usage Control.
  The amount of material which is used in
  each product is also set in determining
  the standard costs. Full allowance is

made for waste at all stages of the
process. If these percentages are
exceeded, the result is shown by the
control system.

- Material Buying Variances.
As standard costs are set up for each
type of material that is bought from
outside sources for subsequent input
to the process, any deviation from the
standards as the materials are actually
purchased is revealed by this aspect
in the control system.

- Wages Control.
In setting up the budget we have shown
for each activity (production) centre
the number of people employed in each
occupation as well as their rates of
pay. Weekly or monthly comparisons
can now be made in relation to the number
of people employed as well as the rates of
pay to determine any deviations that may
occur, corrective action can then be taken
with the least loss of time.

- Expenditure on Different Kinds of Cost.
The actual costs which have been incurred
for the various kinds of expenditure for
the various input factors, excluding raw
materials, are revealed by the financial

control system. These actual ex-
penditures, such as Telephone expenses,
Printing and Stationery expenses, and
so on, are compared with the budgetted
amounts, which have been set out in
determining the operating cost budget.
These differences of expenditure for each
particular kind of factor service input
are revealed against the budgetted amount
both for the month under review and cumu-
latively from the beginning of the period.
By so doing, the deviations are brought to
the notice of management before the end of
the normal annual accounting period.
Inventory levels can also be kept to a minimum by controlling on budgetted requirements.

Control in the Shortest Possible Time.
The various controls which are set out above, are designed to operate with the shortest possible time lapse
between the events occurring and the process of reporting back. For instance, it is desirable that the production utilisation and output variances are revealed
each day for each shift worked. In this way, any
faults which have arisen during the working of a particular shift, are brought to the attention of the shift
supervisors immediately as they come on for their next
shift. Rejects or second grade articles which are
shown up by the checking and inspection processes are
also immediately revealed.

On the marketing and selling aspects it is possible
to use the standard costs which have been calculated
to show up the anticipated profits from orders as
they are received. This means that the average mark-
up against standard cost which is being actually
achieved can be determined in relation to the mark-
up which has been set up in the original sales forecast. This is an example of how this kind of control
operates. As mentioned, the budget as originally set,
is not inflexible; any deviation such as a lowered
mark-up which may have to be taken because of current
trading conditions or the general market position is
revealed immediately. Should there be an increase
in the price of raw material, it is a simple matter
to extract from the data base using a programme designed for that purpose those products which are
affected by the price variation. The new standard
costs can be calculated and the file up-dated to
reflect the affect of these price changes. In this
way it is not necessary to wait until the goods are
actually made and invoiced to decide whether the
general trend or mark-up is acceptable in relation
to the anticipated profit as revealed by the original
forecast. Control is thus exercised as soon as possible after the event has taken place, so that there
is a minimum of delay in bringing about corrective
measures to bear on a particular aspect which is not
meeting the standards already set.

The effectiveness of the efforts of the production
organisation and the marketing organisation as they

go on from day to day in carrying out their tasks
of administering their particular functions, is revealed in the monthly short-term accounting report.
The nature of the efforts and the motives behind
management action is thus directed towards the
critical problem of always trying to achieve the
equilibrium as shown by the forecast budgetted
profit resulting from comparison of standard cost
and selling prices. In this way, as has been
already explained, the budgets which are set do
not thus form inflexible, un-alterable bases which
are upset if there is any deviation. The whole
concept is based on the idea of setting standards
which show an equilibrium or stable position in
relation to the expected nett profit on the capital
employed. <u>Deviations can and do take place</u>. This
is the normal course of business where from day to
day, week to week, and month to month a number of
factors are operating at random to deviate the results from the desired levels. The extent of the
deviation is measured thus by this system and every
single aspect of the managerial action emphasized in
trying to restore the situation to one of stability
towards achieving the desired Plan.

Sales Control.
It is probably clear that the sales forecast and
eventual production budget does, in fact, set up
what could be called a set of quotas which are
expected from the marketing organisation. It is
therefore possible to take all aspects of seasonal

variations into account in setting up short-term
expectations from the marketing effort. We therefore
have means of controlling the sales effort to ensure
that the production capacity is sold. The volume of
turnover must be achieved to use the installed capacity in order to realise the cost structure as set up
in the Standard Operating Costs and the Standard
Product Costs. The Sales Forecast and Production
Budget show that certain profits can be achieved if
specific selling prices are achieved for the various
products. If it is necessary to go below these budgetted selling prices in order to fill the capacity
under given conditions it is as well to know how
this will affect the budgetted profit position. Decisions may then have to be taken by management to
accept lower profits on account of the current trading
conditions. It is essential that full utilisation be
made of the production capacity to prevent a loss, even
if this does mean selling the output at cost.

Projection of New Developments and New Products.
It must be pointed out very clearly that the method used
in Budget setting and Standard Cost Calculations depends
in no way whatsoever on the accounting results of the
previous year in order to set them up. Because they
are based entirely on the technical concepts relating
to the installed plant capacity and the quantity of
each kind of production factor required, it is then
feasible to set-up any kind of scheme for expansion
or diversification which may be contemplated.

Uniformity through Use of the Accounting Framework.
Throughout this system of accounting control, we use
a form of accounting framework which is based upon
the Continental practise in Germany and in France.
The whole of the accounting system, including both
the financial accounts and the industrial accounts,
are coded in a manner which makes it possible to
ensure uniformity in the budgeting and in the classification of actual expenditure when it is incurred.
Coding and arrangements of the accounts makes it
further possible to prepare a concise statement of
the Source and Application of Funds, the Cash Flow,
and the Financial Balance Sheet, each month. As this
accounting framework applies equally to any type or
kind of economic activity, it is apparent that it is
possible to realistically compare the economic viability of a variety of business undertakings and obtain an accurate assessment of the return on the
capital employed.

Subsystems.
The various items of information which have been
collected to set up the Budgets and the Standard
Cost are also used for various other kinds of
applications in the running of an organisation.
The standard data relative to the material requirements for the different products can be used
for the short-term control of waste arising in the
manufacturing processes. Standard production costs
and production time can also be used to prepare
machine loading programmes as well as for the use

of the production planning department in setting up
schedules of delivery and similar purposes. This
programme is expanded to include the procedure which
follows on the confirmation of an order. This could
well include progress control, despatch control,
invoicing and so on.

Code Structure.
It is not possible to over-emphasize the importance
of the code used to identify and categorise any information. If the code is deficient in any important
aspect, it will have a detrimental effect on the computer system.

The structuring and programming of a system is greatly
simplified by constructing a code which mirrors the
levels of a summary required in the system. The
failure to include a logical sequence in the build-
up of a code which follows the pattern of the levels
at which it is necessary to obtain totals will cause
a breakdown in the extraction of the required information.

Having determined precisely the nature of the output
required from any system, it is possible to build a
code which will take into account the relationships
of the data in the various analyses. Any item of
data is likely to have several distinct aspects.
Many of these aspects will only be significant in
summary form. It must also be borne in mind that
allowance must be made for any possible expansion of
the code, otherwise it can cause considerable cost

and inconvenience. A great deal of time and thought has gone into the coding to ensure that the data fed into the system can be successfully used in the various types and kinds of output requirements.

Summary.
It is considered that management initially require basic information that may be considered in terms of four essential subsystems to any Management Information System.

- Management Planning/Control.
- Operations Planning/Control.
- Financial Planning/Control.
- Non-quantitative Information.

The integrated system described, comprises a number of modular programmes which produces the following from calculations performed on basic information held on the Data Base:

- Plant Model.
- Operating Cost Budget.
- Production and Marketing Activity Centre Costs and Process Time Rates.
- Product Standard Costs.
- Sales Forecasts (Budgets) and Production Budgets.
- Financial Budgets.
- Source and Application of Funds Statements.
- Cash Flow Statements and Balance Sheets.

Obviously the only subsystem not covered by the
above is, therefore, the Non-quantitative information, such as employee history, turnover statistics,
etc. and it is felt that before this area is tackled
to produce meaningful information, the integrated
system described covering the first three subsystems
above, can and must be expanded.

Let us consider, for example, the second subsystem
mentioned above

- Operations Planning/Control.

A major planning and control (modular) programme is
built around the receipt of an order to supply goods,
and the processing of this order e.g.

- Confirmation - Standard production item or
  made to order? Price acceptable? Available
  from finished stock? Can it be produced by
  delivery date specified?
- Order Analysis - Raw Material requirements;
  Production capacity and planning; Long-term
  forecasting of material requirements.
- Sales Target Control - Comparison with Budget
- Sales Statistics - Update forecasts; Check
  trends and adjust material and production
  forecasts; Update customer profile analysis.
- Outstanding Order Analysis
- Works Order Routine - Issue works instruction;
  Raw material requirements and comparison with

stocks; Issue of Purchase Order; Machine
or process loading.

To this can be added progress control, waste control,
plant utilisation control, output control, despatch
control, invoicing, statements, credit control and
so on.

Therefore, in this area alone, all arising from the
receipt of the order, there is a major field for
management information, planning and control, without
having to be concerned with Non-quantitative information. Only when all these many obvious fields, which
in turn are related to our central Budgetary concept,
are being successfully and, one might add, scientifi-
cally managed, need one look for further aid to management.

Intuitive management is no longer sufficient in the
modern day fight for survival in the business jungle
and the undergrowth of rising inflationary costs.
Indeed, survival itself is no longer considered adequate, the constant cry is for a maximisation of
profits to show an adequate return on capital employed.

There will undoubtedly be a call for the statistician
and also, no doubt, for the use of esoteric OR techniques. Let us first, however, give management the
practical means to assist themselves in their basic
task of planning and controlling the day to day dynamic
operation of their economic activity.

COST/EFFECTIVENESS ANALYSIS FOR MIS

P. F. Marini
Ing. C. Olivetti & C. S.p.A.
Italy

INTRODUCTION

The need to implement a Management Information System in order to ensure the correct management of a Company is a necessity which is making itself felt more and more as time goes on. However, it is useless to deny that consid erable financial investment is involved and that it may also turn out to be a source of technical problems and difficulties with regard to Company policy.
Therefore, one of the first priorities when implementing a Management Information System is a careful analysis of the parameters which play an important part in determining the financial committment involved.

This article deals with these parameters with regard to an information system but does not pretend by any means to be an exhaustive treatement of the topic; it is rather a compiling, probably incomplete, of the concepts which occur most frequently.

COST ANALYSIS

The various costs to be analysed include:

- Personnel and manpower.

- Raw Materials.

- Equipment.

- Services.

Obviously, these may be of varying importance and predominance; in the case of an information system, the costs which must be given special consideration are the first and the third while the other two are of minimal importance.

The above-mentioned classes may be divided into the following subdivisions and items:-

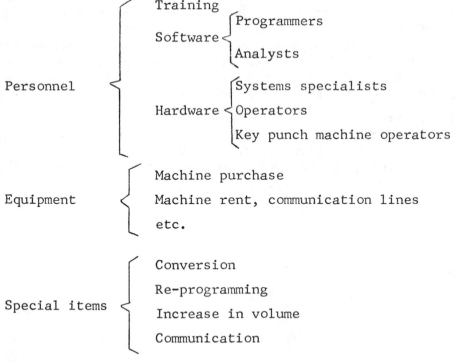

Personnel
- Training
- Software
  - Programmers
  - Analysts
- Hardware
  - Systems specialists
  - Operators
  - Key punch machine operators

Equipment
- Machine purchase
- Machine rent, communication lines
- etc.

Special items
- Conversion
- Re-programming
- Increase in volume
- Communication

Staff training is an item of cost which has been dealt with elsewhere, insofar as it may be of extreme importance and have a decisive influence on the financial side of the system.

It includes in the case of a Management Information Sys tem training courses at all levels, whether for those who are setting up the system, (from the operators to the analysts) or for the Users (from the operative section to top management).

The conversion costs are linked to modifications in the features of the Hardware of the data processing section and are related to the conversion of the files and the parallel systems. These costs are usually separate from the re-programming costs as the latter are more closely connected to the development of new procedures and pro grams regarding a new philosophy of data management. In the case of a Management Information System both these items of cost are important as it is non unreasonable to say that the development of an integrated system implies a re-organization of the files, the extending of the Hard ware and certainly a re-programming of some of the exist ing procedures.

One of the features of all information systems is that the volume of data increases more than proportionally ac cording to their degree of complexity and sophistication. Therefore, when designing and planning a Management Infor mation System, it is advisable to carry out a forecast of the volume of future processing and an estimate of the costs to be borne in such a way as to ensure that the di mensions of the system are the result of an economic choice between alternatives:

a) a well-dimensioned present system but over-loaded in the future with therefore deferred development costs;

b) a system which will be able to meet future requirements but which at the moment is under-loaded with resulting higher costs than are necessary.

An information system, and more particularly a M. I.S. must be characterised by an efficient system of communication between the Users. This is designed keeping in mind such factors as the load to be borne and the acceptable aver age access times.

The problem is, however, not just a technical one but also a financial one. As far as this is concerned, the cost depends very much on the features of the network i.e. the number of Users being served as well as on the number of terminals, on the speed of transmission and other techni cal parameters. It is interesting to discover what is the sensitivity of the number of channels, when there is , a change in the number of Users.

To do this, we consider an organizational structure which is perfectly equalitarian.

This structure is made up of a number of members n and our aim is to link each member to all the rest (n - 1). The total number of couples possible is given by the binomial co-efficient:

$$\binom{n}{2} = \frac{n\,(n-1)}{2} \tag{1}$$

We now consider an increase in the number of members of the group by a factor c > 1

The number of possible couples becomes:

$$\binom{cn}{2} = \frac{cn\,(cn-1)}{2} \tag{2}$$

Dividing (2) by (1) we obtain:

$$\binom{cn}{2} \bigg/ \binom{n}{2} = c^2\,(n^2 - \frac{n}{c}) \,/\, (n^2 - n)$$

Seeing as c > 1 is n/c < n, therefore

$$(n^2 - \frac{n}{c}) \,/\, (n^2 - n) > 1$$

Finally

$$\binom{cn}{2} \bigg/ \binom{n}{2} > c^2$$

From this we conclude that the increasing of the group by a factor c requires an increase in square measurement of the information channels and the corresponding costs.

In conclusion, it should be noticed that, when carrying

out cost analysis, those relating to the new information system are often classified as:-

- recurring (personnel; machine rent; increase in volume; maintenance of the system, etc.)

- non-recurring (installation expenses; design and develop ment; re-programming; conversion, etc.).

The costs of the system to be replaced are on the other hand divided into avoidable and unavoidable. These obviously continue to have an effect on the new system, of which the operating costs are estimated according to its own operating costs plus those of the previous system which could not be eliminated.

QUALITATIVE FEATURES OF THE INFORMATION

The value of the information and its costs depend on a large number of features which determine its quality. These features are influenced in their turn by the system which physically manages the information as well as by the organizational structure which is being served by the system itself. Unfortunately, an analysis of the sensitivity of such features and the costs which derive from them, when there is a change in the second factor, is very complex and is difficult to generalise; therefore, hence forth only those factors which are closely linked to the data processing system will be taken into consideration.

One of the most important features of the information as far as quality is concerned, whether on the operating or strategic level, is its timeliness. Its cost depends on the type of storage support used (tapes, discs, drums), on the way in which the files are organized (sequential, index-sequential, direct) of the access (sequential, ran dom). Long reply time and low costs are typical of the sequential processing of tape files. Short reply times and high costs are a feature of the processing of direct access random organized files. Intermediate times and more reasonable costs may be obtained by an index-sequential type processing in which a group of transactions are proc essed sequentially having been sought on a direct access file.

The volume of the data is another feature which has great influence on the quality of the information. That is to say, that increased availability of data generally ensures more accurate processing and greater flexibility. This should not be confused with an excessive degree of analy sis and detail in the information which on the contrary often results in a falling-off of quality. From an econom ic point of view, the volume of data is influenced by the cost of gathering, transmission, storage, retrieval and processing.

Reference was made earlier to the accuracy of the informa tion. In general, the hardware of an electronic processing system has innate in it the characteristic of precision with a high degree of reliability. Therefore the system is endowed with these features on condition, of course that the software has been designed and implemented in a suitable manner.

One of the main aims of a Management Information System is to improve the quality of the information by integrating the various information channels and by unifying the sources of the data. This entails the clear definition of objectives, elimination of redundancies, clarification of the decision processes, indication of possible alternatives etc.

From what has been said above, we may conclude that the cost of the information depends on the precision and reliability of all the various parts of the system with the exception of the hardware.

The software and the hardware both play an equal part in the _flexibility_ of the information, that is its ability to meet the varied, ever-changing needs of the system. This flexibility can be obtained only if during the design phase of the information system, an accurate forecast of possible future needs is made and if during the set-up phase the modularity of the various component parts is assured with an obvious increase in cost in the two above-mentioned phases.

The feature of _selectivity_ includes, through an ever-increasing degree of complexity and an increase in cost, the possibility of selecting the information, exception reports and analyses, man/machine dialogue, sophistication of the outputs.

To conclude it might be useful to bear in mind that, in the implementation of an information system, a situation often arises like the one indicated in figure 1. i.e. the cost of the information is a function which, beyond a certain limit, increases exponentially according to variations in the quality of the information; this means, for example, that an increase in completeness and precision from 50% to 90% costs less than achieving the final 10%.

Examining this figure, it is possible to deduce that the optimum quality of the information corresponds to the point at which the marginal cost necessary for its improvement is equal to its marginal value.

The optimum point established above is generally influenc

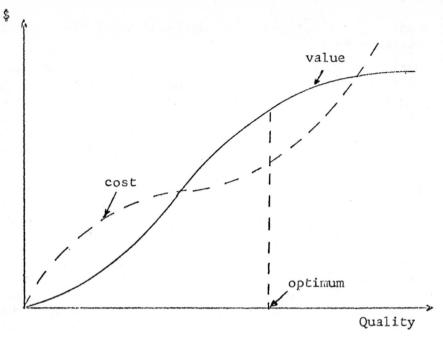

Fig. 1

ed by technical improvements as shown in figure 2, i.e.
a technical improvement brings about an improvement   in
the optimum quality of the information and also, the qual
ity being equal, an increase in the difference (cost-value).

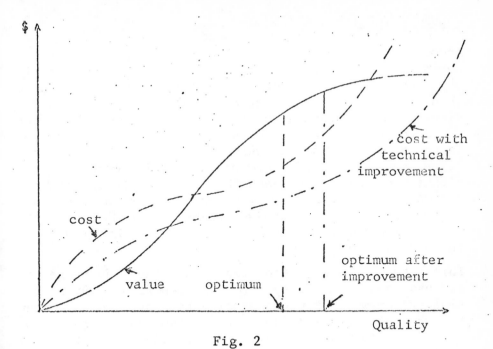

Fig. 2

VALUE OF THE INFORMATION

According to some opinions, the value of information may be defined as the difference in the value of the result obtained when the information is available and the value when the information is not available. Those methods of simulation or "business game" which try to establish what would be the probable results and their equivalent value, in terms of returns and savings, supposing the existence of perfect information, are based on this concept. The difference between this and that relating to the real condition, i.e. imperfect or missing information may provide a limited measurement of the suitability of the investment, when estimating the cost necessary for the improvement of the process being examined.

This method of evaluation clearly has the advantage of expressing as a quantity all those benefits of an information system which cannot normally be expressed as a quantity but on the other hand, it is also characterized by all the approximations which are typical of calculating methods based on models and simulations. However, a quantitative analysis of the sensitivity of a formalized decision process may often serve as a useful guideline when establishing the value of the information. For example, the measuring of the difference in cost of an inventory because of an error in the forecasting of requirements may be a useful indication of how much could be spent to improve the forecasts themselves.

With regard to the value of the information, it has also been proposed that this can be expressed by measuring how much the User is prepared to spend in order to obtain it. This approach does not, however, solve the problem of an intrinsic, objective evaluation as it takes into account only the interest that the User may have subjectively in the use of the information, and it presumes, moreover, that the User is aware of the benefits that the information offers.

In a cost/benefits analysis, the evaluation of a system is based on the preliminary ascertaining of the tangible and untangible benefits.

The tangible benefits are those which can be expressed as

a quantity (for example, returns or savings) and in mone tary terms. The untangible benefits refer to those, direct or indirect, which it is impossible or very difficult to express in terms of money (for example, the improving of the quality of the information, the possibility of making forecasts, the availability of decision alternatives, etc.).

Once these have been classified, the costs of developing a new information system are then compared only to the tangible advantages, thus obtaining (as will be seen in the next paragraph) an indication as to the purely econom ic suitability of the investment.

COST/BENEFITS ANALYSES AND THE EVALUATION OF THE SYSTEM

The cost/benefits analyses of a system require that the costs and the tangible benefits be:-

a) Ascertained according to the class they belong to.

b) Analysed in detail according to the various items.

c) Planned or designed in time.

d) Compared amongst themselves according to the various possible alternatives.

The span of time which these analyses cover is the presumed average lifetime (T) of the system itself. This time must be calculated accurately as it influences the estimating of the required returns on the investment and therefore its suitability or not.

This time total (T) is approximately made up of the partial times:

$$T = T_d + T_i + T_s$$

where:

T_d = the design time of the system (including the preliminary study and the feasibility study).

T_i = set up time (including the development, installation and conversion time).

T_s = the service time.

Usually, it is possible to estimate the T_d and the T_i times with a reasonable amount of accuracy but the calculating of the service time proves to be more difficult.

For the information system of a sector, this is considered to vary from 3 to 5 years. For a Management Information System which is still being developed and of which there is not as yet great experience, the T_s is a parameter which is quite problematical and even risky. However, having indicated with R_t and C_t the costs and returns for a given period t, the value of the system may be expressed as follows:-

$$\alpha_{t_o} = \sum_{t=0}^{T} R_{at} \bigg/ \sum_{t=0}^{T} C_{at}$$

where $\underline{a}$ indicates that the costs and returns are discount
ed at a same point of reference t_o, according to a fixed
Rate of Return.

Without going into the merits of the "Discounted Cash
Flow" technique, through which these cash flows are made
homogeneous, it should be noted that this technique is
usually used in order to ascertain:-

1) once a certain interest rate has been fixed, what is
   the breakeven point at which expenditure and returns
   are equal, that is, when the investment begins to be
   come "active".

2) what is the discount rate which will bring to zero the
   total cash flow at the end of the presumed life of the
   system.

This last value is particularly important because when
considering the suitability or not of the investment, it
is compared to the rate of return fixed by the top manage
ment as being the lowest acceptable limit.

When α is below this limit, the intangible benefits men
tioned in the preceding paragraph have a decisive rôle to
play in deciding whether or not the investment should be
approved.

BIBLIOGRAPHY

- BLUMENTHAL S.C. - "Management Information Systems" - Prentice Hall

- BONNEY M.C. - "Some consideration of the cost and value of information" - Computer J. 12-2 (May 1969)

- DIEBOLD European Research Program - "Evaluating the economic effectiveness of information systems" - E 37

- EMERY J.C. - "Organizational Planning and Control Systems" - Macmillan (1969)

- SCHODERBECK P.P. - "Management Systems" - John Wiley (1968)

- ZANNETOS Z.S. - "On the theory of divisional structures" - Manag. Science, vol. 12, No 4. (1969).

PROFIT VISIBILITY

Albert D. Neveu
Stanford Research Institute
U.S.A.

Managing a business organization involves complex decisions - about people, equipment, facilities, and funds. The decision maker is often faced with obscure alternatives. It is important to select the best of the alternatives, but too often the manager is forced to rely heavily on personal judgement. Managers at all levels need a better means for realistically evaluating existing and probable future conditions, for arriving at policy and investment decisions, and for controlling acts and operations so as to achieve maximum benefits under continual change.

In response to the most difficult of the manager's problems - that of controlling profits - we have now developed a new management science method which is known as "Profit Visibility". We have found that this science can be universally applied to most industrial organizations. The science requires about a week of orientation to be fully understood. This paper therefore represents only a breifing on the fundamentals of the science.

PRINCIPLE FEATURES OF PROFIT VISIBILITY

1. Profit visibility (P.V.) is a management science that provides all levels of management with a new understanding and scope relative to the sources of all profits. It provides a flow of in-depth profit data and information that have hitherto never existed in exposing the dynamics of making profits.

2. P.V. penetrates the executives requirement for information. It brings to the surface the most vital of operating problems. Presidents and directors of companies have repeatedly said that they do not receive any direct benefits from the computer in a form with which they can make decisions. P.V. helps to put every manager, regardless of his level, into the drivers seat.

3. It provides control information that relates to the purpose of the business. Since making profits is the objective of business, it is logical that we should develop control systems to determine our progress and everyone's contribution to the goal. P.V. relates the financial profits to the dynamic occurances which caused them, and it yeilds information as it occurs, hour-by-hour, day-by-day in a management-by-exception form.

4. P.V. helps to develop "Profit Oriented" managers. Managers today have no idea of what their function contributes to profits, nor do they have any idea of what they can do to improve profits in a way that integrates their efforts with those of other functional managers. Their scope, their horizons, and their incentives are placed upon a new plateau with Profit Visibility methods.

5. P.V. was developed to simplify and reduce the great amounts of data generated by a business to action type data that can be understood. It identifies all

conditions graphically to show improving or diminishing
effectiveness.

6. It was developed as a higher order of data retrieval and reduction. It neither interferes with existing
systems, nor does it require reprogramming of computer
runs other than for providing for the insertion of a
few code numbers at the order entry points. It is most
easily applied in firms who have developed order processing
and sales analysis systems.

DEFINITIONS

Profit is defined as Net Profit at standard before tax.
Visibility is defined as the ability to display conditions,
results and trends in graphic form.

INTRODUCTION

Most executives today receive a meager amount of
information with which to evaluate the efficiency of their
operations. They receive financial reports – weeks after
transactions have taken place– which provide summations
of all the transactions of the previous period. Executives
cannot pinpoint a problem from these reports. In fact,
they cannot determine that any problem exists. The real
life enviorment in which every business exists is lumped
together under accounting titles known as Income and
Expense.

The dynamics which involve the customer, the market,
the competition, the facilities, the manpower, the prices,
the organization structure, the policies, and other
considerations are lost with our present techniques of
reporting results.

Financial reports were developed to show the net effect rather than the dynamics of transactions. Accounting is a uniform method of recording data and of reporting results, It is absolutely necessary that accounting methods be used by every firm for tax purposes, and for safeguarding the stockholders interests. Likewise, it is necessary that management be given tools with which to control and improve the results of the facilities entrusted to them. To do this they need more than financial statements – they need dynamic information.

An executive needs to know the answers as to who, how, what, where, and when that concern his profit from operations in order to make decisions and plans that will improve his profit position.

DYNAMIC CONSIDERATIONS

There are many dynamics involved in business trans-- actions. Our concern deal with those that are internal rather than those which are external to the business. The executive can excercise control over the internal dynamics, but has relatively little control over those which are outside of the organization. The profit dynamics of a transaction are shown in figure 1.

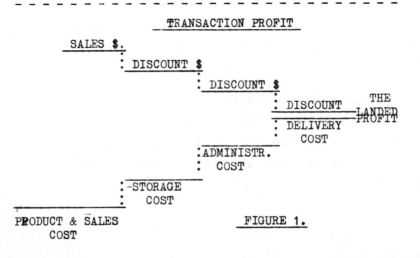

FIGURE 1.

324

Profits occur when a product has been invoiced and
delivered to a customer. This involves on the sales side
of the transaction, pricing and a series of discounts to
meet trade practices in certain industries, and to meet
competition. On the cost side of transactions it involves
a series of incremental costs to produce and market the
product, and each transaction is unique unto itself.

The narrow channel shown in figure 1 between the sales
and costs at the point of delivery is the profit or loss
result for any given transaction.

The profit that any given transaction yields is subject
to three major internal influences. These are:
1. The methods by which a business is organized to
   stimulate and meet demand, and its quality.
2. The qualitative, quantitative, and monetary value
   of our products as they relate to demand and the
   products of our competitors.
3. The policies, systems, and methods adopted.

These three internal influences are illustrated in
figure 2.

INTERNAL INFLUENCES

1	2	3
Salesmen	Product	Policies
Branch	Product Group	Systems
Area	Product Line	Methods
Region		
Department		
Division		

Figure 2.

Weakness or collapse of any one of the influences will
cause a weakness or collapse of the other two. They are

interdependent on each other for success. Each must be measured in context with the other two to determine the effectiveness of the business venture.

Each transaction is unique unto itself by virtue of differing from others in identifying who bought, who sold, what services were involved, what product was sold, when it occurred, where it occurred. The summation of these unique transactions into various categories enable us to determine the following;

. It cost more to sell by one salesman than it does another salesman.

. It costs more to sell one product than another.

. It costs more to sell one customer than another.

. It cost more to use one channel of distribution than it does another

Not only are these factors of concern, but the fact that the costs are continually changing enables us to realize that we must be able to identify these dynamics.

This is the dynamic framework within which Profit Visibility can be of tremendous assistance to the manager.

THE PROFIT VISIBILITY METHOD

1. Seperate manufacturing costs, from marketing and distribution costs. Manufacturing costs are relatively well identified with Job or Process Cost Systems, but marketing and distribution costs require a totally different method of coping with the dynamics involved.

2. Utilize the coordinate costing method for marketing and distribution functions AND account for all products from the end of the production line to their final destination. (Coordinate costing is discussed later in this paper)

3. Illustrate profit results graphically,profiled to executives and managers with a need-to-know.

4. Illustrate the efficiency achieved in all service areas graphically.

5. Train management to use Profit Visibility results.

COORDINATE COSTING

Coordinate Costing is a new method of identifying marketing and distribution costs. It utilizes a two-dimensional matrix for segregating the standard costs of marketing and distribution services performed. Each coordinate in the matrix identifies a unique type of service performed within the various functions, and each coordinate carries with it standard costs, statistics of its usage, and actual cost apportionments.

An example of a coordinate costing matrix is shown in figure 3. Note that the operating expenses are spread horizontally for each major function, and that the various services performed within a function are placed vertically beneath the functional group in which the services are provided.

Each coordinate has a digital position and a number or letter assigned to it to permit ease of identification and to allow it to be retrieved by the computer.

COORDINATE COSTING MATRIX

SELLING EXP	OFFICE EXP	WAREHOUSE EXP	DELIVERY EXP.
0 NONE	0 NONE	0 NONE	0 NONE
1 House Acct	1 Blanket Or	1 Skid Lot	1 City Deliv
2 Inter-Company	2 Data-Phone	2 Bulk Units	2 Suburban
3 Counter Sale	3 System Contr	3 Small Pack	3 Parcel Pst
4 Territory A	4 Consignmnt	4 Unit	4 United Pcl
5 Territory B			

Figure 3

A combination of the various coordinates required to service a customer's order is known as a MOD or Method of Distribution. These codes are written on the order. For example, the number 4322 is the MOD code identifying an order item as comming from a customer in territory A, who has a systems contract arrangement with us, and that requires an item that is packed in bulk units delivered to his suburban plant. The number 5133 is the MOD code for identifying an order item as comming from a customer in territory B, who has a blanket order arrangement, for an item in a small pack to be shipped by parcel post.

The MOD coding is done by order clerks at each distribution location, and when the order or sale data is punched, the MOD codes are punched as well.

The computer deducts the standard cost of the product from the net sales amount to arrive at gross profit, then it retrieves the MOD costs from its table in memory and subtracts it from the gross to arrive at the net profit.

Coordinate Costing is not a complicated process.
It is expandable to any accounting system and to any
number of services performed. It is flexible to any
number of products, any number of facilities, any
number of distribution methods, or to any complicated
pricing schemes your marketing department can desire.
Its power lies in using coordinates.

PROFIT INFORMATION

The computer can calculate 1000 transactions in
less than a second. It can print the result of
1000 transactions in one minute, but then we come
to the big problem — who has the time or patience
to read the data?

To handle voluminous data it is necessary to
reduce it to analytical catagories. We do this
today when we develop sales analyses and obtain
total sales by salesman, by branch, by product,
or by any other catagory for which we have a code
in the original data.

The same type of reduction is done in Profit
Visibility except that we go furthur with the
data and the reduction. The steps are as follows;

1. We profile the information to the needs of
   managers at various levels of the organization.

2. We print reports that show net profit, gross
   profit, costs, and sales by responsibility,
   by MOD, and by product.

3. We filter out exceptional conditions from
   normal conditions and display the exceptions
   in graphic form.(two - dimensional)

4. We process all data for coordinate totals of profits for the current period and over time. This is done in three - dimensional form. The coordinates are as follows;

x	y	z
products	days of month	profit $
MOD	" " "	"
Branch	" " "	"
products	Branch	"
products	MOD	"
Branch	"	"
products	months of year	"
MOD	" " "	"
Branch	" " "	"

CONCLUSION

It has been said that " a picture is worth a thousand words". This is certainly true when it comes to explaining profit dynamics. It is so easy for a manager to look a a curve on a two-dimensional graph and compare it a normal line to see where problems exist. Likewise, it is easy for a manager to look at the mountains and valleys on a three-dimensional graph and see where his problems exist. (These require some imagination on the part of the reader because unfortunately, we cannot show a copy of these charts on this typed report.)

Since the data base contains all of the basic imput, it is easy to retrieve any specific data that the manager may need to investigate to determine the cause of problems shown on graphs.

If we look at profit dynamics from the point of
wiew that they are organizational or people oriented,
product oriented, and/or policy and methods oriented
we begin to see where this type of information should
be disseminated. Obviously,there are specialized
functions in almost every organization that can benefit from P.V. information and that can take action
with the indicators that it provides. There is also
a requirement on the part of executive management to
be sensitive to these indicators, and to play their
part in seeing that policies and practices are modified to meet real world conditions and to coordinate
the actions of all their subordinate managers.

INTERACTION BETWEEN INFORMATION ANALYSIS
AND DESIGN OF CONTROL PROCESSES

Mats Lundeberg
Kungl. Tekniska Högskolan
Sweden

1   INTRODUCTION

1.2   Background

By an <u>information system</u>[1] we mean a system, whose parts
are information sets and information processes[2]. The
information sets are used for decisions and communication (are system connections) in a larger system (e.g.
an administrative control system), in which the information system is a subsystem. An information system contains subsystems for collecting, storing, processing and
distributing information sets.

By <u>information systems work</u> (Swedish: systemering) we
refer to the work with developing information systems.

---

1) A slight revision of the definition in reference (2),
   p. 143
2) Data is defined as means for representing information, see reference (2), p. 193

In order to develop information systems we need different models of the information system, representing different stages of the work. These models are then manipulated in different ways to obtain satisfactory design solutions. There are two principal types of models of an information system: abstract information systems and information processing systems.

By an _abstract information system_ we mean a system consisting of information sets (= parts) and their relations (especially precedence relations).

An _information processing system_ is a system consisting of information sets and information processes and their relations (incidence relations).

1.2 Information systems work methodology

According to Langefors´ fundamental principle of systems work the information systems work itself has to be divided into parts, i.e. method areas or phases. Langefors gives the following four principal method areas of information systems work:[1]

1 Design of control structures and control methods
2 Information analysis
3 Design of information processing system
4 Selection of equipment and implementation

This division of information systems work is suitable for several reasons. Such a complex task as the performance of information systems work has to be partitioned in order to have a fair chance of developing any infor-

---

1) Slightly revised, see reference (5)

mation system at all. It further certainly has to be partitioned in order to develop efficient information systems to meet the desires of the users. Also no single person can today cope with all four method areas in a reasonable way. Different people are differently suited for the method areas in question. The partitioning of information systems work allows for the collaboration between different specialist categories.

In the first method area decisions are made about what the information system is to contain. The design of business administration oriented control structures and control methods forms the foundation for the subsequent information analysis. The information analysis begins with crude precedence and component analysis. The crude phases are followed by more detailed phases, ideally down to the elementary level. The result of the information analysis is documented in form of a basic abstract information system.

The design of the information system is divided into two phases: a principal design phase and a detailed design phase. In the third method area, corresponding to the principal design phase, a structuring is made of the files and the processes that the future system is to work with. Rough decisions are made regarding the automatic and the manual parts of the system to be. The result of the principal design phase is documented in form of an adaptable information processing system, i.e. an information processing system that is possible to adapt to the equipment selected later on.

In the fourth method area, finally, selection of equipment and software takes place and the information processing system is adapted to this choice, which means a detailed design. We assume that the subsequent steps of the implementation follow current practice.

The above is illustrated in figure 1. The arrows pointing upwards indicate that a number of iterations have to be made both within and between the method areas in a practical application situation.

2 DESIGN OF CONTROL STRUCTURES AND CONTROL METHODS

An enlargement of the first method area of information systems work, design of control structures and control methods, is given in figure 2. This and the following enlargements represent a so far promising hypothesis, which currently is being tested within the ISAC[1] research project.

The method area is divided into two main phases, control analysis and control design. The result of the control analysis, the basic control system, is the starting point of the subsequent control design in analogy with the basic abstract information system being the foundation for design of the information processing system. The basic control system shall thus consist of an as design independent description as possible of the control aspects of the future system, while the control system outline is the result of an actual design.

The control analysis is enlarged in figure 3. At first system boundaries and guiding principles are derived. With this result objective and/or activity analysis is performed. We do not have methods for obtaining the

1) Information Systems for Administrative Control

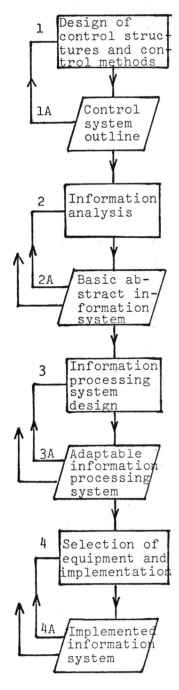

Figure 1

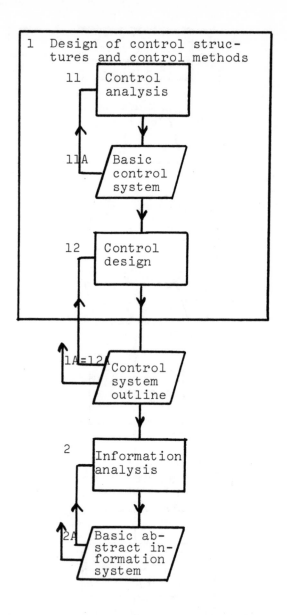

Figure 2

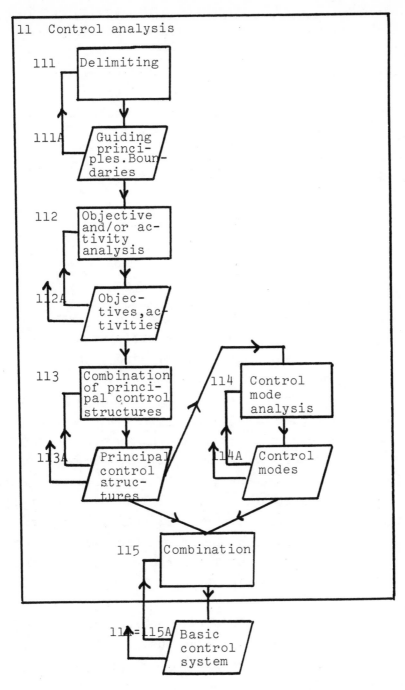

Figure 3

lower-level objectives from the ultimate desires in a
systematic breakdown and analysis procedure. What we can
do instead, therefore, is to start with defining a
structure of objectives, in which the respective goals
are defined intuitively. The appropriateness of the
goals can then be tested and the structure of objectives
adapted as more experience is gathered.

In figure 3 and figure 4 we find the concepts

> control structure
> control mode
> control method
> control process

A control method is associated with control variables
(control information) and how to obtain values for
these. A unique set of information kinds, information
precedents and information succedents, belongs to each
control method. When we apply a control method to an
actual situation we do this in a control process, i.e.
a control process realizes a control method. A control
mode is a class of control methods with the same information kinds as succedents, i.e. the same control variables. A control structure, finally, is a collection of
control modes, control methods or control processes -
which depends on how far the information systems work
has proceeded. Each control structure is put together
to solve a certain problem type.

From the result of the objective and/or activity analysis we are thus able to give an outline of principal
control structures, corresponding to principal problem
types. The analysis of control modes displays the

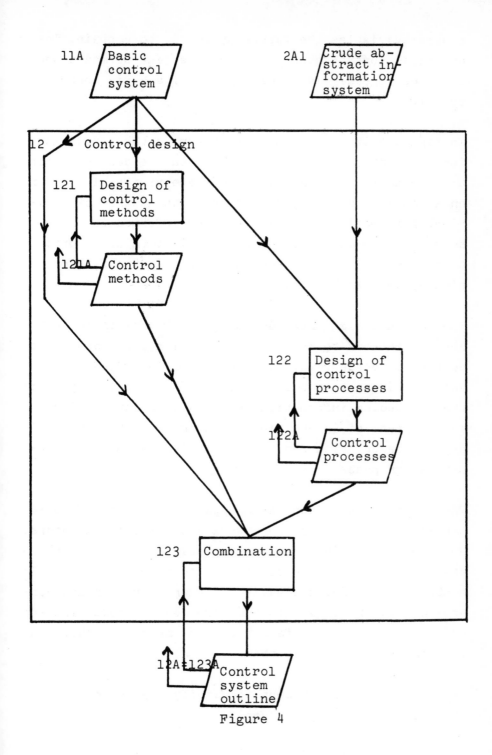

Figure 4

control variables the future system is to contain. The principal control structures and the control modes are combined together in a description of a basic control system.

In figure 4 the basic control system is the foundation for the control design, starting with the design of control methods. The control methods are preferably chosen on a cost/value basis, depending on the degree of ambition. Information analysis is then performed in order to obtain the consequences of this in form of information relations, documented in a crude abstract information system (with information kinds).

The second design phase deals with the application of control methods to the actual situation, i.e. design of control processes. This is analogously based on cost/value estimates. At this point it is suitable to perform the succeeding information analysis with information sets instead of information kinds in order to obtain a precise description for the succeeding information system design phases.

The advocated approach is an application of the fundamental principle of systems work according to Langefors. Note the underlying modularity possibilities. With this design methodology one can decide to start with a simple control method and gradually implement more complex control methods belonging to the same control mode. The same principle goes for different control processes that realize the same control method.

We now end with an attempt to clarify the methodology hypothesis by a simple example.

3   A SIMPLE EXAMPLE FROM THE INVENTORY CONTROL AREA

The outline presented above will be applied to a very simple example concerning an inventory. The numbers in the headings below refer to the corresponding boxes of figures 3 and 4.

111   Delimiting

We are interested in developing an information system for administrative control of Lagerco, a small company in A-town. Lagerco is subsidiary of some larger corporation in A-city.

112   Objective and activity analysis

Lagerco stores products, which are received from the company in A-city and sold to customers in A-town. The operative objective for Lagerco is to minimize inventory costs while keeping a certain service level.

113   Combination of principal control structures

Two principal control structur s were obtained: development and operative control structures. We will in our example enlarge only the latter.

114   Control mode analysis

It is assumed that goal formulating modes, planning modes and implementation modes are regarded. The former two are not discussed further - we accept figures 5 and 6. When it comes to implementation modes we have three different modes to choose from, described in

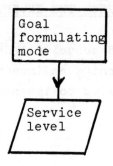

Figure 5

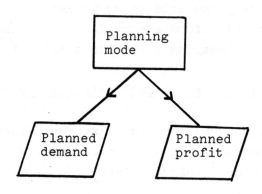

Figure 6

figures 7, 8 and 9. They are described by their control
variables (information succedents) and some properties.
With reference to the actual situation at Lagerco, the
choice was between mode 1 and mode 3. Implementation
mode 1 of figure 7 was finally chosen because of easi-
ness in application.

115   Combination

The result of the combination of control modes and
principal control structures is shown in figures 10, 11
and 12. Figure 10 is a picture giving an overall view.
External information and budgets have been added to the
development and operative control structure to obtain
a more complete overview. The picture shows that operative plans are obtained from development plans and external information and that the operative implementation
is guided by operative plans and budgets.

Figure 11 (picture 3) gives an enlargement of how operative plans are obtained by showing the relations to
the operative goal formulating and planning modes from
figures 5 and 6. In the same manner, figure 12 (picture
6) shows the relations of the operative implementation
mode to inventory handling. These figures thus represent
part of our basic control system, which is to be used
as a starting-point for the control design.

121   Design of control methods

The chosen implementation mode can be realized by a number of control methods depending on degree of ambition
and the actual situation. A number of possible

Control mode 1
Fixed order quantity

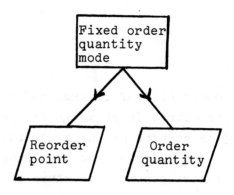

Advantages: Simplicity
Safety
Inexpensiveness
Easy to explain

Disadvantages: Irregular orders

Figure 7

Control mode 2

Periodic inventory order (replenishment)

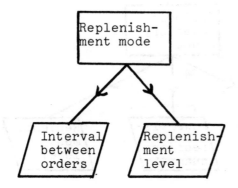

Advantages: Regular orders

Disadvantages: Larger inventory carrying costs
as compared to mode 1

Figure 8

<u>Control mode 3</u>
Periodic inventory count
(optional replenishment)

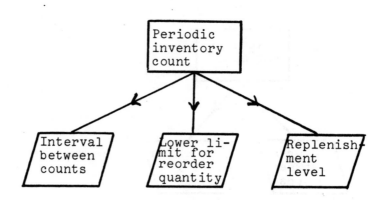

Advantages: It can be shown to give better
results than control mode 1 and
2 for a large range of problems

Disadvantages: More complex to apply

Figure 9

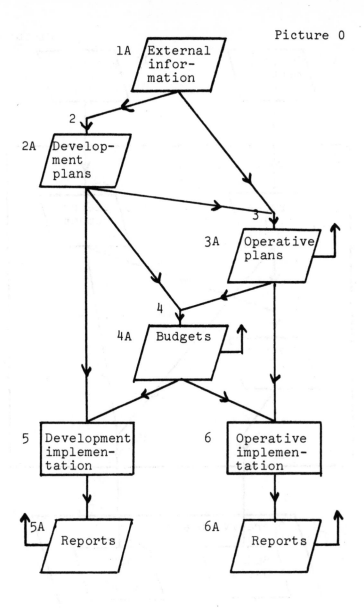

Figure 10

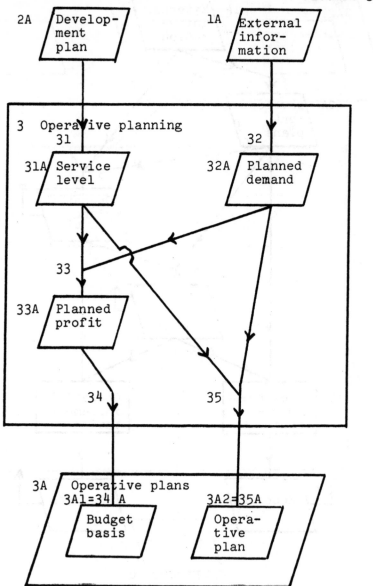

Figure 11

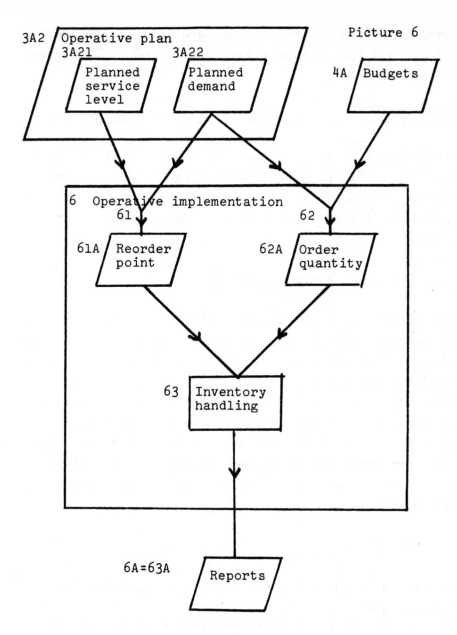

Figure 12

implementation control methods are shown in figures
13, 14 and 15. We assume here that method 1 in figure
13 is chosen.

123 Combination including 21 Information analysis

It is possible to continue with figure 12 (picture 6)
as basis. Enlargements of arcs 61 and 62 are shown in
figure 16 and 17. The information analysis has in this
way been performed a bit more in detail, but it is still
crude.

122 Design of control processes

The exact way of how to apply the chosen control method
is decided. This is done on a cost/value basis. In the
general case there are several ways of applying a control method. The transformation of information kinds to
information sets would in our case involve a discussion
of e.g. if inventory carrying cost and ordering cost
should be calculated for each article seperately or for
some groups of articles. The results of this information
component analysis is documented on forms, which are not
shown here.

4 CONCLUSIONS

It is concluded that there is a strong interaction
between information analysis and design of control processes. At present a computer-aided tool for information
analysis, IA/1 (Information Analysis system 1), is being
developed within the ISAC project in order to facilitate
the testing and application of the presented methodology
hypothesis.

Control method 1

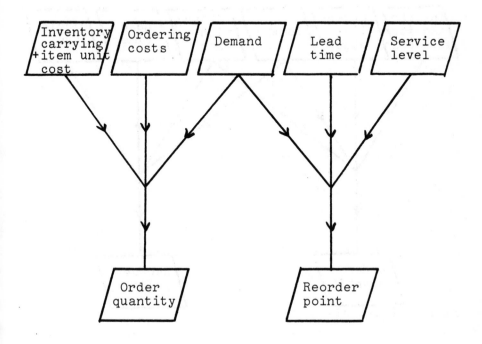

Figure 13

Control method 2

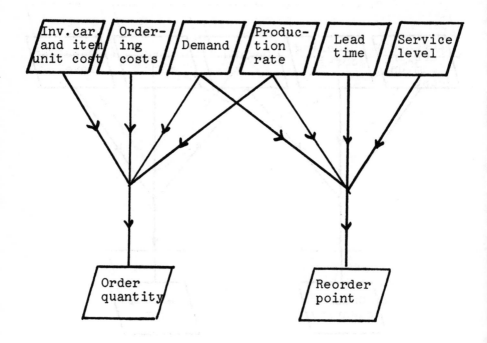

Figure 14

Control method 3

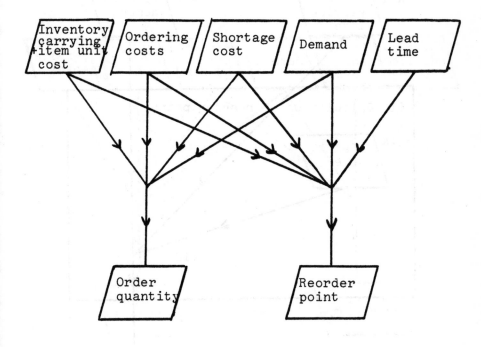

Figure 15

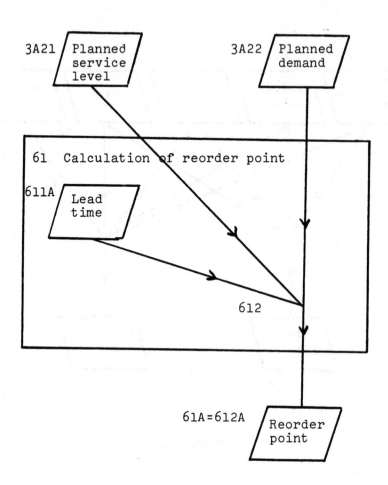

Figure 16

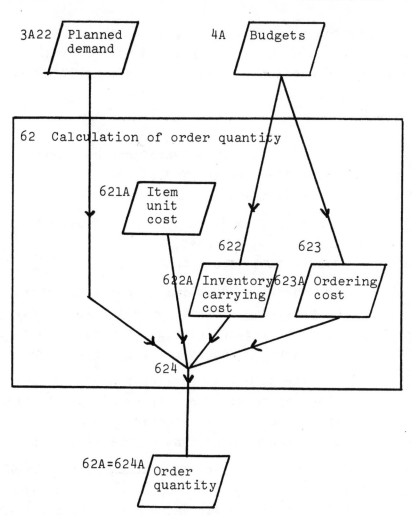

Figure 17

ACKNOWLEDGEMENT

This paper has been written as part of the work with the ISAC project, which is supported by the Swedish Board for Technical development (project no 552 0585).

REFERENCES

(1)   Bubenko/Källhammar/Langefors/Lundeberg/Sølv-
        berg: "Systemering 70",
        Studentlitteratur, Lund, 1970

(2)   Langefors, B: "Theoretical Analysis of
        Information Systems",
        Studentlitteratur, Lund, 1966

(3)   Lundeberg, M: "Outline of possible interac-
        tion between information analysis and design
        of control structures and control methods",
        ISAC Working Report no 1, stenciled paper

(4)   Lundeberg, M: "An application of the present
        ISAC hypothesis for design of control struc-
        tures and control methods",
        ISAC Working Report no 4, stenciled paper

(5)   Lundeberg, M: "On information systems work.
        Further development and practical application
        of a theoretically based information systems
        work methodology",
        ISAC Report 70, no 2, stenciled paper

A MODEL FOR A COMPUTER BASED INTERACTIVE SYSTEM OF CASH MANAGEMENT

F. Zabransky/ G. Duncan
The University of Western Ontario
Canada

INTRODUCTION

This paper outlines a model which has been developed for maximizing the expected rate of return of an investment fund given that specified minimum levels of investment must be made in certain types or classes of assets. Although the model was originally built for the management of bank assets, the system is not unique to this environment and can be readily adapted to other investment situations. The paper has been divided into two main sections, a) the information system surrounding the decision maker, and b) the solution algorithm.

Cash-Management in banks, on a large scale, involves decisions on the allocation of funds into long and short term investments in order to maximize the expected rate of return. The particular problem investigated in this paper is the development of a system to optimize the allocation of funds to day to

day loans, to money market dealers, Government of
Canada Treasury Bills, call loans, short term papers,
etc.

The model developed considers information internal and external to the bank, averaging periods
for primary and secondary cash requirements as specified by the Bank of Canada, probability distributions
of past actions and results and probability estimates
of future events.

The analyst must supply to the model the investment options he feels will be available and the maximum amount he is willing to invest. He is requested
to assess probability distributions for future interest rates, possible future options and the maximum
time periods over which the decisions are to be made.
The model will then indicate the optimum options and
the amount to invest in the current decision process
taking into account strategies for this and future
periods and the corresponding expected monetary gain.

DESCRIPTION OF THE INTERACTIVE SYSTEM

The system is designed for the purpose of
helping the investment analyst in his decision making
process. A summarized flow chart of the information
system is shown in Figure 1. The investment department is designated as the decision centre.

In order to make the system meaningful the model
was designed to interact in real time with a computer
based data bank consisting of the present current
asset position, maturity dates of securities, historical information and probability distributions.
Information concerning political changes, flow of
foreign currencies and other requirements is readily
available to the decision maker.

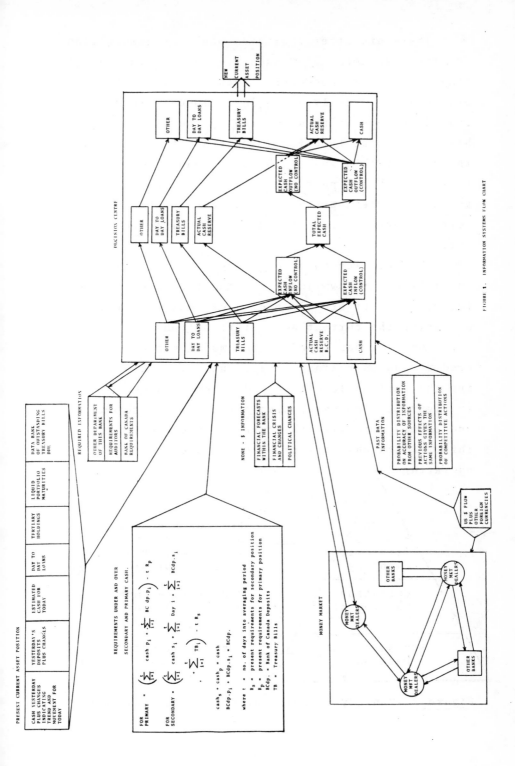

FIGURE 1. INFORMATION SYSTEMS FLOW CHART

There are other chartered banks in competition
for the Government of Canada Treasury Bills and
other short term commercial securities. The former
are sold on a weekly basis in a closed market with
sealed tenders being submitted by the various
bidders. It is, therefore, important to establish
the current thinking of the other banks. Brokerage
houses which are part of the money market are used
as indirect feedback on the current thinking concerning interest rate trends and possible future
outlooks.

The decision maker evaluates this information
in light of his own judgment, and then supplies to
the model a set of parameters for consideration in
assessing the current and future options.

The data base used by the model can be considered at the operations level. One way of classifying the various levels of a data base is depicted
in Figure 2. The daily transactions are recorded
and combined to give the current asset position.
This is data which is to be considered at the
operating level.

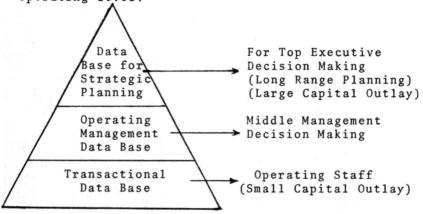

Figure 2. Management Information System Data Base

The strategic data base is used for long range
planning; however, interest has been expressed by
top executives to use the model described herein
at the strategic level.

The system as developed interacts with the
information flow and the data bank and utilizes
system analysis and operations research techniques
to produce an optimal solution.

PROBLEM FORMULATION

As indicated, the problem is one of allocating
limited funds to various investment opportunities
in such a fashion as to maximize the compounded return while simultaneously attempting to satisfy
certain minimum requirements, such as the legal
reserve requirements. Since it is possible that
some minimum requirements cannot be met or could
only be met at the expense of failing to meet others,
the restrictions must be ranked and met according
to an established priority. An investment decision
(or set of decisions) must be made by the investor
and the inability to meet a restriction due to the
lack of funds or investment opportunities cannot
be allowed to render the whole problem infeasible;
rather the solution algorithm, while indicating any
such inabilities, must produce a set of investment
decisions which maximizes the return while satisfying the restrictions as much as possible in the
order of their stated priority. Furthermore, the
algorithm must be sufficiently fast to allow the
manager to interact with the model in a real-time
mode for the determination of the sensitivity of
the overall rate of return to 1) a departure from
the optimal decision, 2) the introduction of new

opportunities or restrictions or 3) the alteration
of opportunities or restrictions already specified
to the model.

The problem can be formulated in mathematical
notation as follows.

$$\text{Maximize } Z = \sum_{t=1}^{T} \sum_{i=1}^{Q_t} C_{i,t} X_{i,t} \tag{1}$$

Subject to:

$$X_{i,t} \leq AV_{i,t} \qquad \begin{array}{l} i=1,2,\ldots,Q_t \\ t=1,2,\ldots,T \end{array} \tag{2}$$

$$\sum_{i=1}^{Q_t} X_{i,t} - \sum_{j=1}^{t-1} \sum_{i=1}^{Q_j} (W_{i,j})(C_{i,j}-1.)(X_{i,j}) = L+\Delta_t$$
$$t=1,2,\ldots,T \tag{3}$$

$$\sum_{i=1}^{Q_t} (A_{i,t,m})(X_{i,t}) \geq N_{t,m}-F_{n,t,m}$$
$$\begin{array}{l} t=1,2,\ldots,T \\ m=1,2,\ldots,M \end{array} \tag{4}$$

$$\sum_{t=1}^{T} \sum_{i=1}^{Q_t} \sum_{m=1}^{M} (U_{i,t,m,r})(P_t)(X_{i,t}) \geq S_r-F_{s,r}$$
$$r=1,2,\ldots,R \tag{5}$$

$$X,AV,L,N,F,S \geq 0 \tag{6}$$

$$PR(F_k) > PR(F_{k+h}) \qquad k=1,2,\ldots,T*M+R \tag{7}$$

where:

T = number of periods

t = period being considered

Q_t = number of investment opportunities available
in period t .

i = identity of option in period t

$C_{i,t}$ = 1.0 + (interest rate of option $X_{i,t}$) (probability of that rate)^{i,t}

$AV_{i,t}$ = maximum size of the opportunity. If this item cannot be purchased in period 't', but rather may only be held over from the previous period (or sold this period), then $AV_{i,t} \leqslant X_{j,t-1}$, where 'j' is the identity of that option in the previous period.

$W_{i,j}$ = 1 if opportunity i,j is compounded in period 't'

$W_{i,j}$ = 0 if opportunity i,j is not compounded in period 't'

L = funds invested in the previous period

Δ_t = expected difference in the available funds in period 't' excluding compounded interest

M = the number of asset classes

m = asset class being considered

$N_{t,m}$ = minimum investment required in class 'm' in period 't'

$F_{n,t,m}$ = amount by which the actual investment in class 'm' in period 't' fails to meet the desired amount $N_{t,m}$

$A_{i,t,m}$ = 1 if $X_{i,t}$ is a class 'm' asset

$A_{i,t,m}$ = 0 if $X_{i,t}$ is not a class 'm' asset

S_r = minimum investment in various groups of asset classes over various periods

$F_{s,r}$ = amount by which actual investment fails to meet desired amount S_r

P_t = length of period t

$U_{i,t,m,r}$ = 1 if opportunity $X_{i,t}$ is a class 'm' asset and class 'm' assets in period 't' contribute to the desired investment S in restriction 'r'; otherwise = 0

$PR(F_j)$ = priority of restrictive equation 'j'. In the event that not all F_j can be reduced to zero, while still satisfying the other restrictions, the above priority relation must be followed, with each F_j being minimized without any regard to any F_j of lower priority and without increasing any F_j of greater priority.

Due to the above requirement that all problems be "feasible" (in the sense that an answer must be produced) and that the constraint equations have a priority, it is not possible to use a standard linear programming approach even though the objective function and all of the constraints are linear.

SAMPLE PROBLEM

In order to illustrate the formulation and the solution algorithm a small sample problem has been included. Figure 3 outlines the various investment opportunities which the manager has felt will be available in the next three periods; a period in this case being one day, however, in general it may be any other multiple day period. Option X_3, the 24 hour call loan to Joe's Brokerage, continues for 3 periods, indicating that if this opportunity is taken in period 1, a decision will have to be made in the next period to terminate or continue the loan; but if the opportunity is not taken in the first period, it will not be available for continuation in any of the subsequent periods. Figure 4 presents exactly the same data in tabular form along with the minimum investment requirements for each class for each period. It is obvious that not all of the requirements in the third period can be met since their sum is 60 units (where a unit could be $1,000.00 or $10,000.00, etc.) whereas, there will only be 45 units available for investment in that period. A standard linear programming algorithm would find the problem infeasible and produce no answers. Figure 5 outlines the minimum investment requirements for the groups of assets taken together.

INVESTMENT OPPORTUNITIES

PERIOD	OPTION SYMBOL	ITEM	CLASS	MAX. AVAIL.	EXPECTED INT. RATE %	LENGTH IN PERIODS
1	X_1	J & D INVESTMENTS	CALL - 5	10	.09	1
	X_2	P & Q DEALERS	DAY - 3	35	.07	1
	X_3	JOE'S BROKERAGE	24 HR - 4	50	.06	3
	X_4	TREASURY BILL JUNE 22	T.B. - 2	30	.04	1
	X_5	GOV'T OF CANADA 1973	OTHER - 6	50	.09	1
	$X_{0,1}$	CASH	CASH - 1	UNLIMITED	0	
2	X_6	TREASURY BILL AUG. 10	T.B. - 2	10	.01	2
	X_7	TREASURY BILL JULY 13	T.B. - 2	5	.06	1
	X_8	P & Q DEALERS	DAY - 3	15	.07	1
	X_9	JOE'S BROKERAGE	24 HR - 4	10	.08	1
	X_{10}	J & D INVESTMENTS	CALL - 5	80	.05	1
	X_{11}	COMMERCIAL PAPER	OTHER - 6	100	.09	2
	$X_{0,2}$	CASH	CASH - 1	UNLIMITED	0	
3	X_{12}	JOE'S BROKERAGE	DAY - 3	10	.03	1
	X_{13}	JOE'S BROKERAGE	24 HR - 4	10	.05	1
	X_{14}	P & Q DEALERS	CALL - 5	25	.08	1
	$X_{0,3}$	CASH	CASH - 1	UNLIMITED	0	

Figure 3. Sample Problem of Investment Opportunities

OPT.	YIELD FACTOR	CLASS	AMT. AVAIL.	OPT.	YIELD FACTOR	CLASS	AMT. AVAIL.	OPT.	YIELD FACTOR	CLASS	AMT. AVAIL.
X_1	1.0009	5	10	$X_{11,2}$	1.0009	6	100	$X_{11,3}$	1.0009	6	0
X_5	1.0009	6	50	X_9	1.0008	4	10	X_{14}	1.0008	5	25
X_2	1.0007	3	35	X_8	1.0007	3	15	$X_{3,3}$	1.0006	4	0
$X_{3,1}$	1.0006	4	50	X_7	1.0006	2	5	X_{13}	1.0005	4	10
X_4	1.0004	2	30	$X_{3,2}$	1.0006	4	0	X_{12}	1.0003	3	10
$X_{0,1}$	1.0000	1	∞	X_{10}	1.0005	5	80	$X_{6,3}$	1.0001	2	0
				$X_{6,2}$	1.0001	2	10	$X_{0,3}$	1.0000	1	∞
				$X_{0,2}$	1.0000	1	∞				

FUNDS MINIMUMS PRIORITY	100 units CLASS	REQUIRE	FUNDS MINIMUMS PRIORITY	130 units CLASS	REQUIRE	FUNDS MINIMUMS PRIORITY	45 units CLASS	REQUIRE
1	1	10	7	1	0	13	1	15
2	2	15	8	2	30	14	2	5
3	3	5	9	3	10	15	3	20
4	4	0	10	4	15	16	4	10
5	5	10	11	5	60	17	5	5
6	6	15	12	6	5	18	6	5

Figure 4. Tabular Form of Investment Opportunities

MINIMUM INVESTMENT IN GROUPS OF ASSET CLASSES

RESTRICTION 1   PRIORITY 19

$$CL_{1,1}+CL_{1,3}+CL_{1,5}+CL_{2,1}+CL_{2,2}+CL_{2,6}+CL_{3,2}+CL_{3,3} \geq 90$$

RESTRICTION 2   PRIORITY 20

$$CL_{1,3}+CL_{2,4}+CL_{3,3}+CL_{3,4} \geq 70$$

RESTRICTION 3   PRIORITY 21

$$CL_{1,3}+CL_{1,4}+CL_{1,6}+CL_{2,2}+CL_{3,2} \geq 60$$

RESTRICTION 4   PRIORITY 22

$$CL_{1,1}+CL_{1,3}+CL_{1,5}+CL_{2,3}+CL_{2,6}+CL_{3,3} \geq 50$$

RESTRICTION 5   PRIORITY 23

$$CL_{1,2}+CL_{1,5}+CL_{2,1}+CL_{2,4}+CL_{2,5}+CL_{3,2}+CL_{3,3}+CL_{3,6} \geq 70$$

where:

$CL_{i,j}$ = investment in class 'j' in period 'i',
weighted by the length of period 'i'.

Figure 5. Restrictions for Groups of Asset Classes

ALGORITHM

MATHEMATICAL FORMULATION

The sample problem can be formulated with forty-four equations as shown in Figure 6. Equations (6.1 to 6.18) establish the upper limit on the investment which can be made in each option. Equations (6.19 to 6.21) restrict the total investment per period to be exactly equal to the funds available in that period. Taken as a group equations (6.1 to 6.21) describe the absolute restrictions on the manager's actions -- he cannot invest more than he has funds and he cannot buy any more of an asset than is available for purchase. On the other hand, equations (6.22 to 6.44) describe the various restrictions in decreasing priority which the investor has felt would be desirable to meet but which may in fact be impossible to satisfy. In the event that two or more restrictions are contradictory the higher priority restriction is to be satisfied first. For this example the priority ranking has been established as:

$$PR(CL_{i,j}) > PR(CL_{i,j+k}) > PR(CL_{i+q,j}) >$$
$$PR(CL_{i+q,j+m}) > PR(Rest_r) > PR(Rest_{r+p}) \qquad (8)$$

where PR = priority of the restriction

$CL_{i,j}$ = class j in period i

$Rest_r$ = the 'r'th cross class restriction.

It must be emphasized that this priority ranking in the example was purely arbitrary and that any priority system could have been employed by merely altering the position of the equations. The algorithm assumes that the equations are in decreasing priority.

Maximize

$$Z = 1.0X_{0,1} + 1.0X_{0,2} + 1.0X_{0,3} + 1.0009X_1 + 1.0007X_2$$
$$+ 1.0006X_{3,1} + 1.0006X_{3,2} + 1.0006X_{3,3} + 1.0004X_4$$
$$+ 1.0009X_5 + 1.0001X_{6,2} + 1.0001X_{6,3} + 1.0006X_7 + 1.0007X_8$$
$$+ 1.0008X_9 + 1.0005X_{10} + 1.0009X_{11,2} + 1.0009X_{11,3}$$
$$+ 1.0003X_{12} + 1.0005X_{13} + 1.0008X_{14}$$

Subject to

$X_1 \leq 10$	(6.1)	$X_7 \leq 5$	(6.10)
$X_2 \leq 35$	(6.2)	$X_8 \leq 15$	(6.11)
$X_{3,1} \leq 50$	(6.3)	$X_9 \leq 10$	(6.12)
$-X_{3,1} + X_{3,2} \leq 0$	(6.4)	$X_{10} \leq 80$	(6.13)
$-X_{3,2} + X_{3,3} \leq 0$	(6.5)	$X_{11,2} \leq 100$	(6.14)
$X_4 \leq 30$	(6.6)	$-X_{11,2} + X_{11,3} \leq 0$	(6.15)
$X_5 \leq 50$	(6.7)	$X_{12} \leq 10$	(6.16)
$X_{6,2} \leq 10$	(6.8)	$X_{13} \leq 10$	(6.17)
$-X_{6,2} + X_{6,3} \leq 0$	(6.9)	$X_{14} \leq 25$	(6.18)

$$X_{0,1} + X_1 + X_2 + X_{3,1} + X_4 + X_5 = 100 \quad (6.19)$$
$$X_{0,2} + X_{3,2} + X_{6,2} + X_7 + X_8 + X_9 + X_{10} + X_{11,2} = 130 \quad (6.20)$$
$$X_{0,3} + X_{3,3} + X_{6,3} + X_{11,3} + X_{12} + X_{13} + X_{14} = 45 \quad (6.21)$$

$X_{0,1} \geq 10$	(6.22)	$X_{3,2} + X_9 \geq 15$	(6.31)
$X_4 \geq 15$	(6.23)	$X_{10} \geq 60$	(6.32)
$X_2 \geq 5$	(6.24)	$X_{11,2} \geq 5$	(6.33)
$X_{3,1} \geq 0$	(6.25)	$X_{0,3} \geq 15$	(6.34)
$X_1 \geq 10$	(6.26)	$X_{6,3} \geq 5$	(6.35)
$X_5 \geq 15$	(6.27)	$X_{12} \geq 20$	(6.36)
$X_{0,2} \geq 0$	(6.28)	$X_{3,3} + X_{13} \geq 10$	(6.37)
$X_{6,2} + X_7 \geq 30$	(6.29)	$X_{14} \geq 5$	(6.38)
$X_8 \geq 10$	(6.30)	$X_{11,3} \geq 5$	(6.39)

$$X_{0,1} + X_{0,2} + X_1 + X_2 + X_{6,2} + X_{6,3} + X_7 + X_{11,2} + X_{12} \geq 90 \quad (6.40)$$
$$X_2 + X_{3,2} + X_{3,3} + X_9 + X_{12} + X_{13} \geq 70 \quad (6.41)$$
$$X_2 + X_{3,1} + X_5 + X_{6,2} + X_{6,3} + X_7 \geq 60 \quad (6.42)$$
$$X_{0,1} + X_1 + X_2 + X_8 + X_{11,2} + X_{12} \geq 50 \quad (6.43)$$
$$X_{0,2} + X_1 + X_{3,2} + X_4 + X_{6,3} + X_9 + X_{10} + X_{11,3} + X_{12} \geq 70 \quad (6.44)$$

Figure 6. Mathematical Formulation of Sample Problem

371

In the above formulation, any interest earned is assumed to be siphoned off and not available for investment in the ensuing period. A relaxation of this assumption can be readily achieved by adding the following coefficients to the various equations.

To equations (6.20) add

$-.0009X_1-.0007X_2-.0006X_{3,1}+.0006X_{3,2}-.0004X_4-.0009X_5$

To equations (6.21) add

$-.0012X_{3,2}+.0012X_{3,3}-.0001X_{6,2}+.0001X_{6,3}-.0006X_7$

$-.0007X_8-.0008X_9-.0005X_{10}-.0009X_{11,2}+.0009X_{11,3}$

From a linear programming viewpoint the problem is infeasible since equations (6.34) to (6.39) as a group, require that:

$$X_{0,3}+X_{3,3}+X_{6,3}+X_{11,3}+X_{12}+X_{13}+X_{14} \geqslant 60$$

yet equation (21) states that:

$$X_{0,3}+X_{3,3}+X_{6,3}+X_{11,3}+X_{12}+X_{13}+X_{14} = 45$$

SOLUTION PROCEDURE

Figure 7 outlines the principle steps involved in the model. Assume that the investment manager wishes to ascertain which assets he should purchase in the sample problem referred to earlier. As his first step the manager types in the information contained in Figures 4 and 5, and requests the program to run.

The model will then accept the typed information, place a duplicate copy in the temporary memory bank for future reference and begin constructing the required equations (Figure 6) automatically. When all of the equations have been built, the priority programming routine is called in to search for a

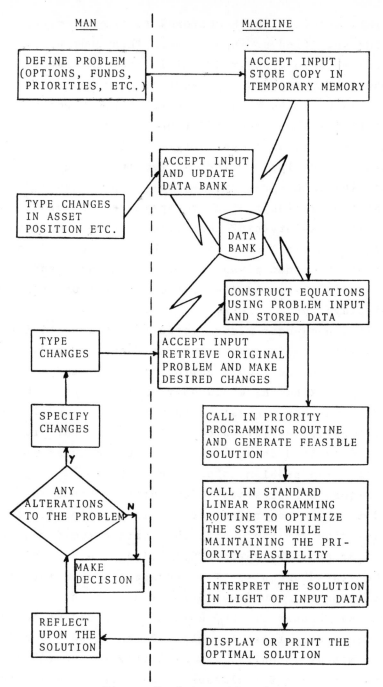

Figure 7. Interactive System

373

feasible solution which conforms to the priority ranking specified at input time. This routine, to be described in greater detail in the next section, automatically adjusts any inherent contradictions or infeasibilities such as the requirement noted above that the desired investment in period 3 be greater than 60 units yet only 45 units will be available. Having obtained as feasible a solution as possible, the program then calls in a standard linear programming routine to optimize the solution while still maintaining the various degrees of feasibility. The final solution is then interpreted in light of the names given with the input data and the results either printed out on the teleprinter or displayed on a screen.

If the manager wishes to perform a sensitivity analysis on the interest rate for future periods, or include an additional option or change the priority ranking, he would only have to supply these changes and then request another run. The model will automatically retrieve a copy of the original problem, make the desired changes, reconstruct the equations and solve the problem as outlined above.

Figure 8 represents a copy of the output supplied to the manager for the sample problem. The optimal solution for the whole time horizon would require that, for example, options 0,1,2,3,4,5 be purchased in the stated amounts. The average expected interest for that period would be 23.7% resulting in a gross operating revenue of .065 units. It should be noted that the restrictions for class 2 in period 2 could not be met by 15 units, and similarly for period 3 the restrictions for classes 3 and 6 are unsatisfied by 10 and 5 units respectively. If the manager felt

```
DETAILS FOR PERIOD      1
************************
ALLOCATIONS
----------

     OPTION              AMOUNT              CLASS
       1                   10                  5
       5                   25                  6
       2                   35                  3
       3,1                  5                  4
       4                   15                  2
       0,1                 10                  1

TOTAL FUNDS ALLOCATED             100.00000
AVERAGE EXPECTED YIELD             23.72496
EXPECTED FUNDS AT END OF PERIOD   100.06499
EXPECTED INCREASE THIS PERIOD       0.06499
LENGTH OF THIS PERIOD (DAYS)        1

AVAILABLE - UNUSED CAPACITY
---------------------------
     OPTION              AMOUNT              CLASS
       5                   25                  6
       3,1                 45                  4
       4                   15                  2
     CASH              UNLIMITED               1


DETAILS FOR PERIOD      2
************************
ALLOCATIONS
----------
     OPTION              AMOUNT              CLASS
      11,2                 30                  6
       9                   10                  4
       8                   10                  3
       7                    5                  2
       3,2                  5                  4
      10                   60                  5
       6,1                 10                  2

TOTAL FUNDS ALLOCATED             130.00000
AVERAGE EXPECTED YIELD             22.18020
EXPECTED FUNDS AT END OF PERIOD   130.07899
EXPECTED INCREASE THIS PERIOD       0.07899
LENGTH OF THIS PERIOD (DAYS)        1

AVAILABLE - UNUSED CAPACITY
---------------------------
     OPTION              AMOUNT              CLASS
      11,2                 70                  6
       8                    5                  3
      10                   20                  5
     CASH              UNLIMITED               1
```
Figure 8.   Sample Output   (con't)

DETAILS FOR PERIOD   3
****
ALLOCATIONS

OPTION	AMOUNT	CLASS
14	5	5
3,3	5	4
13	5	4
12	10	3
6,3	5	2
0,3	15	1

TOTAL FUNDS ALLOCATED	45.00000
AVERAGE EXPECTED YIELD	10.54145
EXPECTED FUNDS AT END OF PERIOD	45.01299
EXPECTED INCREASE THIS PERIOD	0.01299
LENGTH OF THIS PERIOD (DAYS)	1

AVAILABLE - UNUSED CAPACITY

OPTION	AMOUNT	CLASS
11,3	30	6
14	20	5
13	5	4
6,3	5	2
CASH	UNLIMITED	1

SUMMARY INFORMATION
****
AVERAGE EXPECTED YIELD FOR ALL PERIODS   20.83741
ABSOLUTE EXPECTED REVENUE FROM OPERATIONS   0.15699
LENGTH OF OPERATION HORIZON   3
COULD NOT MEET THE FOLLOWING MUNIMUM REQUIREMENTS
OFF BY THE AMOUNT IN BRACKETS
PERIOD NUMBER   2   - CLASS 2(15)
PERIOD NUMBER   3   - CLASS 6(5)
PERIOD NUMBER   3   - CLASS 3(10)
ALL OTHER RESTRICTIONS SATISFIED

Figure 8. continued.

that class 6 period 3 should definitely be met, the priority ranking for that restriction (currently #18) could be altered and the model rerun.

PRIORITY PROGRAMMING

The algorithm used is a modified form of linear programming referred to by the authors as Priority Programming[1]. In standard linear programming a solution to the system of equations is feasible if all of the equations can be met simultaneously and all variables are greater than or equal to zero. If any variable must be negative in order to satisfy all of the constraining equations, the system is infeasible and no solution will be forthcoming. On the other hand, in priority programming the equations are divided into the mandatory restrictions (equations 6.1 to 6.21) and priority restrictions (equations 6.22 to 6.44). The mandatory equations must have a strictly feasible solution according to the above definition whereas for the priority equations, the surplus or slack variables are allowed to assume negative values. Since a negative slack or surplus variable would indicate that the restriction could not be met by that particular amount, the algorithm attempts to have all variables greater than or equal to zero subject, however, to the condition that the attempt to reduce any negativity in equation j will not produce or increase any negativity in the mandatory equations or in the restrictions of higher priority.

Rather than present a formal mathematical

description of the system a small sample will be used to explain the principal concept. For example, we may have the following mandatory equations,

$$X_1 \leq 5 \tag{9}$$

$$X_2 \leq 5 \tag{10}$$

and the two priority equations

$$X_1 + X_2 \geq 12 \tag{11}$$

$$X_1 + X_2 \leq 8 \tag{12}$$

$$X_1, X_2 \geq 0 \tag{13}$$

Obviously the system is infeasible from a linear programming point of view.

Since it is desired to have all slack or surplus variables positive, the equations will be simplified with only the slack variable (SL) on the left hand side

$$SL_1 = 5 - X_1 \tag{14}$$
mandatory
$$SL_2 = 5 - X_2 \tag{15}$$

$$SL_3 = -12 + X_1 + X_2 \quad \text{priority 1} \tag{16}$$

$$SL_4 = 8 - X_1 - X_2 \quad \text{priority 2} \tag{17}$$

$$X_1, X_2 \geq 0 \tag{18}$$

Starting with equations (14) and (15) and with $X_1 = X_2 = 0$, this subset is feasible since $SL_1 = SL_2 = 5 > 0$. The first priority equation is introduced into the system consisting of equations (14), (15) and (16). Since $SL_3 = -12 < 0$ this constraint has not been satisfied and X_1 and/or X_2 must be increased if possible. In order to maintain SL_1 and $SL_2 \geq 0$, while attempting to

reduce SL_3, both X_1 and X_2 will be increased to 5.
SL_3 will still be negative, -2, yet neither X_1
nor X_2 can be increased, therefore the attempt to
improve SL_3 is stopped and the next equation is
introduced. With $X_1=X_2=5$, SL_4 will equal -2, yet
the only method of removing this negativity would
be to reduce either X_1 and/or X_2. Such a move would
decrease SL_3 even further, therefore it would be
inadmissible because of the priority ranking. The
final solution would be $X_1=X_2=5$, $SL_1=SL_2=0$,
$SL_3=SL_4= -2$. Had the priorities been reversed the
solution would have been $X_1+X_2=8$ (in any positive
combination), SL_1 and $SL_2 \geq 0$, $SL_4 = 0$ and $SL_3 = -4$.

MANAGERIAL INTERACTION - A SUMMARY

The managerial interaction (Figure 7) can be
divided into three separate categories -- assessment
of new alternatives, sensitivity to various future
interest rate expectations and sensitivity to different priority rankings. With respect to assessing
new alternatives, the model would run with the
current set of alternative opportunities. The new
alternative would then be added to the system and
the model rerun. A comparison of the two (or more)
solutions with respect to average interest rate,
achievement of priority restrictions and general
deployment of funds would present the manager
with additional information upon which to base his
decision.

The interest rate expectations for the future
are usually uncertain, however, a sensitivity
analysis for today's decision can readily be performed by rerunning the model with various rates
for future alternatives. If today's decision is
relatively unchanged then the uncertainties are

unimportant. On the other hand, if today's decision were to be radically different, then it might be worthwhile investigating the trends further in order to narrow the range of uncertainty.

As shown with the four equation sample, the ranking of the priorities can have a very great bearing on the final solution. If certain restrictions cannot be met, the manager may wish to assess the effect of a priority change. Again this could be readily achieved by rerunning the model with the priorities altered.

The model interacts with the data base in many ways. Firstly an up to date record is available of all of the assets currently owned. If desired, these can be considered in the model without being specifically enumerated at the run time. Secondly, the funds available can be ascertained directly and if desired, incorporated automatically. Thirdly, during the computation of expected values the frequency distribution of past events can be accessed directly by the model without operator intervention. Fourthly, a memory can be retained of the possible options available in the future thereby reducing the amount of information which would otherwise have to be typed in for each run.

In the fully automated system, the investment manager could assess the desirability of a new alternative by merely inputting the new opportunity and requesting the model to obtain all the other pertinent information from the data bank.

1) F. Zabransky & G. Duncan, "Linear Programming with Priority Restrictions," Working Paper Series No. 28, School of Business Administration, University of Western Ontario, London, Canada.

A MANUFACTURING INFORMATION SYSTEM

E. Stewart Lynes
Parsons & Williams
Denmark

SUMMARY

This paper considers the state-of-the-art in computer-based systems for manufacturing planning and control, in terms of a particular system of advanced design which the author has worked with in respect to both development and implementation. The Integrated Manufacturing Planning (IMP) System is surveyed according to key principles and characteristics by which MIS are commonly judged. References are given to more complete presentations of the IMP System available elsewhere in the literature.

INTRODUCTION

In recent years there has been considerable pioneering activity within the area of manufacturing planning systems. Advances in systems technology and the needs of manufacturing management for improved operating controls, as well as the opportunities for

significant improvements in cost performance through use of
management science methods, have combined to bring about
some relatively ambitious undertakings.

In contrast with many Management Information System (MIS)
examples, which are predominantly oriented to better organization of data flow and improved management reporting (often in
financial terms alone), the new manufacturing systems technology
includes a strong measure of what might be termed "applications"
routines. Possibly because engineers have often influenced design
of these systems, they may include substantial analysis and calculation procedures, such as dynamic programming for economic
lot sizing, optimum safety time calculations on inventory replenishment, or statistically determined production start quantities.

Emphasis on functional optimization and scientific method is indeed
characteristic of the more sophisticated manufacturing systems --
of which still today there are but a few operational examples.

The better-designed systems for production management retain,
however, many of the important MIS attributes, e.g., orientation to management processes, integration of related business
functions, and consolidation of transactions handling and file structures.

It is interesting to examine a particular such system and to apply
to it the usual criteria by which MIS are judged. In this way the
status of MIS in manufacturing can be brought under closer scrutiny.

THE SYSTEM CONSIDERED

The system discussed is IMP, the Integrated Manufacturing Planning System. This system has been developed in Scandinavia during

the late 1960's and installed in several different versions for mechanical and electro-mechanical job shops, a steel fabricator, and various other specialized manufacturers. It has been described previously in the literature (References 1-4) and has to date been the object of inspection visits by interested parties from a number of different countries in Europe and North America.

IMP is a total planning system for manufacturing firms, embracing the functions of capacity planning, production scheduling, material control, purchasing and delivery scheduling, shop floor dispatching, and cost control. It directly supports the corresponding management processes through all phases of manufacturing from order entry to final shipment. An overview of the system is given in Figure 1.

The higher level management tasks of product selection and demand steering are not treated; IMP starts from a given order book, but provides some information for delivery date setting and demand steering. A companion system, CORPORAL, which is separately included in these proceedings, assists with the strategic decisions in manufacturing management (Reference 5).

KEY MIS EVALUATION CRITERIA

While MIS are as yet in an early development stage, and even agreement on definition of MIS characteristics is not readily obtained, it is possible to identify a number of features and principles which are commonly associated with the MIS field-of-interest (Reference 6). The following points have been selected for consideration in this paper:

IMP

INTEGRATED MANUFACTURING PLANNING

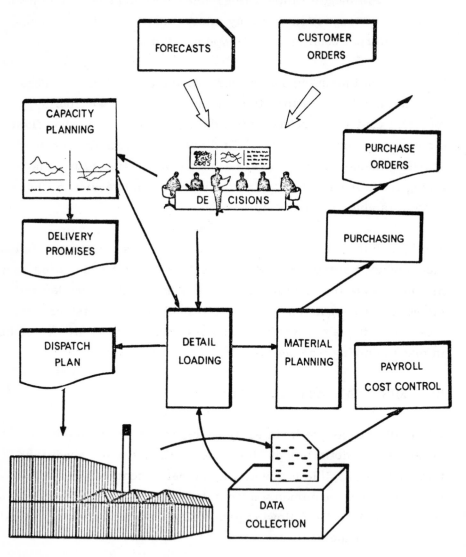

Figure 1: System Overview

1. Functional Composition
   - Breadth of View (Scope)
   - Functional Integration
   - Recognition of Decision Hierarchies
   - Degree of Management Assistance

2. Reporting Characteristics and Usage Modes
   - Types of Reports Produced
   - Timing
   - Types of Interaction Allowed

3. Data Handling Characteristics
   - Transactions
   - Files.

In surveying the state-of-the-art of manufacturing planning systems, as represented by IMP, each of these evaluation criteria will be dealt with. It is suggested that such an approach can bring added objectivity to the process of evaluating manufacturing planning systems in general. Within this paper, principal attention is given to the first of the above three categories.

AN IMP SYSTEM OVERVIEW

The Integrated Manufacturing Planning System is comprised of the following principal modules, arranged according to a hierarchy of planning levels as shown in Figure 2.

Capacity Planning is a simulator for matching long-term sales plans and present order book with capacity needs. It assists management in planning the acquisition of men and machines, and the use of overtime and extra shifts. An adjunct is a model for making optimal buy/make decisions.

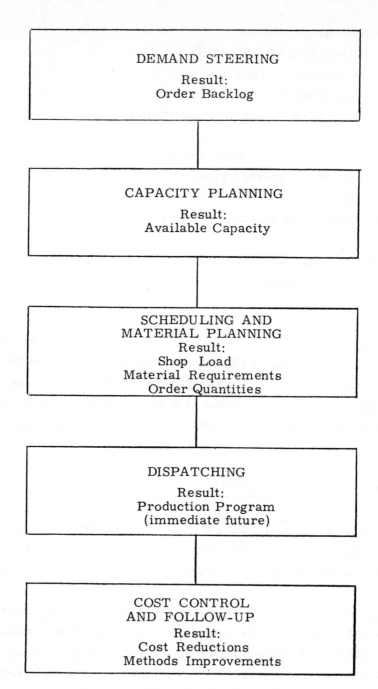

DEMAND STEERING

Result:
Order Backlog

CAPACITY PLANNING

Result:
Available Capacity

SCHEDULING AND
MATERIAL PLANNING
Result:
Shop Load
Material Requirements
Order Quantities

DISPATCHING

Result:
Production Program
(immediate future)

COST CONTROL
AND FOLLOW-UP
Result:
Cost Reductions
Methods Improvements

Figure 2: Planning Levels

Production Planning is comprised of two sub-modules, Scheduling and Dispatching, operating on distinct levels. Scheduling is done by machine loading within the capacity plan established by Capacity Planning; it employs load-smoothing techniques to achieve a schedule which generates minimum work-in-process inventories. Dispatching periodically creates an updated plan of operations to perform at each workcenter, based on the most recent production schedule and the current status of shop activity; it employs optimizing rules designed to maximize capacity utilization and reduce delivery lateness. The final output is a set of Dispatch Plans and complete shop papers for job execution, including material requisitions and suggestions for alternative materials where shortages are expected.

Inventory Management operates on the same planning level as Scheduling, utilizing input which defines exact material requirements to support the established production schedule. Economic lot sizing rules are employed in determining stock replenishment schedules, and safety stocks are optimized to give the desired service level.

Purchasing operates in concert with the Inventory Management module to automate many parts of the Purchasing Department's activities. Suggested purchase orders are generated by the system together with supporting data, such as potential suppliers and their past performance history, for buyer review. Delivery follow-up is performed automatically at various levels and supplier rating measures are maintained.

Cost Control accumulates data regarding actual accomplishment and compares costs to standard prices, generating variances in all affected categories. Performance reports and account transactions are output.

The principal goals of the system are identified as:

- Substantially reduced inventory holding costs
- Shortened delivery times (improved competitive position)
- Increased shop throughput
- Reduced delivery latenesses
- Better management information.

While it is clear that IMP serves principally the middle management levels in a manufacturing enterprise, it is equally clear that it is a MIS. This is so because it is a system which provides essential information for management decision-making processes, and because it is closely aligned with the primary goals of production management, both in a planning and in an operating sense.

These claims will be further substantiated by examining IMP according to the criteria mentioned earlier. As the discussion proceeds, additional aspects of the IMP System are revealed. Readers desiring more explicit description of IMP are referred to the various existing IMP publications identified under References.

FUNCTIONAL COMPOSITION

BREADTH OF VIEW (SCOPE)

A fundamental requirement for a MIS is that it affords management a broad view of the business sector in which used. When that sector is production management, this means a scope which includes management planning and control of all manpower, machines, and material devoted to manufacturing processes.

The manufacturing information system should provide a comprehensive view of current status and future requirements in all the above areas. Ideally it should afford a vehicle for management planning to support the future requirements, and for monitoring actual performance against plan.

The scope of IMP should already be apparent from the earlier description; further sections of this paper will extend that view.

FUNCTIONAL INTEGRATION

To provide meaningful operating and planning support to management over a wide scope, the system must successfully integrate a number of distinct functions.

The classic example is the close coupling desired between production planning (men and machines) and material planning. Information about expected shop loading that does not properly recognize the necessary schedules for production to inventory would be next to useless; and yet the schedules for inventory replenishment depend upon the timing of material requirements, which are determined by order schedules, which depend upon shop loading.

Within IMP, a close interplay is provided between Scheduling and Inventory Management, to recognize the inherent duality of production and material planning.

Other requirements for integration arise from the desire to measure all accomplishment versus plan in a common cost control system, and from the need to regularly coordinate the release of materials and the dispatching of operations.

IMP also provides both these forms of integration. Moreover, it operates from a centralized data base which ensures that common data is utilized within the different system modules.

RECOGNITION OF DECISION HIERARCHIES

For an information system of the scope described, a hierarchy of decision/control spans is also desired, in order to adequately structure the managerial and operating processes involved.

Thus, medium-range planning for properly balancing capacity and order book is placed on a different level from specific scheduling of machine assignments and material requirements. And yet another level corresponds to the very short-term ordering of work priorities at each workcenter. The MIS design should mirror these several gradations of applicable horizon and required detail.

Again taking IMP as an example system, in a typical application environment the following characteristics are found:

Level	Sub-System	Horizon	Extent of Detail
Highest	Capacity Planning	1-2 years	Composite Load Profiles, Critical Materials Only
Middle	Detail Loading (Scheduling)	$\frac{1}{2}$-1 year	Detailed Operation Lists, Complete Material Requirements
Lowest	Dispatching	2-3 weeks	Operations Grouped for Minimum Setup Time and Priority Sequenced with Attention to Remaining Slack; Material Availability Tested for Dispatched Operations and Alternatives Identified.

Corresponding restrictions are seen in the finesse and refinement of decision rules applied at each level and in the precision of the information base afforded. (The manager deciding how much subcontracted capacity to schedule next year does not need to consider which orders will use it, but the decision to transfer individual jobs on next week's Dispatch Plan to alternative loadcenters may call for a large amount of rather specific information.)

DEGREE OF MANAGEMENT ASSISTANCE

In each of the three measures of functional composition discussed above, there is no evaluation of the actual <u>amount</u> of decision-making automation included in a given system; the criteria are strictly qualitative. Systems might rank highly in all three measures but still not really <u>do</u> very much.

Direct Aids

The degree of management assistance provided by a system is influenced by at least two primary factors. One is the extent to which the system releases managers from routine administrative tasks (often of a very time-consuming nature) and thus allows them greater opportunity for creative work. The other is the extent to which the system supports the manager in the pursuit of his creative tasks, i.e., the amount of interplay provided for between the computerized information base and the manager's own work processes.

In IMP, for example, the latter concept is illustrated by the Capacity Planning System. Here a management laboratory, as it were, is provided; experimentation with different load/capacity matches allows the manager to exercise and test his planning approaches to the extent he desires. For each set of order delivery dates studied, a number of capacity plans can be proposed and their effectiveness measured.

The same system provides an example of the former concept, also. Included in Capacity Planning is an inquiry facility which allows a user to automatically establish feasible delivery dates for prospective orders. The computer automates what is otherwise often a

lengthy and tedious process of manually defining capacity requirements for the new order and test-loading these demands against
the disposable future capacity.

A further excellent example of this concept is found in the Purchasing module of IMP; here many routine tasks are taken over
by the system, and purchasing management can better concern
itself with seeking new supply sources, setting up more advan-
tageous agreements, or refining its procedures for coping with
special circumstances.

Optimizing Rules
Management assistance takes a further form within IMP. Extensive optimizing features are included in many sub-systems. The
result of this is a refinement of decision-making which could not
be achieved by manual means alone, and which may often significantly contribute to profitability.

In Scheduling, particularly, the use of sophisticated load-smoothing rules can bring very substantial savings in inventory carrying costs. Or within Dispatching, significant improvement in
utilization of production facilities is gained through priority ranking schemes that govern the suggested sequence of work execution at each workcenter. For instance, by favoring operations
which precede operations due at temporarily underloaded loadcenters, a preventive discipline is achieved.

There are other examples, as the literature indicates.

Altogether a main conclusion is possible: Manufacturing information systems are coming into being which not only qualify as MIS
in terms of alignment with management processes, but which
also -- in some cases -- greatly amplify the manager's effec-

tiveness through the decision aids they provide (Reference 7).

REPORTING CHARACTERISTICS AND USAGE MODES

TYPES OF REPORTS PRODUCED

All of the standard types of MIS reports are included within IMP. These basic types may be identified as Regular (periodic or routine), Exception, Demand, and Planning reports.

Regular reports include the Load Report and Dispatch Plan, as well as Purchase Order Suggestions and Cost Reports. The Cost Reports are structured hierarchically along responsibility lines, with appropriate summarization at higher levels. They included purchasing and loadcenter performance reports, drawn from a foundation of detailed evaluations of variance from standard in all applicable cost categories (purchase price, labor rate and man-hours, material quantity and substitute usage, lot size, alternative loadcenter, reject rate, etc.). There are also Work-in-Process and Inventory Reports, and a Payments List (approved invoices). In addition there is a Planning Variance Report, which identifies for each workcenter the cost of temporary additions to existing capacity, thus providing a basis for evaluating permanent capacity additions.

Exception reports include Invoice Errors, Late Operations, Inventory Differences, Delivery Exceptions, Missing Materials (Shortages), and others. Further, Obsolescent and Surplus Stocks are notified.

Demand reports include Order Status and Feasible Delivery Date Reports, as well as numerous file inquiry facilities.

Planning reports are those which support the manager in exploring "what if" type questions and otherwise aid him in developing his plans. The Gross Load Report produced by the Capacity Planning System is a prime example, but other parts of the IMP System may also be used in a simulation mode.

TIMING

The basic operating cycle for IMP installations to date has been one week, but there are provisions for daily dispatching and work status update; also, current development is leading toward real-time shop floor monitoring and control. Transactions processing (both materials and operations) has been operated daily. Capacity Planning typically operates on a monthly cycle, and Cost Reports occur both on a bi-weekly and monthly basis.

TYPES OF INTERACTION ALLOWED

There are numerous user interfaces to the IMP System, including those areas responsible for order entry, purchasing, shop progress and material movement, and capacity planning (at all levels). One of the more interesting interfaces is that provided to Dispatching. Here a special set of Management Inputs has been developed for use in steering the performance of the Dispatching System. Temporarily underloaded loadcenters are identified and smoothing objectives are specified for both overloaded and underloaded loadcenters. In addition, control is provided over the Pull Ahead feature, which selects future work to be executed ahead of schedule (for load-smoothing purposes).

DATA-HANDLING CHARACTERISTICS

Only brief mention is made here of the data processing details of

IMP. In respect to transactions, automatic data collection terminals are commonly employed and transactions processing is centralized so that edit/checks are more complete and redundancy of information is limited. Files are principally disk-based and random-access is used together with sequential and indexed sequential processing. A specialized Data Maintenance System has been developed for optimum handling of the basic data files, with extensive data control facilities included.

CONCLUSION

One example of the developing sophistication in manufacturing information systems has been given. From this it is seen that MIS is well-established as a practical tool for manufacturing management, including both planning and control aids and highly refined internal decision rules for optimizing key performance measures by which production management is judged.

With these systems, as conditions change, plans can be readily revised and optimality re-established. Through better information and more disciplined processing of that information, planning also becomes more deterministic and less imbued with arbitrary and costly safety factors. Competitive power is thereby strengthened.

REFERENCES

1. Integrated Manufacturing Planning, by the Staff of Parsons & Williams, Studentlitteratur, Lund 1969, Sweden

2. An Integrated Operating System, Robert F. Williams, at NordSAM-66, Vedbæk, Denmark

3. Concepts of Integrated Management Planning, Ole C. Nord, at NordDATA-68, Helsinki, Finland

4. Dispatching Rules in an Integrated Production Management System, E. Stewart Lynes, at NordDATA-68, Helsinki, Finland

5. "MIS Corporate Planning", Robert F. Williams, MIS Copenhagen 1970

6. "What's the Status of MIS?", EDP Analyzer, vol. 7, no. 10, October 1969, by Canning Publications, Inc.

7. Computer-Based Information Systems for Management: A Survey (book), by Neil C. Churchill, John H. Kempster, Myron Uretsky; a Research Study Published by National Association of Accountants, New York, N.Y., 1969.

Part 3 - Data Structure

DATA BASE AND MANAGEMENT
INFORMATION SYSTEMS

John D. Woodward
Rolls-Royce Limited
England

1. INTRODUCTION

This paper is aimed at the wide body of systems designers
who are wrestling with the problems of Data Base and
Management Information Systems.

It attempts to display some of the fundamental principles
and philosophies underlying these areas of design activity
and avoids computer jargon wherever possible.

The paper deals with
a. some fundamentals of data and files,
b. basic types of Commercial DP System,
c. data base,
d. and includes a specification of the functional
   requirements of a suitable software system.

It does not deal with specific access methods, software,
nor hardware, because that approach clouds the essentials,
the understanding of which is a pre-requisite to successful design and implementation.

2. SOME FUNDAMENTALS

a. A FIELD is the smallest meaningful unit of data on a file.

b. A FIELD is meaningless in isolation.   It only acquires meaning in the context of the thing it describes (its KEY) or relates to.

c. A KEY is the label or name by which a field or collection of fields is accessed or referred to.   A Particular KEY VALUE is required to access a particular collection of fields.

d. A KEY in one context can be a descriptive field in another.
KEYS and DESCRIPTIVE fields are analogous to NOUNS and ADJECTIVES.
A Customer's Order, for example, could contain:-
Customer Name and Address.
Customer Order Number.
Customer Item of Order Number.
Our Part or Component Number.
Quantity.
Delivery Date.
Etc, etc.
In any dialogue between the Customer and our Spares Department, it is likely that Customer Order and Item Number will be the KEY or label in terms of which the dialogue takes place.   In this context, Our Part or Component Number is a Descriptive Field.
      On the other hand, in any dialogue between Our Spares Department and our Manufacturing or Supply

Organisation, it is likely that Our Part or Component
Number will be the KEY, and in that context, Customer
Order and Item Number are Descriptive Fields.

It is this changing role of "key" which necessitates different sort orders or cross indexing of the
same data.

e. "CROSS TALK" between files requires that one file
must contain in its records, the search argument
(KEYS) in terms of which the other is either
ordered or indexed.

The search argument may be the KEY field or
a DATA (non-KEY) field in the searching file.

It has been shown above at d, that one set of
data may require to be accessible in terms of
different KEYS.   The traditional approach to this
situation is either

    1. to have separate files, each sorted in its own
        logical order (with duplication of some data)
or 2. to serially search through one file, looking
        for all the records which qualify in terms of
        the "other" keys.

To avoid both these possibilities, and only store the
data once, leads to cross talk in terms of different
KEYS within one physical set of data and gives rise
to the need for CROSS INDEXING.   This concept is
the basis for the definition of Data Base given in
paragraph 11. of this paper.

f. INTEGRATED FILES are files which are CROSS INDEXED
as explained above.

g. CONSOLIDATED FILES are files which contain larger
    collections of data of the same KEY.

3. WHAT IS CROSS INDEXING?
    It is keeping a note of which records in a file conform
    to some criteria other than those in terms of which the
    file is primarily ordered or indexed.

4. WHAT DO WE GAIN FROM CROSS INDEXING?
    a. We avoid the need to create separate files.

    b. We improve the up-to-dateness of the data. If the
        Order Data as shown at 2d is stored only once, no
        matter how many ways there are of accessing it, then
        it can only reflect one state of up-to-dateness at
        one point in time. This would not necessarily be
        the case with separate files.

    c. We save duplication of the fields of data pertinent
        to the CROSS INDEX KEYS.
            It is unlikely, for example, that we would take
        the Customer Terms of Business and Shipping Instructions
        into a separate file for the Manufacturing Department.

5. IMPLICATIONS OF THE USE OF CROSS INDEXING
    a. It is only applicable to DIRECT ACCESS Storage
        Devices.

    b. It will usually cause variable length records to
        be generated for the CROSS INDEX.
            For example, a Part Number may occur in many
        customer orders, whereas another Part Number may
        occur in a different number of customer orders.

c. When one requires to access the data in terms of the cross index keys, the only option then open is to access via the CROSS INDEX. It is not possible to physically sequentially process in terms of the cross index keys, no matter what the activity of the cross indexed records. If the activity is high, access will be slow.

6. METHODS OF CROSS INDEXING
   a. Indirect Addressing.
      Is noting the PRIME KEY VALUES of qualifying records

   b. Direct Addressing
      Is noting the physical addresses of qualifying records.

   c. Record Mapping
      Is keeping a bit map of qualifying records; the Nth bit, or bit set, representing the Nth record.

   d. Chained Listing
      Is linking qualifying records together by embedding physical address links within the records.

7. CONSEQUENCES OF CROSS INDEXING
   a. Maintaining the cross indexes will be time consuming, especially if there is a high volume of change in the data.

   b. Because, by definition, the data records are not in the order of the cross index keys, every qualifying record must be indexed. Therefore there will be an index entry for every qualifying record.

c. With the INDIRECT ADDRESSING technique, the cross indexes need not be re-generated when the data records are re-organised. It will, however, take longer to access than either 6b or 6c. It may or may not, take longer to access than the chain linking technique depending upon whereabouts in the chain, the qualifying records reside.

The other techniques necessitate a re-generation of the cross indexes whenever the data records are re-organised, because indexes are based on the physical location of the records.

8. TYPES OF COMMERCIAL DP SYSTEM
There are two basic types:
a. EXECUTIVE
b. INFORMATION
and each has recognisably different system and file characteristics.

9. SYSTEM CHARACTERISTICS
a. EXECUTIVE SYSTEMS
   1. They tend to run frequently
   2. Processing is repetitive.
   3. Updates the data records.
   4. Are directed towards DOERS.
   5. Decision making is mechanical.

b. INFORMATION SYSTEMS
   1. They tend to run less frequently.
   2. They are RETRIEVAL orientated.
   3. They are directed towards MANAGERS.
   4. Decision making is manual.

10. FILE CHARACTERISTICS

    a. EXECUTIVE

        1. Should be tailored to the job.

        2. Ideally should contain only the essential data.
This is because the information requirements and
output formats are closely defined.

    b. INFORMATION

        1. More opportunity for integration (cross
indexing)

        2. More opportunity for consolidation (large
collections of data of the same key).

This is because the information requirements of
MANAGERS are usually much less well defined.
Therefore he needs access to different data at
different times. His requirements are less
predictable.

11. WHAT IS A DATA BASE?

A Data Base is:

a. A collection of fields of data, which are

b. Related in a meaningful way, and can be

c. Accessed in different logical orders,

d. BUT are stored only once.

It is these last two items together which distinguish
a Data Base from other arrangements of data, and which
give a Data Base the facility to support (many) different
users and their different processing of the same data.

    The application of Data Base Technology in these
terms is not appropriate to all environments. For
example, if one wishes to access more than say 10% of a
total population of records, then it is usually quicker,
in terms of elapsed time to process sequentially against a

separate tape file.   Then one can say that this data base
technology is incompatible with BULK BATCH processing, if
elapsed time is the most important criterion to the user.

At the other end of the spectrum, the technology is
completely compatible with real time systems where direct
access capability is a must because transactions occur at
random.

It is also compatible with SMALL (usually frequent)
BATCH processing via e.g.   Remote Job Entry.   This tends
towards real time.

And it is the ideal support for MANAGEMENT INFORMATION
systems, because characteristically, they need information
at different levels, (say detail component level, and all
the components in a Manufacturing Centre) and the net-
working facilities of Data Base are needed.

12. ADVANTAGES OF DATA BASE
    a.   It conserves secondary storage space for data.
    b.   Greater system integrity; if only stored once, all
         users are given the same data, to the same degree
         of up-to-dateness at one point in time.
    c.   The data base and its sub-sets are always in step.
    d.   It avoids extracting and sorting.

13. DISADVANTAGES OF DATA BASE
    a.   It is fragile - and requires sophisticated back-up
         and checkpointing facilities.

         The data base, while only storing data once,
         may now represent a number of logical data bases.
         It becomes all the more necessary, therefore, to
         ensure we do not lose say, an index, which will
         amount to the loss of a logical data base.

b. It requires complex logical linking.

c. Choice of cross indexing will incur (possibly high)
    overheads for environments where the number of
    records being accessed of a total population, is
    high.   One must take great care in which physical
    order data is stored, and choose the criterion for
    the cross index or chained list wisely.

14. EFFECT OF DATA BASE ON COMPANY ORGANISATION
The traditional approach is separate files and separate
systems serving functional areas of a company.   Usually
in this situation the ownership of data and the
responsibility for its maintenance are reasonably, if
not always wholly, clear.

The data base approach will result in larger
collections of data serving wider areas of a company,
and therefore the divisions will become much less
distinct.

This author therefore sees two new types of manager
emerging in a Company using data base technology:-

a. A Data Accountant - who will have responsibility for
    the ownership and updating of the data.   He will
    not be a DP Technician.

b. A Data Base Administrator - who will have responsibility
    for the physical arrangement of the data base and its
    re-configuring with changing circumstances.   He will
    be a DP Technician.

15. THE PROBLEMS
a. The existing situation
    It is likely that a user considering the creation of
    a data base will already have sophisticated inter-
    dependent systems even though his files are not

integrated. His existing application programs have
an inertia effect on his files; it is difficult to
change the files because of the time and expense of
modifying, re-compiling and re-testing programs, not
all of which will be affected by the changes in the
files. The least a user needs therefore, is a file
handler (an interface package between his application
programs and the files which they access), to achieve
data independence. The initial change to access
via a handler cannot be avoided, but the programs
need to be insulated from subsequent changes due to
an evolving data base, unless their "own" data has
changed.

b. Size and Scope and the Changing Environment
Because Data Base as defined in this paper gives the
ability to support many systems from one Data Base,
the size and scope of the "total" systems and design
effort is likely to be large.

   In the writer's view it is unwise to plan to
implement more than about one year's design work at
one time, simply because the world does not stand
still while we do it. Commercial and Industrial
enterprises must themselves evolve and change, and it
is almost certain that within about one year intervals,
the enterprise itself will have changed, or is wanting
to change. Wise designers and implementors will
therefore try to choose a slice of the whole which
will make a significant contribution toward the
objectives of the enterprise, without having too
many changes stacked up against it when it is
implemented.

   For large systems therefore, it is impractical
to implement at "one shot".

c. <u>The need for the Software Tools</u>

What is needed by the designers of Data Base
Technology Systems is suitable software to handle
network data relationships, and give data
independance of their application programs from
the data base. Only then can the data base be
re-configured and re-moulded in accordance with
the changing environment, to the best overall
operational and cost advantage of the systems
which the data base supports. Such software
should perform the logical to physical storage
translations and vice versa, (and the input/
output transfers from/to secondary storage. It
should not perform any processing of the data.

Anyone who has examined in detail, the design
and implementation of such software, rapidly
becomes aware of the large investment in time and
money which is required. In the writer's opinion
users who are not in the software marketing.
business cannot afford the necessary investment.

For the large body of normal users therefore,
there is a pressing need for suitable Data Base
Management Software.

16. <u>FUNCTIONAL REQUIREMENTS OF DATA BASE MANAGEMENT SOFTWARE</u>

a. It must be accessible from a procedural language,
so that application programmers can write their own
processing procedures.

It must therefore have an interface with the
procedural language(s) of the installation.

b. It may have a non-procedural language enhancement so
that non-programmers can write their own retrievals.

c. It must have a Data Definition Language so that complex data relationships of the network and tree form can be described to it.

It must also be capable of handling simple data relationships.

d. It must provide data independence such that the user is unaware of the storage devices on which the data is resident, and other data which he does not need in the data base, as far as is practicable.

e. The file handler (the logical to physical translator) which is at the core of the software, should be accessible to the user so that he can describe his own storage organisations to it. Too often it seems to be taken for granted that the physical storage organisations available in the software are the best. This is not necessarily true and yet data independence is still needed by the user in many cases.

f. It must be able to create and maintain cross indexes or embedded chain address lists to enable the handling of network and tree relationsjips.

g. It must be able to create new or delete old cross indexes without re-loading the data base. This is because a characteristic of data bases is change. New data relationships may become apparent, or be now needed where they were not needed before, or not needed where they were needed before. In this event a re-load of the data base should not be imposed. The data Base Manager must have the option.

h. It must perform efficiently in batch and real time
    mode.
    To achieve this it must operate by generating
    executive code when in batch mode, and interpret
    each input/output request when in real time mode.

i. It must maintain adequate statistics as to usage
    of the separate components of the data base.
    These statistics will be part of the tools of
    the Data Base Manager's trade. They will enable
    him to re-configure the data base with changing
    circumstances.

j. It must provide acceptable security of access to
    data.
    In the data base environment the meaning of 'file'
    and 'record' become rather obscure. It is likely
    that "field level" security will be necessary.

k. It must provide back-up and checkpointing. Because
    the data base will be updated in place, a "before"
    and "after" update image of each physical block of
    data will need to be created on some other secondary
    storage device (probably magnetic tape) for each
    physical transfer of data between core storage and
    secondary storage, if the data has been subject to
    update.
        The application program should also have the
    facility to dump its core partition and save the
    content of registers and buffers at appropriate
    intervals.
        These facilities are even more necessary in the
    data base environment because many logical data bases

may be represented in one physical set of data.
The loss of a cross index or a break in an address
link chain may cause the complete or partial loss
of a logical data base.

h.   And, of course, it must be compatible with the
user's operating system.

17. SUMMARY

a.   The pressing need for normal users is suitable Data
Base Management Software. In the writer's opinion
such a user, who is not in the software marketing
business, cannot afford the large investment of
writing his own. He needs a package deal, either
from a computer manufacturer or a software house.

b.   Designers, whose experience is in traditional systems
design, have a lot of basic re-thinking to do. In
the traditional approach one tends to think, like a
programmer, in terms of records and file organisations
at an early stage.

In the data base approach, the essential first
step is to analyse and understand the data to
establish all the network and tree relationships
among the data. This must be done without any
reference to particular hardware and storage organisations. Only then can one think about configuring
the data base.

c.   Because of the changing environment, large systems
can only be sensibly implemented step by step.
Information Systems will thus evolve step by step

from wherever the user happens to be now, and will always be changing.

d. Because a true data base will exert an influence over wide areas of a company, Management will have to be prepared to partially erase the traditionally drawn boundaries between functional areas of their organisations.

The true aim of Data Base and Management Information is to store the data once only, and make it accessible to all authorised users.

ACKNOWLEDGEMENTS

The author wishes to acknowledge the help given in the preparation and editing of this paper by K. W. S. Lewis, of Rolls-Royce, Ltd., Aero Engine Division.

Much useful information in this field will be found in the following publications.

DATA STRUCTURE DIAGRAMS by Charles W. Bachman (DATA BASE, Volume 1, Number 2, Summer 1969).

THE LARGE DATA BASE, ITS ORGANISATION, AND USER INTERFACE Transcript of a Panel Session (DATA BASE, Volume 1, Number 3, Fall 1969)

STORING THE DIRECTORY FOR AN INVERTED LIST SYSTEM by John H. Spitzer (DATA BASE, Volume 1, Number 4, Winter 1969)

INFORMATION MANAGEMENT SYSTEM - IMS/360. (IBM Publication - Application Description Manual, H20-0524)

INTEGRATED DATA STORE (General Electric Information Systems Publication - CPB-481B)

A NEW CONCEPT IN DATA MANAGEMENT (General Electric Information Systems Publication - CPB-483A)

GENERALIZED DATABASE MANAGEMENT SYSTEMS FOR MIS

Denis M. Manelski/ Henry C. Lefkovits
General Electric Company
U.S.A

Introduction

The creation of a MIS consists of establishing a database and set of procedures to operate on it; the database can be viewed as a model of a business. This model serves as a record of the logical structure and information contents of the more vital aspects of the organization. The procedural portion of an MIS serves to update this database, produce status and planning reports and provide for unanticipated queries against the database.

The mission of an MIS cannot be successfully fulfilled without a database system capable of modeling the complex data structures inherent in any large organization. It is not only necessary to incorporate explicit relations in the data structures, but careful planning is required to insure that evolving requirements of the database will not be restricted when new data requirements and relationships are identified.

The remainder of this paper considers the elements of database management systems, the functions they perform and their role in providing the appropriate environment for the MIS user.

Components of an MIS System

The main components of an MIS, as illustrated in Figure 1, have the following characteristics:

1. The User - interfaces with a collection of user systems and the environment. The user systems provide him with information about the environment. This information is subsequently utilized in controlling and manipulating the environment.

   Several important user parameters must be noted:
   (i) There is a wide range in the scope and detail of his information requirements.
   (ii) No substantial computer expertise can be assumed. However, differences can be expected in the effort and investment he will make in learning how to utilize an MIS system.
   (iii) On the other hand, the user can be expected to be relatively knowledgeable concerning the information contents of the environment. Thus, while it is unwise to expect the user to be aware of the system's computer-derived conventions, sophisticated knowledge and demands can be derived from his involvement with the information contents of the environment.
   (iv) The functional capabilities required by an MIS user substantially reflect his position in the organization. The following broad categories, although not universally applicable and subject to exception, define the needs in terms of level within the organization:
   a. Operations Personnel - are mainly concerned with transaction processing. The user chooses a message with a predefined format; this message has a specified destination and is processed according to established rules. This category involves relatively simple tasks. It covers, for example, recording completion of a production run in a manufacturing plant and inquiry of an airline passenger's status. The transaction processing provides a record of events in the organization.
   b. Lower and Middle Management - utilize the MIS to monitor

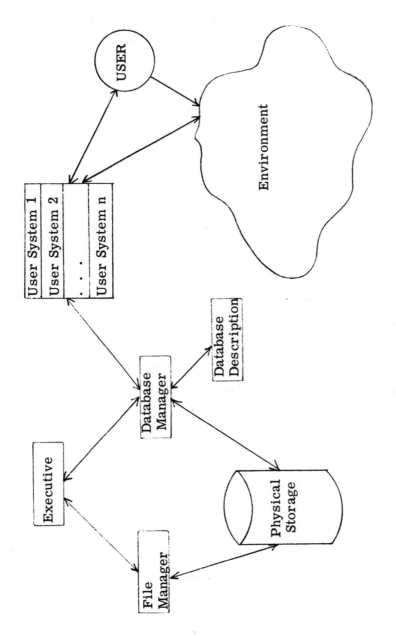

Figure 1 — Structure of a MIS

417

and report the status of the environment. At this level, it is necessary to aggregate and summarize transaction information. The criteria that determine report generation may be quite complex but stable.

    c. Middle and Upper Management - requires unanticipated reports that involve substantial aggregation of transaction data. More emphasis is placed on planning and signalling of exceptional conditions; hence the procedural abilities of the MIS will be more thoroughly exercised.

In general, the discreation associated with the reporting function increases with the level of the organization. Operations personnel are required to record and examine certain events while upper management structures its information requirements in terms of its perceived needs.

2.   User Systems[1] - the variability of requirements leads to a wide range of systems, languages and functional abilities. The user distinguishes two main categories:

    (i)   A General Query Capability - allows for the extraction of information from a database. This includes the class of non-procedural data retrieval languages permitting unpredictable or unanticipated queries, and systems specifying formatted reports such as those provided by an RPH.

    (ii) An Applications-Oriented Facility - required to provide for more complex procedural requirements.

3.   Executive - is responsible for allocating, dispatching and controlling the resources of the information system. Consequently, the MIS re-

---

1) See also Reference 2.

quests services of the executive; principally these requests concern the file manager and the database manager.

4. File Manager - manipulates files as entities, and consequently is not concerned with the organization or contents of files. It is used to map a file name to physical storage space, control file access and handle the recovery and restart system. The control of file access and the recovery and restart functions can best be handled in conjunction with the database manager.

5. Database Manager - performs its functions in light of its knowledge of the logical structure of the database. These include mapping from an address in the logical structure of the physical structure and providing structure dependent access control and the recovery and restart capability.

6. Database Description - provides the logical structure of the database. It is conceptual mechanism to aggregate and organize the data. The database description shields the user from concern with the physical storage mechanism.

7. Physical Storage - includes what the user conceives of as data, structural information defining data relationships and control information for the database manager. The files may be spread over a number of media, such as disc, removable disc, etc.

8. Environment - provides the information which after some selection or processing is placed in physical storage. The concept of an MIS, as shown in Figure 1, permits the system to provide data to the MIS, however the control of the MIS on the environment is indirect. The user, acting upon results from the MIS, can make changes upon the environment.

419

There are various other aspects of MIS requirements not specifically identified in Figure 1, which do have a significant impact on its characteristics. The expenditure of resources required to implement and maintain an MIS can only be justified in a multi-user environment. Thus, a number of other facilities, such as a terminal manager and a message manager, are required to handle communications. In addition, the multi-user environment requires the solution of new problems, particularly the deadlock problems arising from the situation where many users share the database and are permitted to update it concurrently.

File Manger: Access Control

As stated previously, access control is a principal function of the file manager. The function should involve three parameters[1]:

(i)   The users who may access the file.
(ii) The access rights associated with the user.
(iii) The process dependent access rights given to the user.

Each of these methods of control is more circumscribing than the previous one. Multiple user systems validate file access on user-name and provide various types of memory access. Combinations of read, write, execute and append are examples of memory access modes.

It is customary to specify access control to level (ii). However, the ability to control file access to procedures or groups of procedures[2] would substantially impede the misuse, intentional or otherwise, of the file. A

---

1) Discussion and implementation of the Multics "access control by procedure" is found in Reference 1.
2) Discussion and implementation of the Multic "access control by procedure" is found in Reference 1.

database might be readable to all users, but only by procedures that have been tested and permit reading of non-sensitive information.

Database Manager: Access Control

The access control of the file manager treates the file as an entity more discriminating selectivity requires the database manager since it is there that the awareness of the database structure and contents resides. Various levels of control can be specified, the effective cost of checking increasing with the level of detail. These are:

(i) At the record level - we can distinguish two cases:

    (a) Data control

    (b) Data and path control

In the first case, only the data of a record type is restricted. In the second case, control for the paths associated with the record can also be specified. In the file, shown in Figure 2, a user may be permitted "department sales" data (in the "department record") and "orders received" (in the "orders record") without giving him access to "employee-salary" (in the "personnel record"). This requires that the database manager permit the user access to the "department record - personnel record" relationship and the "personnel record - orders record" relationship without allowing him to retrieve any data from the "personnel record".

(ii) At the field level.

(iii) At the field content level - in the file of Figure 2, clerical personnel might be permitted access to "employee-salary" only when "employee-level" < 13.

A database manager permitting the detailed control of data access would substantially increase the willingness of an organization to store their data in a multiple user environment.

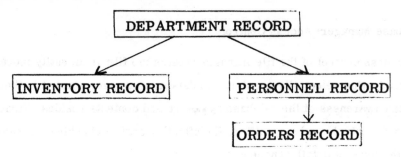

Figure 2

Database Descriptions: Logical Structure

Database descriptions may be implemented in many ways; the data division of a program may be compiled into object code, or stored as a file, consequently not only are there variations in implementation strategy, but also in the structures that can be described.

The logical structure of a database can be modeled in terms of items and relationships. The items, shown as boxes in Figures 3, 4 and 5, are connected by directed line segments, each one representing a relationship.

Associated with an item are attributes. These include name, length, data type, etc. The example in Figure 3 shows a simple inventory file with items named "amount in stock", "amount on order", "inventory location", "item description" and "item name".

Similarly, relationships have attributes. The attributes of a relationship discriminate on the ordering disciplin (e.g., LIFO, FIFO, sorted, etc.) and between mapping (1-1 or 1-n). When multiple relationships exist bet-

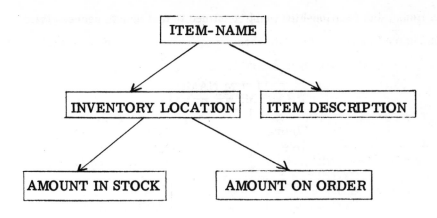

Figure 3

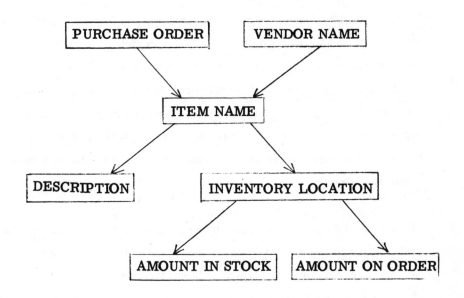

Figure 4

ween items, the relationships must be named to distinguish between them, as in Figure 5.

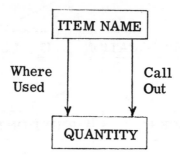

Figure 5

When the model is restricted so that items are only referenced by one relationship, the logical structure consists of trees. An example is given in Figure 3. More general structures are shown in Figures 4 and 5; such structures are known as graphs, and they both violate the conditions of a tree. In Figure 4, "item name" is referred to in two relationships. Each purchase order is made up of a series of items and each vendor supplies a series of items; these are examples of 1-n mappings. The example in Figure 5 shows the parts-explosion relationship, with "where used" giving the quantity of items in the sub-assembly and "call out" determining the component items.

The ability of graphs to express complex relationships permits data items, even when used in multiple contexts, to appear only once in the database. Not only does this provide for probable reduction of physical storage, but also simplifies maintenance procedures and access control, particularly when many users are sharing the database. The ability to provide graph structures is particularly important in a multi-user environment that must encompass a wide variety of response requirements. It is common that data will be shared between users who expect economical sequential access to their data and those whose on-line examination of small portions of the database can only be achieved by random access. This wide range of needs can be realized with data structures implementing rich data relationships.

Furthermore, it is not necessary that a unique database description exist for a database. It is often desirable to use multiple database descriptions, each one presenting an aspect of the database that is relevant to a particular user community. This can greatly simplify the task of the user who need concern himself only with the database description that is structured for his requirements[1].

User Systems: Some Aids

It is desirable that data entered in the physical storage of the database be relatively primitive in terms of its probable use. When the transactions themselves are recorded, it is possible to aggregate this primary data according to the needs of the various levels of management.

A system that allows data transformations in an entirely transparent manner would encourage the use of primary data. This transparency can be achieved by providing a dictionary or extending the file description so that what the user treats as a data item consists of a call to procedure that generates the equivalent data item.

Thus, addressing "shipments overdue" would produce a comparison between "shipment date" and "due date " to produce the list of overdue items.

---

1) The concept of sub-schema is explained in Reference 3.

Similarly, results could be aggregated from primary data producing the most current version without the user noting the procedural requirements. This type of facility can substantially reduce the amount of database updating and produce timely information.

Summary

This paper has examined the elements of database systems in terms of MIS requirements. After delineating the principal components of the MIS, attention was focused on aspects whose enhancement would significantly improve its capabilities. In particular, the following areas were discussed:

(i) Increasing the control of data access by extending the role of the file manager and the database manager.

(ii) Providing data structures that permit the database to adequately reflect the complexity of the organization being modeled.

(iii) Extending the user's concept of the database by embedding procedures in the database description.

BIBLIOGRAPHY

(1) Belmont, P.A., "Access Control to the Multics Virtual Memory",
     General Electric TIS R69LSD4, 1970.

(2) Lefkovits, H.C., "Characteristics of Database systems in a Compu-
     ter Network Environment". Interdisciplinary Conference on Multiple
     Access Computer Networks, April 1970, Austin, Texas.

(3) CODASYL Data Base Task Group, October 1969 Report
     (Available from ACM).

MIS ENGINEERING IN A MANUFACTURING COMPANY

Torben Dybkjær
International Business Machines A/S
Denmark

SUMMARY

*This is a paper around SYSTEMS ENGINEE-
RING in relation to the ORGANIZATION and
COMMUNICATION of MANAGEMENT INFOR-
MATION after the concept: all relevant data
could be management information some day. The
outline is wellknown but the contents are new
built around the new version of INFORMATION
MANAGEMENT SYSTEM/360 and the new computers for the 70'ies. It includes a CASE from
the MANUFACTURING ENVIRONMENT - a
fundamental case attaching importance to the
DATA BASE/DATA COMMUNICATION SYSTEM
with only few references to the exact outline
of management information. Its chiefest purpose
is to give you a useful plan of action for
IMPLEMENTING MIS.*

1. THE MANUFACTURING ENVIRONMENT

THE MANUFACTURING MODEL

Let's start traditionally by showing a functional model (figure 1) with the wellknown areas of purchasing, engineering, production, finance and sales. The purpose of this model is in addition to give the leitmotif in the next chapters to illustrate some of the basic single modules in a MIS. This gives us opportunity for drawing up the following objectives with the paper:

* give topmanagement an approach to develop a MIS fitting the company's short and long range plans and objectives
* show how a modular MIS can be implemented by composition of submodules without wasting ysterday's work - this openended modular approach permits the company to start big or small, move fast or slow, have a total or partial commitment
* illustrate the elimination of internal redundancy primarily in connection with the construction of a central data bank
* draw the attention to the elimination of external redundancy by using ready-made program products and thereby eliminating investments in the development of application programs already made.

The paper does not apply only to people from manufacturing companies. The contents of the paper concerns every type of company although the sample

casually is from the manufacturing environment -
more closely from a single large, but not too gigantic,
manufacturing company with an organization as above
(figure 1).

MANAGEMENT CONTROL

The management control module contains the short
and long term planning that combined with ideas
and facts from every function (communicated through
current reports, totals, details, exceptions) results
in masterplans and budgets for these functions.

As regards the MIS it is the management's primarily responsibilty of creating an environment for
acceptance and implementation. Management must
establish objectives for the level of automation,
the degree of integration and the scope of computerization (litt. 1) and through these objectives
develop masterplans and budgets for the approach to
a large common data base environment from one or
more of a number of different directions.

PROJECT MANAGEMENT

Project teams with qualified project members assigned
for a limited period to loose a given problem play
a vital role in the modern organized company. And
the project management (including activities as
time planning, resource allocation, budgetting,
costing and performance evaluation) has been an
important discipline (litt. 2).

In relation to the MIS an information system will
only be as successful as its implementation plan
and it is imperativ to analyze grossly both the
company decision system plus the present organization and the management information requirements
before embarking on an installation program. But do
not get too intrigated in this analysis - the next
chapters will show how far you should go.

2. DATA BASE SYSTEMS ENGINEERING

THE ELIMINATION OF REDUNDANCY

For getting a better use of resources you eliminate
redundancy - apart from these situations where you
from a security point of view want a substitution.
Considering the data in the company it therefore
would be adventageous to:

*   collect all relevant data in one common data
       base, the data bank
*   manage this data bank as far as possible in-
       dependent of the users
*   minimize the programming effort around this data
       bank by using general ready-made program products
       with a modular and openended form permitting an
       individual ongoing program development for the
       company.

Regarding the first point you should make a file study
by investigating the current files in the company.
These files should be combined, and some eliminated,
in satisfying the management information requirements.
Finally you get an idea of the company data bank

with files accessible for every MIS module, but
with only one definitely module as the generator
of new entries in a file (figure 2) - the lines
illustrate the relationship file/generating module.

Regarding the second point you should simplify the
users communication with the data bank. This could
most significantly be done in the programming made
by extracting all redundant file descriptions from
the application programs and submitting this with a
single data base description (figure 3).

Regarding the third point one answer could be the
Information Management System/360 version 2 (IMS/360)
for the IBM System/360 and the IBM System/370
(litt. 3).

IMS/360

IMS/360 comprises two major components: the data base
facility and the data communication facility
(figure 4). It has four major objectives:

*   to provide data organization methods that are
        conducive to the creation, interrelation, and
        maintenance of large common data bases and the
        multiapplication use of these data bases
*   to provide the means to develop and maintain
        a data base system in the batch processing
        environment
*   to provide the ability to easily extend data
        base processing to the teleprocessing or data
        communication environment

*   to provide an efficient data communication sub-
    system to support the development of a high
    volume/rapid response online application sys-
    tem.

Data Language/1

The data base processing capabilities of IMS/360
are provided by a facility called Data Language/1
(DL/1). DL/1 provides application program independence
from access methods, from physical storage organizations, and from the characteristics of the devices on
which the data of the application is stored. This
independence is provided by a common symbolic program
linkage and by data base descriptions external to the
application program. The application programmer only
uses few DL/1 statements to manipulate with segments
of the data bank and his program is independent of
changes in the data bank environment. With the combination of PL/1 and DL/1 you have a very serviceable
programming tool also usable for non-programmers.

The storage organizations and access methods employed
by DL/1 facilitate data integration with a minimum of
data redundancy. However, if analysis of a company's
data shows that it is not practical to place all data
in a single data base - for example from a security
point of view - DL/1 gives the additional capability
of physically structuring the data over more than one
data base.

An important capability of DL/1 that protects each
application of a multiapplication data base is the

concept of data sensitivity. When operating against
a DL/1 data base, <u>only the data that is predefined as</u>
<u>sensitive is available for use in a particular appli-</u>
<u>cation.</u>

Physical structure

Physical refers to the manner in which the data is
stored on a direct access storage device or tape.
Physical storage is accomplished through the use of
two unique DL/1 storage organizations:

* hierarchical sequential provides the basis for
  the hierarchical sequential access method
  <u>(HSAM)</u> and the hierarchical indexed sequential
  access method <u>(HISAM)</u>
* hierarchical direct provides the basis for the
  <u>hierarchical direct access method</u> <u>(HDAM)</u> and
  the hierarchical indexed direct access method
  <u>(HIDAM)</u>

The physical parent-child-twin relationships (figure 5)
may be indicated by physical juxtaposition of segments
for the hierarchical sequential or by direct addresses
in the prefix of a segment for the hierarchical
direct.

As mentioned above the application program is insensitive to the particular organization or access
method and it has therefore no interest to continue
in this context (litterature 3 is recommended for
further studies).

Logical structure

Logical refers to the manner in which the application program sees the data. A logical data structure is always a hierarchical structure of segments (figure 6) - a segment is a data element of fixed length, containing one or more logically related data fields. Programs written to process logical data structures can be independent of the physical data structure.

A segment of information need not be a part of only one logical structure. The physical storage techniques of IMS/360 allows a segment of information to participate in more than one logical data structure through the use of pointers indicating logical parent-child-twin relationship by direct addressing. Direct address relationships may be bidirectional and make inverted structures possible. By allowing a segment to exist only once but yet participate in a number of logical data structures, IMS/360 allows elimination of redundant data and facilitates processing requirements. In addition to having a pointer, a pointer segment may also contain user data called inter-section data, that is data unique to the relation-ship between a specific pointer segment and a target segment.

THE MANUFACTURING DATA BANK

In the manufacturing sample the data bank is made up of 8 physical data bases (figure 7), where a physical data base means a family of physical data base records where all have a common hierarchical segment structure. The physical data bases are connected in a logical relationship via several logical pointers and create in this way many logical data bases. Though IMS/360 allows orderly expansion with new segments it is advisable in a MIS survey to make this overall picture of the expected logical relationship between the physical data bases to ensure that no existing search argument chains later have to be modified and thereby prevent current programs from running. The logical relationship between all the segments in the data bank would be too detailed in this relation, but has been explored (litt. 4).

The first application using IMS/360 requires a detailed analysis of the logical data structure, the segments and the fields within a segment as earlier illustrated (figure 6). With this logical relationship within the overall data base picture this basic application can be expanded to become a multi-application environment. Furthermore, this application can begin as batch and be moved to online status as required - and this is the subject for the next chapter.

3. DATA COMMUNICATION SYSTEMS ENGINEERING

ONLINE REQUIREMENTS

The major requirements for a smooth transition from batch to online include:

* extensive editing and verification checks for data to be created and updated online
* procedures for backup and recovery of online files in case erroneous data is introduced into the data base or a physical disaster occurs
* coding programs in a modular form to keep the size down
* coding programs so that a call to read a batch input transaction can be replaced by a call for a transaction from the teleprocessing terminal in the same or similar format.

A high level of automation - the first management objective stated in chapter 1 - should be converted into a picture showing the terminal requirements for each MIS submodule and in this way illustrate the transition from batch to online (figure 8). The second management objective, the degree of integration, should be illustrated by showing the information flow for each function, that is the communication with other functions and the connection with the data bank, which as an example is indicated for one of the seven functions (figure 9).

IMS/360 DATA COMMUNICATION FACILITY

IMS/360 makes a smooth transition from batch to online possible with a minimum of user involvement. A system generation function called system definition allows the user to specify the communication lines and terminals, message types, programs, and data bases particular to the user's environment (figure 9). This

information enables IMS/360 to tailor a system
for efficient use of message processing and message
switching (figure 10). Message processing may result
in both data base inquiry and update activity. And
conversational terminal operation is also possible.

Checkpoint and restart

Periodic checkpoints of IMS/360 are required in order
to provide the ability to restart after loss of
core memory, disk message queue, or data base
information. There are many conditions under which
IMS/360 may require a checkpoint to be taken.
These conditions, in general, can be grouped into
four classifications

* system-scheduled checkpoints based upon message
  volume
* master terminal request to checkpoint the system
* master terminal request to orderly terminate
  the system
* master terminal request to produce a current
  copy of the data from a data base.

IMS/360 can be stopped or restarted daily or at explicit intervals. Restart provides for system re-
construction after a controlled stop, an emergency
stop, or a data base destruction.

The checkpoint and restart functions are dependant
upon message queuing on direct access storage and
the recording on the system log of all messages
and data base modifications.

Security

Connected with the data sensitivity in the data
base environment two types of security verification
may be designated in the data communication environment:

*   terminal security ensures that a secured trans-
    action or command may be entered only from spe-
    cific designated terminals
*   password security ensures that a transaction or
    a command message will not be processed unless
    a user-defined password is appended to the trans-
    action code or to the command verb.

4. MANAGEMENT INFORMATION SYSTEMS ENGINEERING

PRIMARILY A MATTER OF ORGANIZATION

A business success primarily depends on its organization and the people within it - and it is indeed
the same for the success of management information
systems engineering.

In relation to the management of the data bank should
two important functions be realized: the physical
data base management and the logical data base management.

The physical data base controller

The physical data base controller should be occupied
with:

*   structuring the IMS/360 by the creation of a

control block for each communications line,
terminal, message type, message processing
program and data base
* restructuring these control blocks as the operating environment changes
* defining security requirements
* establishing and supervising restare procedures
* supervising all daily activities through the
activity log especially making reorganization of
a data base when needed due to performance
* educating and advising the logical data base
controller and the application programmers in
optimizing their use of IMS/360.

The logical data base controller

The logical data base controller should be occupied
with:
* structuring the data base in relation to the
aspects of a total system
* defining all the fields and segments in every
data base eliminating redundancy and territorial
property of data
* supervising the creation of new fields and segments
* defining processing programs, transaction
types and processing priority, communication
lines and terminals in relation to IMS/360
* defining and supervising security requirements
* educating and advising the application programmers
in the development of data processing applications that use the facilities of IMS/360 and
optimize this use.

The overall DP organization

The organizational trend by using IMS/360 is a
relative drastic reduction of application programmers partly on behalf of some more DP specialists
and systems programmers (figure 11). This trend
illustrates the progress against the direct communication between non-programmers and the computers.

NEXT A MATTER OF PROJECT MANAGEMENT

A successful installation of a MIS will probably
include as much education as possible, a solid plan
and a generous amount of time. But to get started
with the education and get experience with the
planning without involvement of too much time a
pilot project would be helpful (figure 12). A project group composed of a user and the later physical
and logical data base controllers should get the
task in few weeks to go through the phases from the
correspnding computerization level to a mini data
base in the DL/1 environment and by this way be
familiar with IMS/360 before starting a real MIS
project.

Particular emphasis should later on be
placed on systems design to allow movement from
batch processing to online processing through the
design of small, modular and single - transaction
oriented programs. Especially care must be placed on
file organization, recovery and reorganization
procedures.

Extensive care on data accessibility is necessary
to protect certain data from unauthorized access.
When an application programmer needs data, he should
make a request to the logical data base controller.
If the data exists in the file and there is a legitimate need the logical data base controller supplies
the required segment search argument to obtain it.
If not the logical data base controller establishes
a new segment and again provides the required segment
search argument. Under either circumstances a record is made of the usage of data. Future changes
of the data bank can then be analyzed, and the impact on existing programs assessed on the basic of
usage.

BUT AN OVERALL QUESTION OF MANAGEMENT INVOLVEMENT

In the first chapter we stated "the managements
primary responsibility of creating an environment
for acceptance and implementation". And we de-
scriped the initial tasks of setting the objectives
and developing the masterplans and budgets for
the MIS project.

The next chapters have shown how to realize a MIS
with a minimum of investments. The paper could in
fact be taken as a guide for the outcome of a MIS
survey and should as such only be supplied with
information about volumes and a company plan of
action including implementation priorities for
every MIS module.

To control these activities, the management must
recognize their need for
*   education
*   participation
*   evaluation.

The need for education varies but should start with
a general course about the scope of MIS followed
by external workshops considering the structure and
modularity of information systems and internal
workshops reviewing approaches and ambitions in the
development of MIS, especially defining the management information requirements (litt. 4).

The need for participation should manifest itself
via checkpoint meetings in the steering committee.
This means quite often meetings in the survey phase
and later on review meetings for each application
when it enters the frozen zone and when it is to be
installed.

The need for evaluation should as concerns the projects be obliged by a sober project budgetting and
cost evaluation. The evaluation of the benefits of
an application in a IMS/360 environment should
especially be concentrated on the time requirements
of the application, in other ways what is the most
profitable: real time communication or periodical
reports. The evaluation of a large common
data base system should chiefly be occupied with
the possibilities for a dynamic extension of the
physical and logical data bank including a minimi-

zing of the program development costs both in the batch, under the transition and in the online phases. Finally the evaluation in relation to the third management objective, the scope of computerization, has to do with the physical aspects where the out-looking price/performance for the new systems for the 70'ies especially make the development of data base/data communication systems profitable.

Figure 1:   THE MANUFACTURING MODEL
* 14 MIS modules — 27 submodules

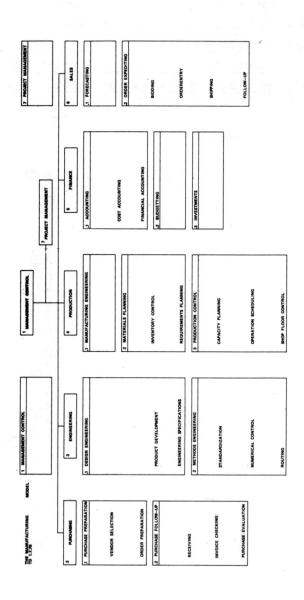

Figure 2:   THE MANUFACTURING DB MODEL
  * 16 files
  * 800 mill. char. pr. disk storage

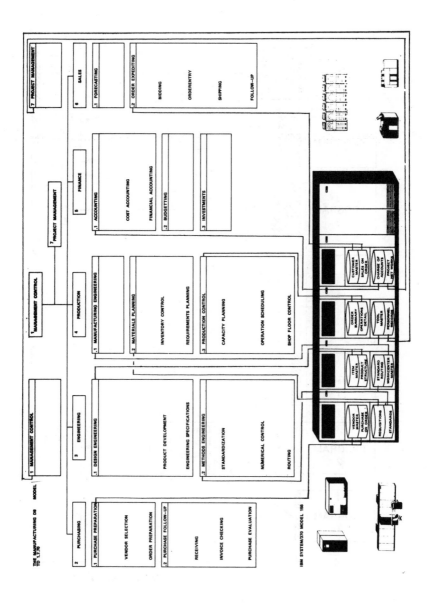

447

Figure 3:   a) TRADITIONAL REDUNDANCY
                b) THE DATA BANK IDEA

a)

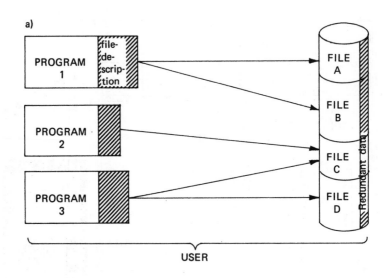

b)

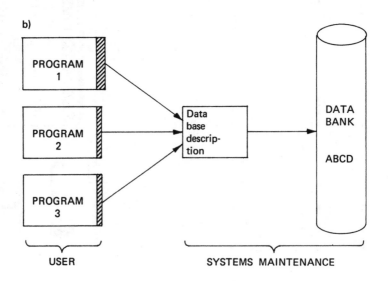

Figure 4:   IMS/360

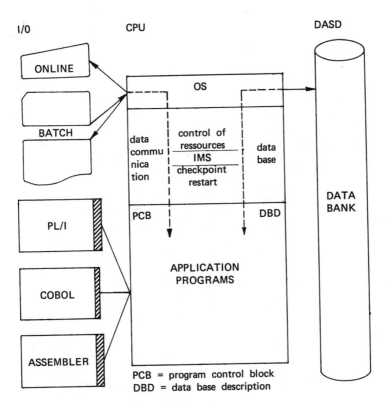

PCB = program control block
DBD = data base description

DL/I:

GET UNIQUE (retrieve a unique segment)
GET NEXT (retrieve the next sequential segment)
REPLACE (replace the data in an existing segment)
DELETE (delete the data in an existing segment)
INSERT (insert a new segment)

449

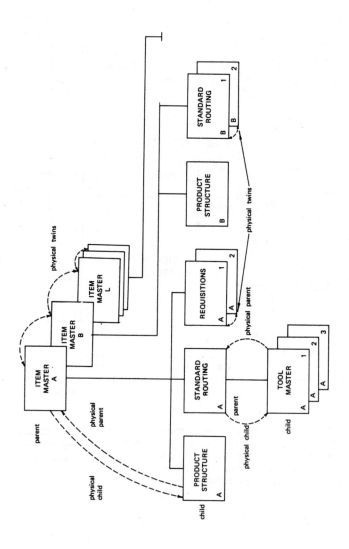

Figure 6:   a) TRADITIONAL RECORD
              b) LOGICAL DATA BASE RECORD

a)   one file

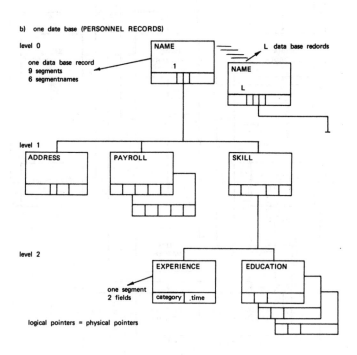

NAME	ADDRESS	**PAYROLL**		EDUCATION	EDUCATION

variable recordlength

b)   one date base (PERSONNEL RECORDS)

level 0   NAME   L data base redords

   one data base record   NAME
   9 segments   1   L
   6 segmentnames

level 1
   ADDRESS   PAYROLL   SKILL

level 2
                          EXPERIENCE   EDUCATION
   one segment
   2 fields   category   .time

logical pointers = physical pointers

451

Figure 7: THE MANUFACTURING DATA BANK
 * logical pointers

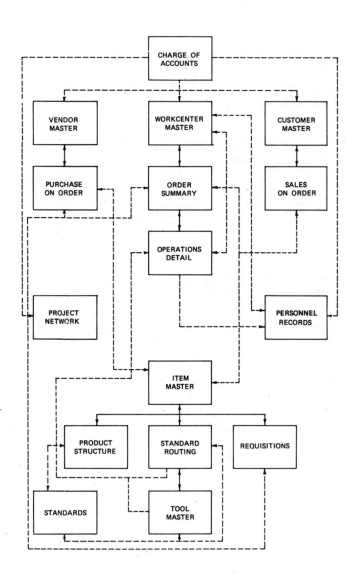

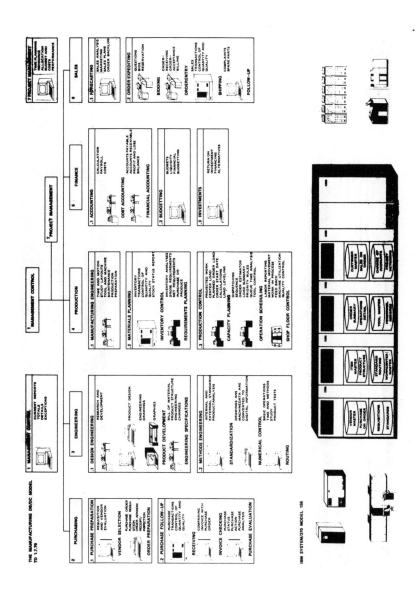

Figure 8: THE MANUFACTURING DB/DC MODEL
* realtime environment

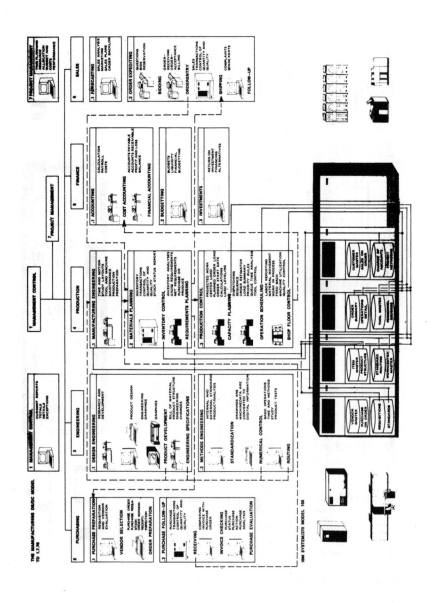

Figure 10:   THE TELEPROCESSING SYSTEM

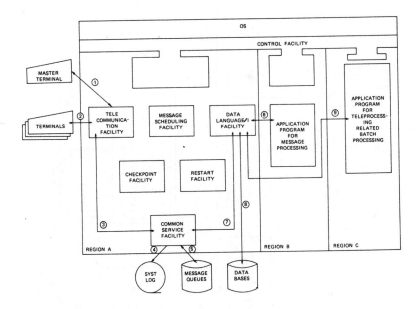

OS initialize the regions and this system flow occurs:

①   TF requests restart from MT

②   after restart MT open the T and input come

③   TF invokes CSF

④   input message is logged

⑤   and queued, control to MSF and then APFMP

⑥   APFMP requests the input and/or data base

⑦   control to DL1F for message reference through CSF

⑧   or for data reference

⑨   during execution event 5,7 and 8 can occur

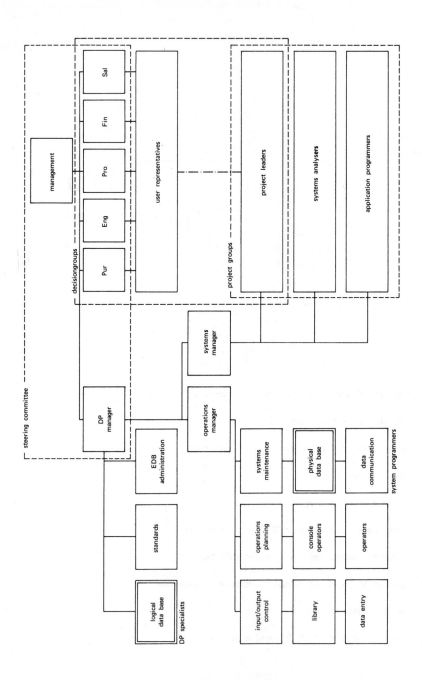

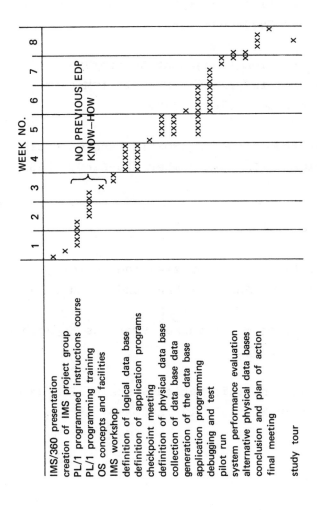

Figure 12:   IMS/36o PILOT PROJECT
         ✳ a company DL/1 sample

457

List of references:

1. The Successful Computer System, Joseph Orlicky,
   New York 1969, McGraw-Hill Book Company.

2. Project Management System/360 version 3
   Application Description Manual, IBM form
   number GH20-4004, 1969.

3. Information Management System/360 version 2
   General Information Manual, IBM form
   number GH20-0765, 1970.

4. The Production Information and Control System
   (PICS), IBM form number E20-0280, 1968.

Additional literature:

*   Creating and Organizing the Corporate Data
    Base, EDP Analyzer Feb. and March 1970.

*   Databases - databanks, Sveriges Mekanförbund,
    March 1970.

*   Management Information Systems, IBM Nach-
    richten No. 191, 192 and 193, 1968.

THE NIMMS FILE HANDLER

A.P.G. Brown
International Computers Limited
England

1. INTRODUCTION

NIMMS (Nineteenhundred Integrated Modular Management System)
consists of suites of programs for Production Control, Stock
Control, Payroll and so on, covering between them many
different data processing applications.   The data required
to run the programs comprises a Data Base whose structure
and format is not known to the programs; so the data base
may be developed without the need to re-program, re-compile
or re-test the application programs.   Implementation of
NIMMS can start at any one of the applications with re-
organisation of the files in the data base each time new
applications are implemented.

The separation of programs and data is achieved by the NIMMS
File Handler, which is a special housekeeping system designed
to present data to the program in the way the program expects
it regardless of the method of storing the data in the
physical files.   The implications of this development are
broad and far reaching.

1. The life of program is lengthened since it is not
    necessary to change them when files change.
2. Since file formats can be continuously changed systems
    development can evolve instead of proceeding in periodic
    'great leaps forward'.   The upheaval caused by making
    sweeping changes in operational systems has been a
    major barrier to progress.
3. The data base can be continuously 'tuned' to meet the
    requirements of the organisation.   The need to duplicate
    data to avoid changing 'old' systems disappears - so does
    the need for allowing blank spaces for expansion in data
    records.
4. Development of new data storage techniques or new hard-
    ware devices does not render programs obsolete.

In our view flexibility in the design of files and the
ability to change file formats is a requirement of any
organisation developing integrated systems.   In our
experience the biggest problem has been the reconciliation
of data used by different systems which one would expect to
be the same.   Often both systems can 'prove' that their data
is correct and the causes of differences have to be traced
and understood.   If the systems are not integrated then each
manager has his own information system and managers find they
are increasingly discussing the accuracy of figures instead
of their interpretation.

As data processing applications are transferred to a computer
the user has a chance to integrate them with existing systems.
However, this has often not been done because of the
difficulty of changing applications programs.   Changes of
file design usually result in re-writing or re-compiling
programs.

In the development of NIMMS a number of applications have been
developed in parallel by separate applications teams.   These
have been co-ordinated and integrated through their use of the
common data base, which is controlled by a separate team.
The physical placement of data on storage media is not the
concern of the applications teams although this does play a
part in feasibility studies.   The co-ordinator ensures that
the data in the data base is understood by the teams and that
data is not 'logically' duplicated.   Elements of data are
given unique names and no element should have two names.

Ideally when the physical data base is designed no data should
be duplicated.   However, in practice, duplication is sometimes
necessary if the efficiency of application programs is not to
be impaired.   Inconsistencies in duplicated data are possible
if the applications programs change data so, as far as is
practically possible, data base maintenance is handled by a
suite of Data Management Programs which do not themselves
belong to any application.   In this way the Data Management
Programs can be made to control data in the data-base and help
to ensure that duplicated data is kept self-consistent.

Data is important in its own right and the data that is used
by the applications of an organisation is the soundest base
of a Management Information System.   File Handler makes the
applications programs independent of the physical placement of
data so that the data base can be more easily tuned to the
changing requirements of the organisation.

2. USING THE FILE HANDLER

A program using the File Handler to access or write data is
said to handle Logical Files.   The logical file is a
software data interface and is used both to define the data
requirements of the program and to pass data to and from the
data base.   The logical file consists of an hierarchy of
logical entities, where an entity is any thing or relationship about which data is defined.

This is best explained by an example.   Fig. 1 shows a
Logical Stock File which contains the entities needed for
a stock control application.   Each entity has a key which
identifies it and attributes which are properties of the
entity.   For example the key of the Item could be a part
number or a catalogue reference number.   Attributes of
the item would include an item description and possibly
standard costing or pricing data.

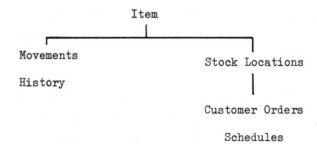

Figure 1. Structure of a Logical File.

The structure of the hierarchy indicates three things.
Firstly the relationships between the entities is one of
higher level entities owning lower level entities.
Secondly the method of accessing the entities is defined.
Customer orders, for example, will be accessed by first
finding the Item entity, then the Stock Location entity.

Thirdly the sequence of processing is defined. The program
will find an Item entity, then process the Movements History
entities, then process Stock Locations, processing the
Customer Orders of the first before proceeding to the second
Stock Location entity and so on.

The Logical File is defined by a table which is preset in the
program. The table is divided into areas, one for each entity.
The entity key and those attributes that the program wishes to
process are specified by field mnemonics in the entity area.
The relationships between the entities are indicated by the
sequence of the areas and pointers which link entities to their
owing entities. The Logical File Table for fig. 1. is
outlined in fig. 2.

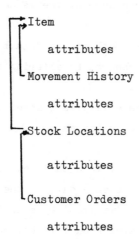

Figure 2.   Layout of a Logical File.

The entity handling functions consist of calls to File Handler
subroutines. Each instruction indicates an entity in the
Logical File table by supplying the address of the entity
description. The preset description of the file is used once
only by File Handler at the start of the program. When the
physical files have been opened, the area occupied by the

attribute mnemonics is used to contain pointers to attribute
values.   This is true if the values have been read from the
data base and are being made available to the program, or if
the program is giving File Handler data to be stored in the
data-base.

The functions available are explained briefly below.

1. READ - This reads an entity defined by a key value.
2. READN - This reads the first or next entity of the given
    type belonging to the same owning entity.   It will not be
    successful if there are no more entities of the given type.
3. CREATE - This creates a new entity belonging to the same
    owning entity but does not store it in the data base.
    Thus the program can change some of the values in it before
    it is written away.
4. WRITE - Stores an entity back in the data base.   Its
    attributes may have been changed by altering the pointers
    in the Logical File Table.
5. DELETE - Ensures that an entity is removed from the file,
    together with all its owned entities.

When the program has read an entity which is owned by another
entity it may still access and change data in the owning entity.
If the owning entity has been 'written' by a WRITE instruction
its attributes may still be referenced but they cannot be changed.

The user is not concerned with physical data transfers at all.
The WRITE instruction, for example, merely informs File Handler
that the data can be written back.   The user should write all
data as soon as possible as failure to do so can lead to core
store constipation which slows the program.

In addition to the five conventional functions there are also
routines for re-allocating entities to different owning entities.

For example in fig. 1. Customer orders are allocated to stock
locations and it may be necessary to re-allocate them. These
functions are performed by a series of list-processing routines.
Each entity can have a list of entities temporarily dissociated
from the data-base. The routines are for removing entities
from the logical file and adding them to the list and vice-versa.

If it is not possible to finish processing an entity before
reading the next entity of the same type it is possible to 'Save'
it and read more entities of the same type. A 'Restore'
function restores the file to its 'Saved' condition so that
processing of the entity can be completed. Reading would
result in entities being presented for a second time unless
they were unlinked during the look ahead phase.

3. THE DATA BASE

The NIMMS data base is not a huge direct access file held on-line
to a computer. We define the data base as consisting of all the
files necessary to run the applications. These may be arranged
in a complicated structure on discs or they may be serial files
with data arranged primarily for the efficiency of the
applications programs.

For these two approaches two types of file are allowed. For a
highly structured direct access data base the files used are
PLUTO (see reference 1). Briefly, a Pluto Data Base consists of
Master and Structure files which are linked by Direct Access
addresses.

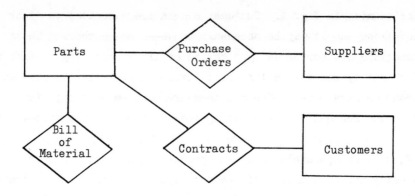

Figure 3.   A Pluto Data-Base.

In fig. 3 the squares are Master Files and these are indexed on
key name.   The structure files express relationships between
the entities on Master Files.   Processing can start at any
Master File record and follow direct access links to other
files.   For example, if a Supplier went out of business one
could retrieve the Parts affected via the Purchase Orders
File.   The Bill of Material file could be used to find the end
Products affected and the contracts file could show the
Customers affected.   All this processing is done by following
direct access address links and no irrelevant records are
retrieved.

Note that this type of structure can reflect very accurately
the true structure of the data.   We have found the type of
diagram shown quite useful in analysing the structure of data.
However for applications processing purposes some of the links
are essential and others can virtually be ignored.   The
program that could use all the links shown in a single run
is practically impossible to conceive.   In practice, we
find that the processing needs of an application can be
expressed quite satisfactorily by a Logical File.   The power
of the PLUTO structure is that so many different Logical Files

466

can be regarded as sub-sets of the same physical structure and therefore the same data can satisfy the needs of several different application systems.

The second type of file is called a Generalised File. This is hierarchical, consisting of entities owned by other entities. In fact is is as close as one can get physically to the logical file described in section 2.

Fig. 4 shows a hierarchy and the sequence of the entities in the file.

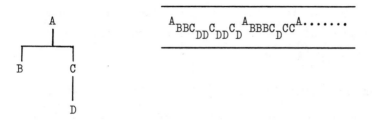

Figure 4. Generalised File Structure and Sequence.

Each entity can have variable length fields. Any entity can own a variable number of 'owned entities' of up to eight types. This can be repeated down to eight levels. A generalised file may be a serial file on disc or tape, or it may be indexed sequential on disc.

The file is organised into physical records for the highest level entities, with all owned entities considered as repeatable sections or sub-sections of the record. Since this method means some records will be very large, they can be split into a start record with continuations. It is not necessary to hold a complete record in core in order to process it.

This method of organisation involves considerable packing and
unpacking of records but it does compress the data into the
minimum amount of media space.   This in turn minimises transfer
time.

The specification of generalised files is currently being
enhanced to allow (optionally) owned entities to exist as
separate records on the file.   This increases the size of the
file but saves unpacking time and increases the efficiency of
indexing.   The enhancement was found necessary because some
files had very few top-level entities.

Many simple files can be regarded as generalised files since
they are hierarchical but with top-level entities only.
This is the degenerate case.

A very important feature of File Handler is the fact that the
physical fields in the data base do not have to be in one-to-
one correspondence with the attributes in the logical file.
In fig. 1, for example, we said that pricing data was held
at the Item Level.   This may be so in the data base but a
forward looking systems designer would recognise that it is
logically at the Customer Order level, since this is where the
data is used.   Thus if it became necessary to hold different
prices for different locations the data base only would need
to be changed, not the programs.   Any data which is not
changed by a program can be held physically on an 'owning'
entity.   It may even be defined in a physical file
description and not held on file at all.

4.   STRUCTURE OF THE FILE HANDLER

The File Handler is (like Gaul) divided into three parts.
The Pre-processor processes the Logical File Tables at the
start of a program and maps them onto the Data Base.
The Interpreter processes the Entity Handling functions
described in section 2 and, using the results of the Pre-
processor, calls housekeeping routines.   The third part,
the Housekeeping System, is a function of the type of
physical files being processed.   In the present
implementation housekeeping routines for Pluto and
Generalised Files are available.

The 'Keys' to the working of File Handler are tables which
are set up in core by the pre-processor and which are
subsequently used to interpret the program's entity transfer requests.   These Physical File tables are constructed
by matching Physical File descriptions which are held on a
Control File, with the Logical File Table in the program
area.   When the matching is complete Physical File Control
Areas are set-up, buffers are allocated and the files are
opened.

Any remaining core is allocated to a File Handler Buffer
which holds all current data, i.e. all data the program is
aware of.

Figure 5 shows an example of a Logical File Table with a
Physical File Table which describes a file containing the
data required.   The Physical File Table is divided
firstly into sections corresponding to the Logical Entities
– the Logical Entity Equivalents.   A Logical Entity
Equivalent may be split into groups to cater for the case
when the program is not processing a particular entity
(as in the example which is explained below).   A Group
can contain references to more than one physical file and

will often do so when links are to be followed between PLUTO
files. The use of the table is explained for the Read Next
function.

Logical File Table   Physical Table
Item Entity   –   Item Entity Equivalent, not owned.◄──┐
    Item number,   Group   │
    Item description   Item Entity (indicates F.C.A.) │
                                         Item Number   │
                                         Item Description   │
                                         Item Price   │
Order Entity   –   Order Entity Equivalent, owned by ───┘
    Location Code   First Group
    Customer Number   Location Entity (indicates F.C.A.)
    Order Number   Location Code
    Quantity   Location Address
    Item Price   Transport Charge
    Transport Charge   Second Group
    Location Address   Order Entity (indicates F.C.A.)
                                         Customer Number
                                         Order Number
                                         Quantity

                 Note: FCA = File Control Area – used by the
                        Physical File Housekeeping Routines.

Figure 5.   A Logical File Table and Corresponding Physical
            File Table.

From studying the Logical File Table we see that the program is
processing Orders for Items.   Note that the Item Price is an
attribute of the Order whereas physically the field is held
with the Item.   From the Physical Table we see that orders
are grouped into Locations and that some logical Order
attributes correspond to fields of the Location.

The method of processing is to read an Item entity followed by the Order entities. When a request to read the next Order is received processing is as follows:

1. The File Handler follows the pointer from the Order Entity to the Order Entity Equivalent and checks that there is a Current Item Entity.
2. It then identifies the Groups and, if and only if there is no current one it reads a new Location and sets the Logical File Table to the appropriate values using the field descriptors.
3. File Handler attempts to read the next (or first) Order Entity; if successful the Logical File Table is set up and the routine exits.
4. If there is no next Order Entity the routine tries the next location (2). When there are no more locations the routine exits with a negative reply. The program must then read another Item.

The physical Read Next instructions given by File Handler to its files are made by using Physical File Control Areas whose addresses are held in the Physical File Tables.

The Physical File Table is not used just for reading. It is a map which indicates what the Logical File corresponds to on the Data Base and is used by all the functions.

5. CONCLUSION

The NIMMS File Handler was developed initially for NIMMS which required complex data structures for its earliest applications. Its use to date has been restricted to programs written in house and to certain customers who are field testing NIMMS.

Programs using File Handler have been easier to write because of its powerful housekeeping facilities. Testing has been straight-forward except in the earliest days when File Handler itself was fragile. It now has its own monitoring system as a de-bugging aid. Programs written to run directly from large data bases can be efficiently tested using serial files specially constructed for the purpose so that there is no danger of corrupting data.

Since most applications operate in batch mode, this was the method chosen for the first file handler.   Future versions will have to work in an on-line mode, which poses special problems of data privacy and multi-access to files.   This work will be closely linked with operating system developments.

File Handler is capable of being enhanced in two ways. Firstly the interface with the program can be extended to allow more types of instruction and secondly the physical file standards can be relaxed to allow greater freedom to the data base designer.

Other file handling systems are being developed in the U.K. and the U.S.A.   The power of the NIMMS File Handler is the degree of data independance between the program and two different file systems and the fact that this independance is achieved without the need to re-compile programs.   .

Acknowledgement

The author wishes to thank International Computers Limited for their co-operation and for permission to publish this paper.

Reference 1.   S. Sem-Sandberg and E. Odmansson.
               File Organisation by PLUTO.
               File 68. Working Papers.

THE DATA BASE OF THE DAISY PRODUCTION
CONTROL INFORMATION SYSTEM

John F. Sprong
NV Philips Electrologica
Holland

DAISY stand for Domestic Appliances Information System,
the information system which has been developped for
the Domestic Appliances Division of the Philips
Gloeilampenfabrieken N.V. at Drachten, Holland.

DAISY is designed to control production and perform
detailed planning functions for some 20.000 products,
subassemblies and parts. There are well over 100.000
relations between these products and parts in the
bill of material section of the system.

The main characteristic of the system is however
not so much the size as the complexity of the interrelations between the seperate files. Any file in
the system can be reached either direct or via the
central product master file from any given other
file. There are more than 50 independant chains and
a number of these have been designed in such a way
that all their components are within the same cylinder.
For a number of files the PRINSYS standard software
package has been used.

For purposes of description the data base can be split
in three main parts:

1. the product related files containing information
   on the products and parts and their relations.
2. the supplier related files containing information
   on suppliers and machines plus their relations
   with the products in the form of orders and
   production plans.
3. the files related to the stock keeping funtion.

A separate database has been build for the commercial
department of the industry group. It is linked to the
production control data base through a cross-index
on both product master files. On the next pages all
the sections will be discussed shortly.

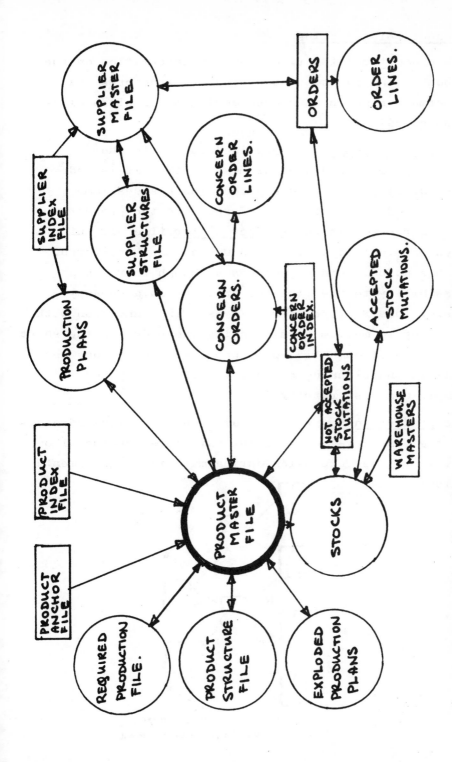

PRODUCTION CONTROL FILES IN DAISY.

Product related files

The product related files contain information on the products and parts, on the product structures and information which is needed during material requirement calculations.

The product index file provided access to the directly organized product master file. It is index sequentially organized and contains besides some status indicators only a reference to the product master record. In the product master file all information relevant to a given product or part is stored. It has no build-in structures although there is a possibility to tie finished articles in a one-way chain. This feature is mainly used in connection with the long to medium term planning where due to the short life span of domestic appliances two generations may fall in one planning period. It allows then for simple and fast retrieval.

The product anchor file contains the starting addresses of the same level chains. The same level chains allow level by level explosion during material requirements-calculations.

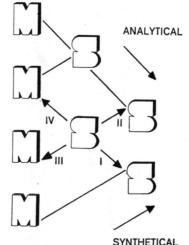

Figure 7: References in a product structure record.

In the product structure file all product relations
are stored. The usual bill of material information and
references allow both analytical and synthetical
analysis (see figure).

The production plans required to maintain planned
sales which form the input for the material requirements calculation are stored in the required production
file. The results of the material requirements calculation again per article per period stored in the
exploded production plans file.
While usage of the files in this section is extremely
complicated, the file structures themselves with the
exeption of the product structure file are relatively
simple.

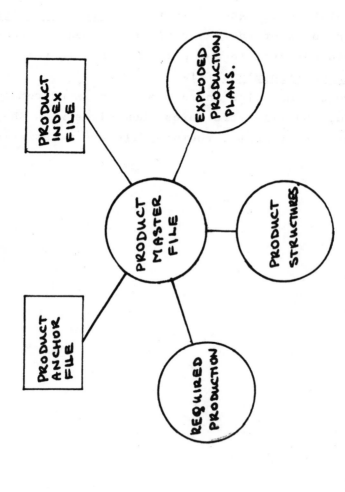

FILES CONTAINING INFORMATION ON PRODUCTS,
PRODUCT STRUCTURES AND MATERIAL REQUIREMENT
CALCULATIONS.

Diagram labels:
- PRODUCT INDEX FILE
- PRODUCT ANCHOR FILE
- PRODUCT MASTER FILE
- EXPLODED PRODUCTION PLANS.
- PRODUCT STRUCTURES.
- REQUIRED PRODUCTION

Supplier related files

All files which are related to both a product and a
supplier are grouped together as the supplier related
files.

Amongst them are the supplier structure file, the
file containing the production plans and two on-order
files.

The supplier file itself consists of two parts; the
master file and the index to the master file. The
index file uses the index-sequential organization
and contains besides some status indicators only two
references; one to the supplier master record and one
to the production plan record for the first planning
period.
The supplier master file contains all the permanent
information on external and internal suppliers.
There are nine different record lay-outs in order to
allow the user to select the one best suited for the
information he wants to store. Lay-outs are preformatted
for production departments, production units, machines,
two external and two different internal suppliers.
All contain a hierarchical structure (see figure) and
references to the supplier structure-, the order-
and the concern order files.

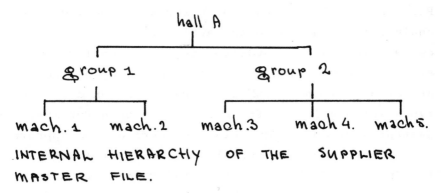

INTERNAL HIERARCHY OF THE SUPPLIER
MASTER FILE.

The <u>supplier structure file</u> contains structural information on the relation between the product and its suppliers. It contains references which allow storing and retrievel of where-used and alternative supplier information (see figure).

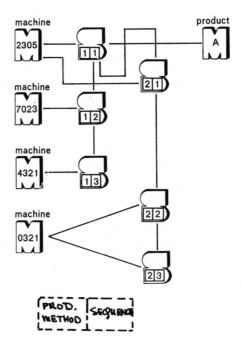

RELATIONS BETWEEN PRODUCTS AND SUPPLIERS.

<u>Production plans</u> are filled for consecutive periods. Per product all records for a series of periods are chained in sequence to the article. For capacity calculations all records for a given capacity group and pertaining to the same planning period are also chained together. There are seven different types which allow differentiation between for instance past/present and future planning periods and approved or pending plans. A special variety are the short term plans for the current period which form a ringlike structure attached to the current period (see figure).

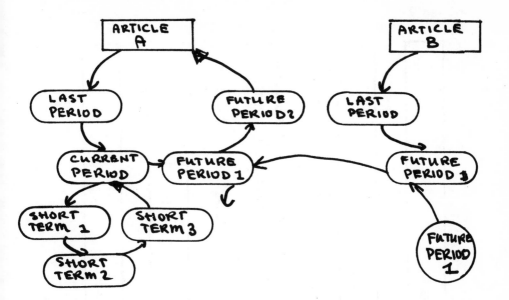

INTERNAL STRUCTURE OF THE PRODUCTION PLANS FILE.

The order files contain the common order information for a given order. Order lines are stored in a special order line file. Retrieval can be either from the product file, from the supplier file or direct. Orders to suppliers can be approached directly by means of a key-conversion routine. For concern orders for parts the build-up of the key does not allow useful conversion and therefore a special index file to these orders is maintained.

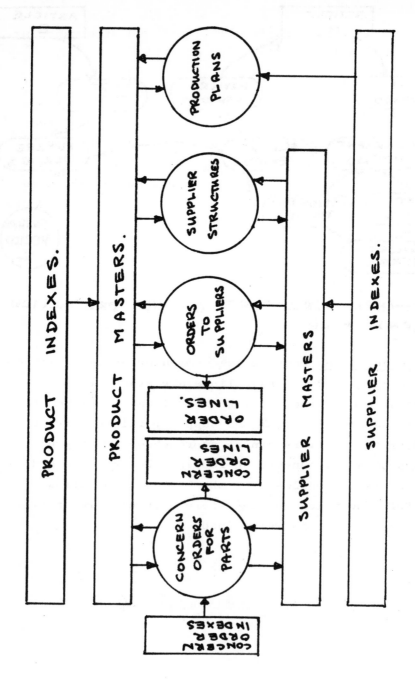

SUPPLIER RELATED FILES.

Stock related files

All information connected to stocks and stock keeping is stored in these files.

Main files are the actual stock file and the file of not accepted stock mutations.
Articles can be kept in stock in several warehouses simultaneously. As a rule required products are obtained from a preferred warehouse. In out of stock situations, however, alternative warehouses are used. This necessitates the structure sketched in the figure for the <u>stock</u> file.

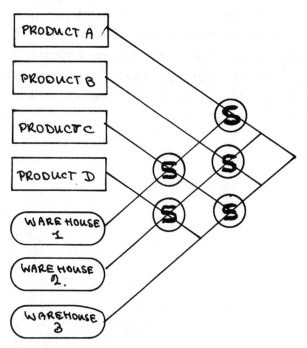

RELATIONS BETWEEN WAREHOUSES AND ARTICLES.

Some stock mutations are not accepted by the screening
of the stock keeping. They are stored in the
not accepted stock mutations file. While pending
they can be retrieved either through the article
file or through the order file. There is also a
reference from the stock record to its future yet
pending mutations.
In order to allow corrections using turn around
documents the records can also be addressed directly
using a key conversion routine.

Accepted mutations are related to a given stock using
a simple push down chain and stored in the accepted
stock mutation file. They are used for accounting and
checking purposes. For every warehouse there exists
a master record containing basic information about
the warehouse. From this warehouse master file a single
chain connects all stocks in a given warehouse which
allows stock surveys per warehouse.

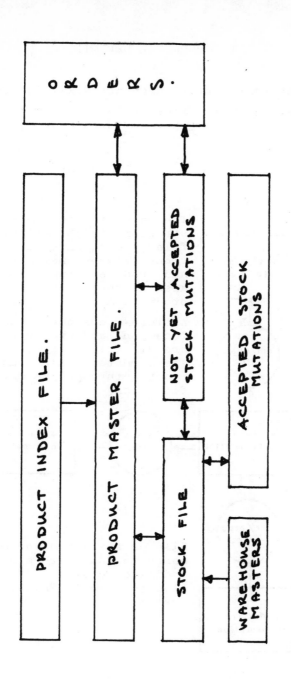

STOCKS · RELATED FILES.

THE DATABASE FOR THE COMMERCIAL DEPTMT.

The files contain information on articles, customers and producers. The main files are an article file, a customer file, a producer file, and relation files between these.

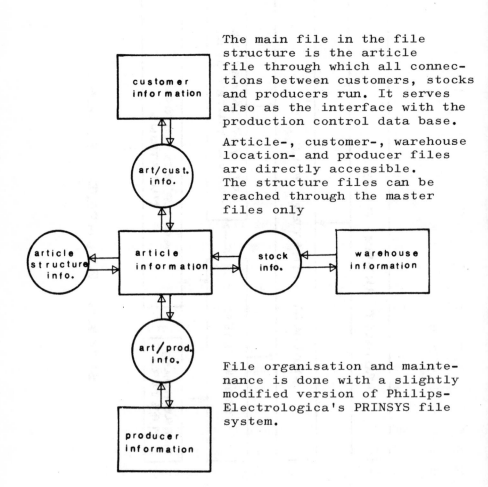

The main file in the file structure is the article file through which all connections between customers, stocks and producers run. It serves also as the interface with the production control data base.

Article-, customer-, warehouse location- and producer files are directly accessible. The structure files can be reached through the master files only

File organisation and maintenance is done with a slightly modified version of Philips-Electrologica's PRINSYS file system.

FILE SECURITY IN AN INFORMATION INDEPENDENT
DATA MANAGEMENT SYSTEM

P.A.D. deMaine and N.F. Chaffee

The Pennsylvania State University

USA

1. INTRODUCTION

The SOLID System[1] is a high-speed, fully automatic, Information
Management/Retrieval System. It is information independent, self-
organizing, and (within the framework of the assigned descriptors
(or indexes)) it is independent of the kind of question asked. The
SOLID System can be easily used to organize any collection of
information items (e.g. documents or business files) that have been
assigned unique descriptor sets. There are provisions for
incorporating Text Processing Components, which would extract
descriptors from natural language texts. To use the SOLID System the
user-manager has usually, at most, only to code a TRANSLATOR Component,
which rearranges the assigned or extracted descriptor sets to a
special JOBLIST Task form. These linear JOBLIST Tasks are used by
the SOLID System to trace, purge or delete, update, or create
information paths to the referenced information. The absolute

---

[1] Self-Organizing Large Information Dissemination System.

integrity of each separate item of information is assured by an optional system of "security locks" that are entered by the user-manager, when the files are updated, and/or by the individual users.

The SOLID System was described before implementation began [1], and at various stages during implementation [2,3]. The COPAK Compressor [3,4,5,6,7,8] and the Global Memory [3,9] subsystems have already been described. The fully implemented SOLID System will be described in a five volume set [10].

The principal purpose of this paper is to describe the SOLID System and its several stand-alone subsystems. Special emphasis will be placed on the File Security facilities.

2. OVERVIEW OF THE SOLID SYSTEM

In the SOLID System there are three distinct, separate files, the AUXILIARY, RECORD, and MAIN FILES. The descriptor sets (or indexes) are associated with the AUXILIARY FILE. The "referenced information", which is never searched directly, is stored in the MAIN FILE in a highly compressed form. The AUXILIARY FILE can be viewed as a maze of "information paths" that terminate with a symbolic address(es) in the RECORD FILE (RFILE). Each symbolic address contains the address in the MAIN FILE of the first one of a linked set of items of compressed referenced information (see Figure I). The assigned or extracted descriptor sets are rearranged by the TRANSLATOR Component(s) to the unique linear JOBLIST Tasks, which are descriptions of "information paths" in the AUXILIARY FILE.

The structure of the JOBLIST Tasks is described in Section 5. Here it is noted that the simplest form of JOBLIST Task is:

$$\text{JOBLIST Task} \equiv (M/J/LD_0/LD_1/.../LD_N*) \qquad\qquad ....(A)$$

M is the prime index (viz., 1,2,...); J is a screen that discloses the subclasses of the descriptors in the screen LD_0; LD_0, LD_1 ... are screens which contain the assigned or extracted descriptors.

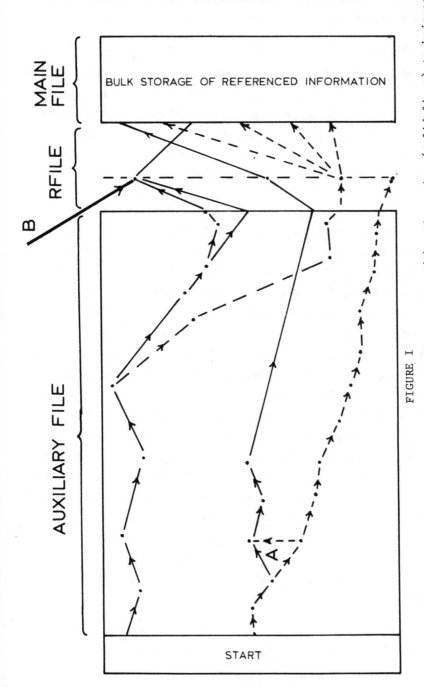

FIGURE I

Illustration of the path creating (broken lines), updating (A) and tracing (solid lines) techniques that are a part of the SOLID System. The points represent decisions that are made with the information path description (viz., JOBLIST Task). The length of a path is determined solely by the number of decisions. Registry Number searches (B) enter the RFILE directly.

The asterisk indicates that the information path terminates in the RFILE (see Figure I).

The JOBLIST Tasks are used to create, purge, update, or trace the information paths (subpath by subpath) in the AUXILIARY FILE to the RFILE. Subpaths are never duplicated, and they are only created when they are needed. Except for a single retrieval command (MODE), which has eight options [10a], all storage, retrieval, purge, and update operations are fully automatic. The AUXILIARY, RECORD and MAIN FILES are fully self-organizing within their allocated storage resources.

In many respects the scheme that is being described is analogous to an evolving communications network. Each telephone number (or calling code) can be viewed as a unique description (viz., JOBLIST Task) of a path (or channel) from the transmitter substation to a receiver substation in the network. A call is aborted if any link (or subpath) of the path cannot be found. In the SOLID System the prime index, M, and the first two screens (J and LD_0) together fill the function of the "area-code". The prime index, M, and all the screens (J, LD_0, LD_1, ..., LD_N*) can be viewed as descriptions of links (or subpaths) between the substations that are linked for the telephone call. However, unlike communications networks, which are bi-directional, the SOLID System is normally uni-directional [10a]. The receiver substations are the terminal locations of the information paths, which contain a symbolic address in the RECORD FILE (RFILE). The symbolic address contains the address in the MAIN FILE of the first one of a linked set of items of compressed referenced information. The transmitter substation, which can be linked to terminals, contains the TRANSLATOR Component(s) that produce the unique JOBLIST Tasks from the assigned or extracted descriptor sets.

The analogy with a communication network breaks down when the following facets of the SOLID System are considered.

(a) Unlike telephone numbers, which are somewhat arbitrarily assigned to each subscriber, the JOBLIST Task actually describes both the path (in the AUXILIARY FILE) and the referenced information, which is stored in the MAIN FILE. This means that the SOLID System is a self-registry system and that the assignment of "idiot numbers" (like Registry, Ascension, Acquisition, or Inventory Numbers) can serve no meaningful or useful purpose. In fact, the automaticall assigned symbolic RFILE address(es) in the terminal locations of information paths can be viewed as a "Registry"for whatever collection(s) are organized by the SOLID System. There are provi for using the Registry Numbers to access the automatically assign MAIN FILE address(es) (in RFILE), without tracing information paths (see Figure I)

(b) The fully implemented SOLID System will have a capability for "browsing", "fragment", "substructure", and other non-explicit searches that have no parallels in any communications network.

(c) Unlike communications networks, whose new branch and substations must be created at quite rigidly prescribed locations, the SOLID System automatically creates new information subpaths (or sub-stations) whenever they are needed and wherever storage is available.

Evolving conventional libraries, cities, or roadway networks can also serve as useful analogies of the SOLID System. For example, the TRANSLATOR Component(s) performs those indexing and/or cataloguing functions which include the expansion and use of the conventional card indexes (viz., author, subject and cross reference files). The JOBLIST Tasks that are produced by the TRANSLATOR Component(s) are, like the Library of Congress or Dewey Decimal Systems, descriptions of path(s) to the location where the referenced information is stored. It should be noted that the mere assignment of an Acquisition or Library of Congress number does not by itself mean that the referenced information is in the library and available to users. In the conventional library "browsing" can occur when the card indexes are searched, and while the path(s) are being traced. These functions are performed in the SOLID System by the TRANSLATOR Component(s), which can produce partially specified JOBLIST Tasks, and by the MOBILE CANONICALIZATION Package which is used when tracing or updating information paths with partially specified JOBLIST Items [10a].

The AUXILIARY FILE is divided into two parts. One of these parts, which resides permanently in the computer, is associated with the prime index, M, the screen J, and the Continuance Tables. The second part is divided into memory-blocks and stored in the global (or virtual) memory. The RETRIEVAL Package uses the JOBLIST Tasks that are produced by the TRANSLATOR Components and a single input command (MODE), which has eight options [10a], to automatically execute all tracing, purging, creating, and updating operations in core-storage. The Internal GLOBAL MEMORY transfers the memory-blocks between the virtual memory and core-storage when they are needed. The function of the Continuance Tables is to restrict all information paths within single memory-blocks. This insures that each explicit[2] storage, update, retrieval, or purge request can be executed with, at most, the transfer of a single memory-block.

The MAIN FILE, which contains the compressed referenced information, is supervised by the stand-alone GLOBAL MEMORY (SGM), which uses the RFILE to find and allocate the MAIN FILE addresses. The SGM compresses[3] new referenced information, and then stores it at the automatically assigned address(es) in the MAIN FILE. It retrieves and decompresses[4] referenced information also [10a,11]. The retrieved, decompressed, referenced information is disseminated to the user(s).

---

[2] Here defined as an operation that involves only one information path.

[3] The recently implemented INTEGRAL Family of Compressors [12,13] will replace COPAK in the SOLID System. The INTEGRAL Compressors are channel programs that can be used either as additional instructions or as an integral part of the operating system. They require very substantially less storage than COPAK does and are significantly faster and yield higher savings.

[4] INTEGRAL decompression speeds of more than 470,000 bytes/second have been observed on the IBM 360/67.

The specifications of the fully implemented SOLID System are summarized in the next section. The data structure, computer implementation, and file security are discussed in subsequent sections.

3. SPECIFICATIONS OF THE SOLID SYSTEM

The design specifications for the SOLID System were discussed [1] before implementation began. These specifications will be fully met when the System is fully implemented. In this section the principal features and performance characteristics of the RETRIEVAL Package are summarized.

(a) Except for the single input command MODE, all storage, retrieval, updating, and purging operations are fully automatic.

(b) The RETRIEVAL Package is independent of the data-base and the meanings of the assigned or extracted descriptor sets. This means that the SOLID System can be used to organize any collections that have been assigned descriptor sets. The TRANSLATOR Components, which are embedded in the TRANSLATION Package [10a], rearrange the assigned or extracted descriptor sets to the JOBLIST Task form (see Section 5). The SOLID System is designed so that only a TRANSLATOR Component and the SECURITY macro-instruction might have to be coded for each new collection.

(c) The RETRIEVAL Package is capable of handling any questions that can be asked about any part(s) of any descriptor set. This means that there is a full capability for automatically handling all browsing, fragment, class, and intersecting (or inverted) file type searches. The seven override codes and the MOBILE CANONICALIZATION Package together make this capability possible [10a].

(d) The maximum search time for any explicit request is independent of the size of the collection, and it can never exceed the time it takes to fetch a single memory-block from the global or

virtual memory.[5] The average search time, which is determined
by the memory-block size and the amount of request queuing [10a]
is substantially less than the maximum search time. For large
retrieval systems (viz., A National Retrieval System) the average
search time will be between 0.01 and 0.0001 seconds for each
explicit request.[6]

(e) Because the maximum search times are independent of the file
size, there is no need to create subfiles. In fact the
resultant loss of interface and/or duplication are compelling
reasons for not creating subfiles.

(f) Because subpaths are never duplicated and they are only created
when they are needed, the AUXILIARY FILE requires a small
fraction of the storage that is needed for the index parts of
conventional retrieval systems.[7] It should be noted that the
AUXILIARY FILE is never compressed. The INTEGRAL family of
compressors,[3,4] which has replaced the COPAK Compressor
[3,4,5,6,7,8], is used to compress the referenced information
that is stored in the MAIN FILE. Savings of storage between
60 and 70 percent are commonly obtained by both COPAK and
INTEGRAL [13].

---

[5]In the SOLID System the maximum search time (M_t) can be computed
exactly (see Chapter XI of [10a]). An approximate equation is:

$$M_t = A_t + C_t + C_t \sum_{i=1}^{I} \alpha_{1i}.$$

Here: A_t is the time it takes to access and transfer a memory-block;
C_t is the average machine cycle time per byte (or character). α_{1i}
is a function of the number of subpaths originating in the ith
substation [10a]. Normally α_{1i} is 1. I is the number of subpaths
in the information path. The exact equations are given in [10a].

[6]Computed on the basis of a memory-block size of 500,000 bytes and a
request queue of 1000.

[7]With the Continuance Tables implemented it is estimated that this
fraction will be between 0.05 and 0.25.

494

(g) Storage that is released from the AUXILIARY FILE during purging operations is automatically reused when new subpaths are created, without reorganizing the files in any way. The Linkhole Facility [10a] manages the "holes" that are created during purge or delete operations.

(h) The SOLID System is a self-registry system. This means that Registry Numbers[8] are automatically assigned and that they can be used to store or retrieve items of referenced information.

(i) The SOLID System has twelve System Parameters which must be selected before it is compiled. These System Parameters (see Chapter III in [10a]) can be easily tailored to fit virtually any IBM 360 or 370 configuration. In fact the System has operated on IBM 360/40 (128K core), IBM 360/50 (512K core), and IBM 360/67 (3000K core). Moreover, by slightly modifying selected macro-instructions in the Internal (IGM) and stand-alone (SGM) GLOBAL MEMORIES any new hardware component can be used.

(j) The absolute integrity of both the AUXILIARY and MAIN FILES are easily assured in a natural way (see Section 7).

(k) The fully implemented SOLID System will be machine independent also. The ALLOCATE Translator [10a], which is now being implemented, will eventually produce the System in a machine independent higher level language such as Pl/I.

(1) The fully automatic purge and update facilities [10a] of the SOLID System permit the user-manager to collect information stored under several paths and store it under a single new information path at any time. This capability permits the reclassification of information without reorganizing the files in any way.

These specifications together mean that the SOLID System is several orders of magnitude better than any other retrieval/management system.

---

[8] Registry Numbers are identified with the National Compound Registry, Payroll, Acquisition, Ascension, Inventory and any other assigned numbers.

These claims are made with respect to speed, file security, automatic operations, efficient use of storage, expandability, versatility, and independence with respect to both the data-base and the question type. For example the DIALOG [14], MEDLARS [15], and Chemical Abstrac Services [16] Systems, which are all very inefficient with respect to storage, have <u>average search times</u> for medium sized collections (viz., 50,000 to 500,000 items) that are substantially greater than th <u>maximum search times</u> for the SOLID System. Moreover, in the SOLID System, the maximum search times are not measurably altered even if th file is expanded to contain information for 100,000,000 items. Of course, it is supposed that the machine configuration that is used has sufficient direct access storage for the entire AUXILIARY FILE.

The structure of the SOLID System is discussed next.

4. STRUCTURE OF THE SOLID SYSTEM

The design of the SOLID System is based on the concept of a system that contains two subsets of instructions. In one subset are all the assembly language instructions. The second subset, which is entered in the macro library (SOLID.MACLIB), contains all those components of the SOLID System and certain selected service macros. Components are entered as macro-subroutines with their own base registers so they may be placed anywhere in the system. Independently compiled components are stored in a partitioned data set, SOLID.LOAD.

Since both subsets of instructions are processed by the same compiler, the programmer can code with any arbitrarily selected combination of assembly language and macro-instructions. A "level of coding" or "coding level" refers to one such arbitrarily selected combination of instructions. At every coding level, the programmer can add, delete, or override instructions in the second subset whenever he wishes. New instructions can be coded at any previously defined coding level. In its final form the SOLID System, which is coded at the highest level (in the language ALLOCATE), will be

496

independent of the machine used.[9] In its final form the language
ALLOCATE has less than fifteen instructions, drawn from the two
subsets mentioned above.[10]

The two-part, open-ended design that has evolved for the SOLID System
(see Chapter II in [10a]) consists of the various components and
service macros, MACROPAK[11] and a control routine (CONTROL). The
control routine, which is coded in the higher language ALLOCATE,
assigns tasks to the various packages of the SOLID System when an
input, output, translation, search, compression, or decompression
job is executed. These packages, which consist of one or more
components, can be viewed as inter-dependent subprograms that can
also be used on a stand-alone basis.

The service macros in MACROPAK perform specialized tasks such as the
bit, byte, and string manipulation which are necessary for an
information system. Also included in this group are macros used for
input/output operations, the calling procedures for branching from
the control routine (CONTROL), and other specialized macros. The
components are coded in a hierarchical fashion with extensive
nesting. The kind of hierarchical arrangement that has been
achieved is illustrated in Figure II.

The open-ended, two-part, design just described permits optimum
machine language coding while giving rise to a "machine independent"
language whose structure can be preserved in a transportable language
in a conventional higher encoding.[9] Moreover, examination of the
"missing instructions" in the second subset discloses the weakness of
the computer that is used, and suggests ways in which existing

---

[9] The ALLOCATE Translator, which is now being implemented, will
eventually produce ALLOCATE in FORTRAN IV [10a].

[10] Only four of these fifteen instructions are drawn from the first
subset of instructions.

[11] MACROPAK has currently 206 entries.

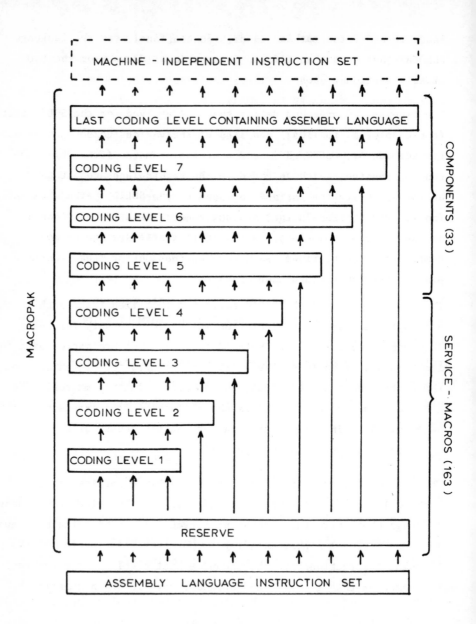

FIGURE II

Diagram illustrating the hierarchical arrangement in the design
selected for the SOLID System. The arbitrarily selected coding
levels are discussed in the text. RESERVE defines global
variables.

hardware can be modified. In this connection it is certain that the IBM 360 and 370 machines should be modified by microprogramming if they are to be used for large scale retrieval/management systems (see Chapter XV in [10a]).

At the present time there are eleven packages in the SOLID System (TABLE 1). Each package consists of one or more of the twenty-two components in MACROPAK. Seven of the eleven packages can be viewed as service-packages because they are used by the remaining four (COMMUNICATION, RETRIEVAL, SGM, and TRANSLATION). Three of seven service-packages, (NORMALIZATION, TRANSFORMATION and MOBILE CANONICALIZATION) are used when the JOBLIST Tasks, which are produced by the TRANSLATION Package, must be rearranged to one or more of their equivalent forms (see Section 5). Both the MOBILE CANONICALIZATION (MCP) and the NORMALIZATION Packages use the TRANSFORMATION Package, which contains the three transformation rules.[12] These three packages transform the information path description and, in effect, reorganize the AUXILIARY FILE without altering a single item in any way [10a]. They will not be considered further here.

The SOLID System is divided into two distinct parts, FRONTEND and RETRIEVAL (see Figure III). These two parts can be implemented in different CPU's or partitions, or they can be implemented together in a single partition (See Chapter XV [10a]). The FRONTEND uses three (COMMUNICATION, TRANSLATION, SGM) of the four primary packages and it is the information dependent user-machine interface. The RETRIEVAL part is information independent. It uses the JOBLIST Tasks that are produced by the TRANSLATION Package to automatically execute operations in the AUXILIARY FILE. A brief description of the principal parts of the SOLID System follows.

----

[12] These are the Cyclic Shift, Reflection, and Interchange Rules (see Chapter X in [10a]).

Package	Function
COMMUNICATION	Reads all input for the System and disseminates answers to users.
COMPRESSOR	Compress and decompress the referenced information in the MAIN FILE.
GENERATOR	Produces random JOBLIST Tasks for tests.
GLOBAL MEMORIES:	
(a) Internal (IGM)	Supervises the AUXILIARY FILE.
(b) Stand-Alone(SGM)	Supervises the RFILE and MAIN FILES.
MCP	See Text.
NORMALIZATION	See Text.
RETRIEVAL	Uses the JOBLIST Tasks produced by the TRANSLATION Package to trace, purge, update, or create information paths in the AUXILIARY FILE.
TRANSFORMATION	See Text
TRANSLATION	Reads the descriptor sets then uses the TRANSLATOR Components to produce the JOBLIST Tasks.
STATISTIC	Collects data about the performance of the RETRIEVAL Package.

TABLE 1

Packages of the SOLID System. Packages are inter-dependent subprograms that can be used on a stand-alone basis.

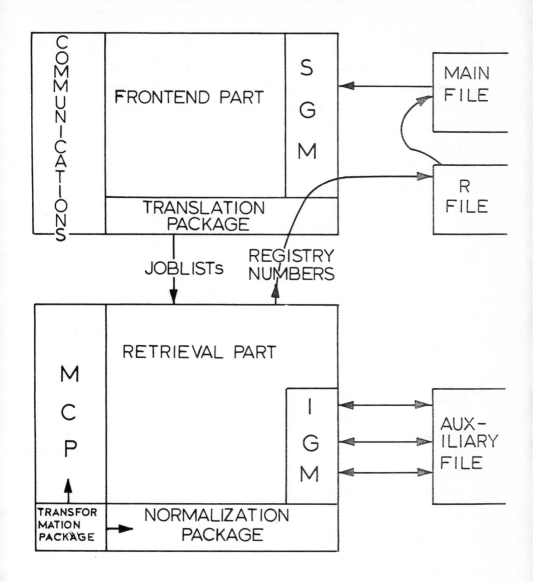

FIGURE III

Two-machine design of the SOLID System. The Internal (IGM) and Stand-
Alone (SGM) GLOBAL MEMORIES supervise the MAIN FILE and AUXILIARY FILE
respectively. The TRANSLATION Package produces the information independ
JOBLIST s that are used by the RETRIEVAL Part to retrieve (or assign) th
Registry Numbers (or Symbolic Addresses) in RFILE. The compressed item:
of referenced information are stored in the MAIN FILE.

501

Commands:

There are twenty-seven commands for the SOLID System. Thirteen of
these are associated exclusively with the TRANSLATION Package.
The remaining fourteen commands specify the I/O communications
devices and the path that is to be taken through the system. The
retrieval command (MODE), which is used in the RETRIEVAL Package, and
the output command (OUTPXT), which is used in the OUTPUT Package, are
the only ones active in normal retrieval operations.
Note: Every command is assigned a "safe" default option, which
is executed if a wrong or no value is entered or an error occurs.

COMMUNICATION Package:

This package reads all commands and input for the system. It also
disseminates retrieved information to the users.

TRANSLATION Package:

This package uses the translation package commands to rearrange the
assigned descriptor sets to the JOBLIST Task form. Its function
is fully described in the next section (5. TRANSLATION PACKAGE).

Stand-Alone GLOBAL MEMORY Package:

The stand-alone GLOBAL MEMORY (SGM), which is now being implemented,
will have two forms, simple and extended (see Chapter XII in
[10a]). Both forms will contain the new ultra high-speed INTEGRAL
family of compressors [10a, 12, 13]. Information is compressed
before it is stored at an automatically assigned address by the SGM.
Retrieved referenced information is decompressed before dissimination
to the user(s). The symbolic or RFILE addresses that are retrieved
(or assigned) by the RETRIEVAL package and the RFILE are used by the
SGM to find (or allocate) the MAIN FILE address(es). The extended form
of the SGM will contain its own paging system and it will allocate new
storage automatically. The potentials of the SGM are considered in
Chapter XVI of [10a].

RETRIEVAL Package:

This inordinately complex package has an estimated twenty-six
overlapping and interlocked signal systems (see Chapter XI in
[10a]). It uses a single command (MODE) and the JOBLIST Tasks

that are produced by the TRANSLATION Package to automatically
execute any purge, storage, retrieval or update operation in the
AUXILIARY FILE. The RETRIEVAL Package uses the Internal GLOBAL
MEMORY (IGM) part of the GLOBAL MEMORY Package to fetch and store
the memory-blocks of the AUXILIARY FILE. It can also use the
MOBILE CANONICALIZATION Package (MCP), which in turn uses the
TRANSFORMATION Package, to transform the information path
description (viz., JOBLIST Task).

In the next section the TRANSLATION Package is considered. The
TRANSLATOR Components are discussed in Section 6, and the File
Security mechanisms are described in Section 7.

5. TRANSLATION PACKAGE

The TRANSLATION Package produces the descriptions of information
paths (viz., JOBLIST Tasks) that are used by the RETRIEVAL Package
to execute storage, retrieval, updating, or purging operations in
the AUXILIARY FILE. It uses the TRANSLATOR Component(s) and the
GENERATOR, NORMALIZATION, and TRANSFORMATION Packages (see Figure IV).
The TRANSLATOR Components actually rearrange the descriptors to their
JOBLIST Task form. They are normally the only part of the SOLID System
that might have to be coded by the user-manager.

There are thirteen translation package commands and they are read from
two cards (see Chapter V and [10a]). Six of these commands are
associated exclusively with the GENERATOR Package, which is used to
produce random JOBLIST Tasks for debugging and tests. The other seven
commands are defined next. Two of these commands (JLINPXT and
JLRSKIP) specify the location of the descriptor sets that are to be
rearranged to the JOBLIST Task form. JLTRAN specifies which
TRANSLATOR Component is to be used. There are provisions for easily
incorporating additional TRANSLATOR Components. Another command,
(NFORM $\equiv$ JLNORM), specifies whether or not the NORMALIZATION and TRANS-
FORMATION Packages are to be used. KLENGTH is the number of characters
(or bytes) in each descriptor of the descriptor sets. It has a maximum
value of 255. NJOBS is the maximum number of items of referenced

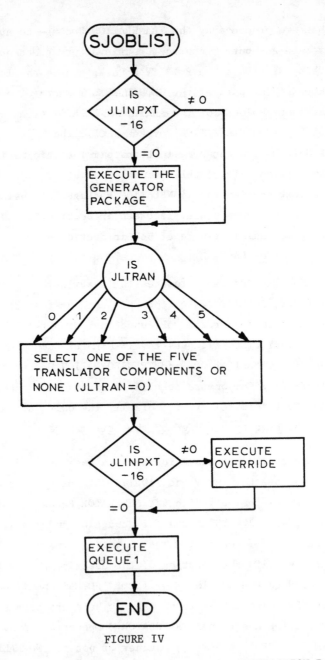

FIGURE IV

Flow-chart for the supervisory component of the TRANSLATION Package.
JLINPXT, JLTRAN, and JLNORM are commands that are read in COMMUNICATION
(not shown). If the GENERATOR Package is used, JLTRAN is set to zero.
The macro-instruction OVERRIDE counts override codes and executes the
SECURITY macro-instruction (see Section 7) QUEUE1 queues the search
requests.

information that are to be stored or retrieved. The last command (SECURE) is used to designate a protected path (SECURE $\neq$ 0).

For well structured data the TRANSLATOR Components simply rearrange the descriptors in each set to the JOBLIST Task form. This will be the case for most business, government, military, and scientific collections of data. For quasi-amorphous information like natural language texts or digitized pictorial data the TRANSLATOR Component must also extract the descriptors (or classifiers). The recently implemented AGISAR System [17], which is now being interfaced to the SOLID System,can be viewed as an inordinately complex TRANSLATOR Component. The English language text processor that is now being developed in our laboratories is based primarily on the logical-analysis method of Hillman [18]. In the remainder of this paper it is supposed that the items in the collections that are to be classified have been assigned unique descriptor sets. This means that the TRANSLATOR Component(s) will be simple rearrangement routines that can be easily coded by any programmer. The structure of JOBLIST Tasks and the rules for coding TRANSLATOR Components are discussed next.

6. TRANSLATOR COMPONENTS

A TRANSLATOR Component and the SECURITY macro-instruction are the only parts of the SOLID System which might have to be recoded for a new application of the system. The SECURITY macro-instruction, which processes questions about classified (viz., restricted access) information is discussed in Section 7. To code a TRANSLATOR Component the programmer must know the following:

(a) The format of the descriptor sets that are to be converted to JOBLIST Tasks.

(b) The structure of a JOBLIST Task and its relationship to the structure of the AUXILIARY FILE.

(c) The eleven translator commands (BITSCREN, ITEMUNON, JLTRAN, KLENGTH MARKUSH, NFORM JLNORM, NOSCREEN, NTASKS, PRINCPAL, QUEUE1, and TASK

Several of these commands (BITSCREN, ITEMUNON, PRINCPAL, QUEUE1 and TASKUNON) are not read. All translator commands can be reset in the TRANSLATOR Components. The commands JLTRAN and QUEUE1 can be used to couple two or more TRANSLATOR Components.

A detailed knowledge of the SOLID System or any of its parts is not required.

(i) Structure of JOBLIST

A JOBLIST consists of NTASKS Tasks, each of which is used by the RETRIEVAL Package to trace, purge, update, or create information path(s) in the AUXILIARY FILE. A JOBLIST Task contains one or more Items. A JOBLIST Item consists of a prime index, M, and one or more screens. These screens are combinations of the descriptors in a set that is associated with a particular item of referenced information. The mathematical basis of the SOLID System, which is the Information Representation (IR) and its two Bit-Maps (B_1 and B_2), has been fully described [1,2,3]. An IR is a square array organization of a descriptor set that is associated with a particular item of referenced information. The elements of the IR are the individual descriptors. The first Bit-Map (B_1) contains the prime index (M), which is the rank of the IR, and the J screen. The J screen is M bytes (or characters) long and it contains the ranks of the nested Information Representations in the IR (see [1]). The second Bit-Map (B_2) is a square array whose elements are binary numbers. It is a binary bit projection of the IR with zeros for null (i.e., no information) descriptors.

The IR and its two Bit-Maps (B_1 and B_2) are combined into a linear JOBLIST Item thus:

JL-Item $\equiv$ (M/J//LD$_0$//BD$_1$/LD$_1$//BD$_2$/LD$_2$//...//BD$_N$/LD$_N$*)   ...(B)

Here M and J are from the first Bit-Map (B_1), LD_i and BD_i are diagonals taken from the IR and the second Bit-Map respectively, and the asterisk indicates that the path terminates with a symbolic address in the RFILE. The order of the diagonals (BD_i and LD_i) in the

506

JL-Item has been given in [1,2,3]. Zero descriptors in the IR screens (viz., $LD_0, LD_1, \ldots$ etc.) are omitted and the JOBLIST Item is terminated with the last non-zero IR screen. The / and // have been inserted for clarity. They do not appear in the computer representations. New TRANSLATOR Components can be coded without any knowledge of the machine form of JOBLIST. A single macro-instruction, BUILDJLT, constructs the self-defined machine representations from the IR screens and six of the translator commands (BITSCREN, KLENGTH, MARKUSH, NFORM≡JLNORM, NOSCREEN, and NTASKS). Details of the computer representations will be found in Chapters VII and IX of reference [10a].

The IR can be used to describe logically complex relations of descriptors [10a]. For any such organization of descriptors, the NORMALIZATION Package of the system can select a unique NORMAL FORM of the IR from the class of logically equivalent organizations of the descriptors. The MOBILE CANONICALIZATION Package is used to automatically interconvert between members of a class of equivalent forms. Both the NORMALIZATION and MOBILE CANONICALIZATION[13] Packages use the transformation rules that are coded in the TRANSFORMATION Package [10a]. For example, if the order of the N^2 descriptors in a set is not significant[14] then there are $N^2!$ ways that they can be arranged into IR form. There are $N^2!/N!$ non-equivalent classes, each with N! <u>equivalent</u> <u>JOBLIST Items</u>. The programmer of a TRANSLATOR Component must select one of the non-equivalent classes. While the search times are insensitive to the class that is choosen, a poor choice can result in the inefficient use of storage.

JOBLIST Items can also be constructed without reference to any Information Representation. In this case the Transformation Rules

---

[13]The MCP consists of two parts (SMATCH and SMOBILE) and it is used only if Override codes are present in the JOBLIST Item. SMOBILE uses the TRANSFORMATION Package.

[14]For example, the line formulae for chemical compounds.

cannot be used because each JOBLIST Item is a NORMAL FORM. For
example, suppose that a collection of referenced items have nine
descriptors, and that the set of descriptors that is associated with
a particular item is A,0,B,0,C,0,E,0,F. The 0 specifies that there is
no information for the indicated descriptor. One of the many
possible[15] JOBLIST Items is:

JL-Item $\equiv$ (1/3//A0BC//2/E//1/F*)   ...(B)

Here the M(=1) and J(=3) values are arbitrarily set. The first "IR"
or descriptor screen contains the null element because it does not
have a binary-bit projection. The second screen (2 or binary 010)
indicates that the E in the next screen is preceded and followed by
zero (i.e., 0E0). The asterisk indicates that the information path,
which is described by the JL-Item, terminates with a symbolic address
in the RFILE (see Figure I).

The TRANSLATOR Component, which is coded once for each collection,
will produce the same form of JOBLIST Item for each descriptor set
in the collection. The particular form that uses the least amount of
AUXILIARY FILE storage can usually be selected by applying the following
two simple rules:

(a) The descriptors should be taken from the descriptor set in
     increasing order of their ranges in the entire collection.
(b) The descriptor or "IR" screens should be constructed from
     descriptors which have approximately the same frequency of
     occurrence in the collection.

Thus, to construct the most suitable form of JOBLIST. Task for
explicit questions, the programmer usually need only determine the
frequency of each value of each descriptor in a sample of descriptor sets
for the collection. If the most suitable form is not selected the search
times are virtually unaffected. However, the storage needed for the

---

[15]Another non-equivalent JOBLIST Item is:
   JL-ITEM$\equiv$(1/3//A//3/BC//1/E//0/0//1F*)

AUXILIARY FILE can be greatly increased. The eleven translator commands
(BITSCREN, ITEMUNON, JLTRAN, KLENGTH, MARKUSH, NFORM=JLNORM, NOSCREEN,
NTASKS, PRINCPAL, QUEUE1, and TASKUNON), which have been assigned default
options, can be reset in the TRANSLATOR Components. They are discussed
in the next subsection. Here it is noted that KLENGTH is the number of
characters (or bytes) for each descriptor. Nine codes (0,1,2,3,4,5,6,7,
and 8), which can be used for any descriptor, are reserved. Their meanings in
retrieval operations are given next:

'0' means that the descriptor has no meanings.

'1' means that any non-zero value will be acceptable
    for the designated descriptor(s).

'2' means that any value will be acceptable for the designated
    descriptor(s).

'3' – the gate override – means that any value in a stipulated
    range will be acceptable for the designated descriptor.

'4' – the not override – means that any value except those given
    will be acceptable for the designated descriptor(s).

'5' – the first markush override – means that any non-zero number of
    contiguous non-zero descriptors will be accepted.

'6' – the second markush override – means that any number of contiguous
    descriptors will be accepted.

'7' – the third markush override – will be used to specify the sub-
    structure or polymer unit.

'8' – designates the location of a Dynamic Security Lock (see Section 7).

The seven override codes (1,2,3,4,5,6, and 7) and the Dynamic Security
Lock indicator will be inserted by the TRANSLATOR Components. They are
automatically counted, and their locations are recorded by the
macro-instruction OVERRIDE (see Figure IV). However, it should be noted
that security locks can be overriden only with special permission. In
storage, update, and purge operations, the meanings of the override codes
are determined by the value of the retrieval command, MODE.

In retrieval operations the override codes permit the automatic
processing of browsing, fragment, substructure, class, group, and other
intersecting file type questions. In these cases the SMATCH component[13]

of the MOBILE CANONICALIZATION Package automatically performs sequential searches of local areas of the AUXILIARY FILE. In storage and update operations the override codes are used to indicate that basic operations like purging; collecting and purging; collecting without purging; and creating of alternative paths are to be performed. These basic operations are automatic. They can be used to change the paths or add new ones. For example, suppose that a file has been created by using JOBLIST Items of the form (B). If a frequently asked non-explicit question is:

$$JL\text{-}Item \equiv (1/3//12BC//2/E//1/F*) \qquad \qquad \ldots (C)$$

Many information paths (including the one created by (B)) will satisfy the request (C). This means that each time question (C) is asked, many information paths will be traced simultaneously. By using the update facility, (C) can be used to create a single information path that will point to all those items of referenced information that are normally retrieved when the non-explicit question (C) is asked. After this update operation is performed the JOBLIST Item (C) is processed as an explicit question and a single information path is traced. The update and purge operations have been fully described in [10a]. They cannot be considered further here. The five translator commands are considered next.

(ii) Translator Commands

In this subsection the following definitions are required:

An unsigned JOBLIST Item has the end asterisk omitted, e.g., the unsigned form of (B) is (1/3//AOBC//2/E//1/F). It describes an incomplete information path which terminates before the RFILE is reached (see Figure I).

A signed JOBLIST Item describes a complete information path which terminates in the RFILE. (A), (B), and (C) are examples of signed JOBLIST Items.

A JOBLIST Task is constructed from one or more JOBLIST Items, which may be signed and/or unsigned (see concatenation indicator below).

A <u>JOBLIST</u> consists of NTASKS Tasks.

For illustrative purposes the following notation will be used:

$$JL\text{-}I_i \equiv (M_i/J_i//LD_{0i}//BD_{1i}/LD_{1i}//\ldots//BD_{Ni}/LD_{Ni}) \qquad \ldots(D)$$

Here $JL\text{-}I_i$ is the unsigned JOBLIST Item i.

$JL\text{-}I_i{}^*$ is the corresponding signed JOBLIST Item.

The eleven translator commands are a vital part of the TRANSLATOR Components. They have been assigned the default options indicated below. Normally they will be reset in the TRANSLATOR Components.

BITSCREN (Default Option = 1) is the bit-map screen indicator. If BITSCREN equals zero, then bit-map screens are not used in any JOBLIST Task.

ITEMUNON (Default Option = 0) is the JOBLIST Item union indicator. If ITEMUNON is not zero, the macro-instruction ITEMUNON is executed after each Item in a Type III concatenated JOBLIST (see NOSCREEN below) has been used.

JLTRAN (Default Option = 0) is the command which normally designates the single TRANSLATOR Component that is to be used for the application. However, it can be changed in any TRANSLATOR Component and used in conjunction with QUEUE1 to process assigned descriptor sets on different TRANSLATOR components.

KLENGTH is the number of characters (or bytes) in each descriptor. The maximum value of KLENGTH is 255 and its default option is 1.

NFORM≡JLNORM (Default Option = 0) is the normalization indicator (see Figure IV). If NFORM is zero, the NORMALIZATION Package is not used.

NOSCREEN (Default Option Type I) is the so called concatenation indicator. There are the following three kinds of concatenation.

(a) <u>Type I</u>: The JOBLIST Task consists of interleaved NOSCREEN (=I) unsigned JOBLIST Items thus:

$$JL\text{-}T \equiv (M_1/J_1//LD_{01}//LD_{02}//\ldots//LD_{0I}//BD_{11}/LD_{11}//BD_{12}/LD_{12}//\ldots$$

$$//BD_{1I}/LD_{1I}//\ldots//BD_{N1}/LD_{N1}//\ldots//BD_{NI}/LD_{NI}{}^*)$$

JL-T describes a path which terminates in the RFILE, where the address(es) of the referenced information is stored. If NOSCREEN = 1, then JL-T contains one signed JOBLIST Item. If BITSCREN = 0, all the Bit-map screens (BD_{11}, BD_{12}, etc.) are omitted.

(b) Type II: (NOSCREEN = 0). The JOBLIST Task contains a single unsigned JOBLIST Item thus:

$$JL\text{-}T \equiv (M/J//LD_0//BD_1/LD_1//\ldots//BD_N/LD_N)$$

JL-T describes an incomplete information path that terminates before the RFILE is searched.

(c) Type III: In this case NOSCREEN (=I) is a negative integer. The JOBLIST Task (JL-T) consists of -I chained unsigned JOBLIST Items and it is terminated with an asterisk thus:

$$JL\text{-}T \equiv (JL\text{-}I_1/JL\text{-}I_2/\ldots/JL\text{-}I_{-I}*)$$

These three kinds of concatenation can be used in many different way

For example, a Type I (with NOSCREEN=1) followed by a Type II produc

a Type III with NOSCREEN=-2. The concatenation indicator can be use

to extend information paths. The Type II and Type III concatenatior

can also be used to create families of equivalent information paths.

Each path in such a family can be used to locate parts or all of the

referenced information that is associated with the entire family of

paths (see Chapter VIII in [10a]).

NTASKS (Default Option = 1) is the number of Tasks in each JOBLIST. Each Task is processed as a separate job.

MARKUSH (Default Option = 0) is the markush indicator. MARKUSH $\neq 0$ means that nested pairs of Information Representations are inter-connected by single connectors at the junctions of each pair.

PRINCPAL (Default Option = 2) is the principal screen in each JOBLIST Task. This information is used when new information paths are created in storage and update operations. PRINCPAL = 2 means that the first "IR" or descriptor screen (i.e., LD_{0i} in (D)) is the principal one. In the latest version of the SOLID System this faci has been extended so that the sizes of all arrays associated with a screens can be arbitrarily set.

QUEUE1 (Default Option = 0) specifies the number of JOBLIST Tasks tha will be queued before the RETRIEVAL Package is used. The macro-instruction QUEUE1 is executed after each production of a JOBLIST Task of QUEUE $\neq 0$.

TASKUNON (Default Option = 0) is the JOBLIST Task union indicator. If TASKUNON $\neq 0$, the macro-instruction TASKUNON is executed after each Task has been used.

7. FILE SECURITY

In the SOLID System there are two different classes of security

mechanisms. The first of these is fully automatic and is designed to insure the absolute integrity of the System and its files against all machine, program, and operator errors [10a]. It will not be considered further here. The second class of security mechanism is designed to insure the absolute integrity of every item in the MAIN FILE, which contains the referenced information, and the information paths in the AUXILIARY FILE, which are described by JOBLIST Tasks, against all unqualified users. This class of security mechanism can be easily used, by the user and/or the user-manager, to prevent all unqualified users from ever accessing information that they are not entitled to have.

Any number of "security locks", which prevent illegal access to information, can be inserted in a JOBLIST Task when it is constructed by the TRANSLATOR Component. They may also be inserted at the head of the compressed referenced information when it is stored in the MAIN FILE.[16] The two different kinds of security locks are identified next.

(a) Static Security Locks are unique codes that are a part of the JOBLIST Task. They are inserted as additional descriptors when the Task is constructed by the TRANSLATOR Components. The entire JOBLIST Task, which includes the security locks, is used by the RETRIEVAL Package to trace, create, purge, or update an information path in the AUXILIARY FILE. In retrieval operation the search will be aborted if any one of the security locks is not correct. It is supposed that the user-manager of the installation will be exclusively responsible for all storage, update, and purging operations. The automatically assigned Static Security Locks would be disclosed only to qualified users.

(b) Dynamic Security Locks are unique codes that notify the TRANSLATOR Component that additional information must be supplied by the user before a JOBLIST Task can be completed. The additional information is inserted in the JOBLIST Task, then it is processed as if it were a Static Security Lock. The user is interrogated by the TRANSLATOR Component. If the interrogation is not successful (e.g., if the user supplies the wrong additional information) the search will be terminated as unsuccessful. Unlike the Static Security Locks, which will

---

[16] The stand-alone GLOBAL MEMORY (SGM), which supervises the MAIN FILE, will be responsible for inserting and checking security locks at the head of each item of referenced information.

be inserted by the user manager, the Dynamic Security Locks can be inserted by the user.

The Security Lock Command (SECURE) is used to specify a protected path. If SECURE ≠ 0, the macro-instruction OVERRIDE (see Figure IV) inserts the right three bytes of the command SECURE at the head of the screen and increments M by 3. The SECURITY macro-instruction, which i executed in OVERRIDE, contains the interrogation routine (for Dynamic Security Locks) and checks for permission to override Security Locks. SECURITY must be coded by the user-manager.

Two examples of the Security Locks are given next. It is supposed that the unprotected information path is described by the JOBLIST Task:

$$JL-T \equiv (M/J//AOBC//2/E//1/F*)$$

Suppose that two Static Security Locks (L_1 and L_2) are to be inserted thus:

$$JL-T \equiv (M+3/SJ//AOL_1BC//3/EL_2//1/F*)$$

Here S is the right three bytes of SECURE.

For new storage operations the TRANSLATOR Component will automatically assign and insert values for L_1 and L_2 when the JOBLIST Task(s) are constructed. In retrieval operations L_1 and L_2 must be supplied by the user as a part of the descriptor set. However, it is obvious that L_1 and L_2 can also be obtained from look-up tables by the TRANSLATOR Component.

Suppose that whenever the special code 8 (assigned for the Dynamic Security Lock) occurs the interrogation routine, which is part of the SECURITY macro-instruction, asks the question: What Language can you speak? Further suppose that the four correct answers are English (L_1), Zulu (L_2), Swahili (L_3), and Afrikaans (L_4) (In that order). In new storage operations these descriptors might be inserted thus:

$$JL-T \equiv (M+3/SJ//L_1AOBC//7/L_2EL_3//3/L_4F*)$$

In retrieval operations the special code (8) would be inserted in the

JOBLIST Task thus:

$$JL\text{-}T \equiv (M+3/SJ//8AOBC//7/8E8//3/8F*)$$

The interrogation routine would use look-up tables to determine
whether or not the correct Dynamic Security Locks are known to
the user. If they are not the search will be aborted. If the
interrogation is successful then the four Dynamic Security Locks
(English, Zulu, Swahili, and Afrikaans) can replace the special codes (8)
in the JOBLIST Task and be processed as if they were Static Security
Locks, or the special codes (8) can be left in. The second alternative
may be perferred because it permits the user-manager to change the
interrogation procedure without altering the AUXILIARY FILE. In this
case the Dynamic Security Locks would be analogous to the conventional
military pass word - counter pass word system.

It should be noted that it is the responsibility of the programmer of the
SECURITY macro-instruction to make certain that the override codes are
never used by unqualified persons to override security locks. Security
Locks will normally be overriden only in maintenance operations.

Security Lock Combinations:

Several security locks can be used in conjunction with the Type II
and Type III concatenation (see (ii) above) to arrange a hierarchical
security lock combinations with groups of equivalent information
paths that correspond to a graduated scale of "security clearances".
For illustrative purposes it is supposed that the Type II and
Type III concatenations have been used to create four families of
information paths that are associated with the following prototype
JOBLIST Tasks:

$$(JBItem_1/JBItem_2/JBItem_3/JBItem_4*)$$
$$(JBItem_2/JBItem_3/JBItem_4/JBItem_1*)$$
$$(JBItem_1/JBItem_3/JBItem_4/JBitem_2*)$$
$$(JBItem_1/JBItem_2/JBItem_4/JBItem_3*)$$

Here $JBItem_1$ and $JBItem_1*$ are unsigned and signed JOBLIST Items. Each of these four families has sixteen information paths [10a], e.g., for the first family the JOBLIST Tasks for the sixteen paths are:

$(JBItem_4*)$

$(JBItem_3/JBItem_4*)$

$(JBItem_2/JBItem_4*)$

$(JBItem_1/JBItem_4*)$

$(JBItem_1/JBItem_2/JBItem_4*)$

$(JBItem_2/JBItem_1/JBItem_4*)$

$(JBItem_2/JBItem_3/JBItem_4*)$

$(JBItem_3/JBItem_2/JBItem_4*)$

$(JBItem_1/JBItem_3/JBItem_4*)$

$(JBItem_3/JBItem_1/JBItem_4*)$

$(JBItem_1/JBItem_2/JBItem_3/JBItem_4*)$

$(JBItem_2/JBItem_1/JBItem_3/JBItem_4*)$

$(JBItem_2/JBItem_3/JBItem_1/JBItem_4*)$

$(JBItem_3/JBItem_2/JBItem_1/JBItem_4*)$

$(JBItem_3/JBItem_1/JBItem_2/JBItem_4*)$

$(JBItem_1/JBItem_3/JBItem_2/JBItem_4*)$

The translator command ITEMUNON and the macro-instruction ITEMUNON can be used to specify the connection(s) between the JOBLIST Items in the multi-item JOBLIST Tasks (see 6(ii)).

Each of these JOBLIST Tasks describes a single information path, and all sixteen paths terminate in the same part of the RFILE. Thus the same items of referenced information are associated with every path in a family.

If the four unsigned JOBLIST Items ($JBItem_i$, with i = 1,2,3, and 4) each contain one or more security locks then the 64 information paths have four "security clearances" (e.g., one per family), each described by sixteen different JOBLIST Tasks. One such JOBLIST Task

for the first "security clearance" in the above example is $(JBItem_4, *)$.
The formulae for computing these data are:

Number of Security Clearances = Number of signed JOBLIST Items times
the number of different security lock combinations in each item.

$$\text{Number of equivalent paths/Security Clearance} = \sum_{i=1}^{N} P_i \cdot C_i$$

Here: $P_i = (N - i)!$ and $C_i = (N - 1)!/[(N - i)!(i - 1)!]$,
with $(N - i)$ unsigned JOBLIST Items.

In the above example this means that there are four different
"security clearances", each with sixteen equivalent information paths
(or combinations). From the above illustration it should be clear
that numerous security locks can be easily designed into the system
without substantially increasing the file storage requirements.
Because the AUXILIARY and MAIN FILES are separated, additional
natural points for introducing security locks are:

(a) in the MAIN FILE addresses which are stored in the RFILE (see
     Figure I). These addresses are entered directly in Registry
     Number Searches [10a]. This can be used to provide file
     security for this type of search.

(b) at the head of each separately referenced item of compressed
     referenced information in the MAIN FILE.

If the Security Lock Indicator (SECURE) is not zero, then Security Locks
are automatically attached to the Registry Number (in RFILE) and inserted
at the head of the compressed items of referenced information (in MAIN FILE).

References

[1] P.A.D. deMaine and B.A. Marron, The SOLID System I. A Method for Organizing and Searching Files, in G. Schecter, ed., "Information Retrieval: A Critical View" (Thompson Book Co., Washington, 1967).

[2] P.A.D. deMaine, "File Structure of the SOLID System", in FILE ORGANISATION, Amsterdam, Swets and Zeitlinger N.V., (1969).

[3] P.A.D. deMaine and G.K. Springer, Details of the SOLID System - July 1968, Pennsylvania State University, University Park, Pa., (1968).; Also P.B. 182 476 from the Federal Clearinghouse, U.S. Department of Commerce, Springfield, Virginia 22151 (Price $3.00).

[4] P.A.D. deMaine, K. Kloss and B.A. Marron, The SOLID System II. Numeric Compression, National Bureau of Standards Technical Note 413 (1967).

[5] P.A.D. deMaine, B.A. Marron and K. Kloss, The SOLID System III. Alphanumeric Compression, National Bureau of Standards Technical Note 413 (1967).

[6] B.A. Marron and P.A.D. deMaine, "Automatic Data Compression", Comm. Assoc. Compt. Machinery, 10, 711-715 (1967).

[7] P.A.D. deMaine, G. K. Springer, and G.M. Campbell, "Software Packages for Increasing "Traffic" in the Communications Channels of Networks", Proc. Amer. Soc. Inf. Science 5, 109 (1968).

[8] P.A.D. deMaine and G.K. Springer, "The COPAK Compressor", in FILE ORGANISATION, Amsterdam, Swets and Zeitlinger N.V., (1969).

[9] G. K. Springer and P.A.D. deMaine, "The SOLID System Global Memory Component" in FILE ORGANISATION, Amsterdam, Swets and Zeitlinger, N.V., (1969).

[10] (a) P.A.D. deMaine, J.T. Perry, and G. K. Springer, "The SOLID System. Volume I. Design Philosophy, Basic Frame, and Compressors", Compiled at Pennsylvania State University, University Park, Pennsylvania, 16802 (1970). Approximately 1100 pages.

[11] P.A.D. deMaine and G.K. Springer, Global Memories I. Simple Form (In preparation).

[12] R. Overbeek, "Manual for the INTEGRAL Family of Compressors", Report No. 2, Computer Science Department, Pennsylvania State University, University Park, Pennsylvania, 16802 (1970)

[13] P.A.D. deMaine and R. Overbeek, "High Speed, Reversible Compressors", (In preparation).

[14] R.K. Summit, "DIALOG - An Operational, On-Line Reference Retrieval System", Proceedings of the 22nd Conference of the ACM, Thompson Book Company, Washington, D.C., 1967, pp. 51-56.

[15] (a) Kent, A. "Computers and biomedical information storage and retrieval", JAMA 196:927-32, June 1966.

(b) Kenton, C. "MEDLARS -- program of the National Library of Medicine; searching operation", Presented at the 3rd Annual Institute of Technical Literature Abstracting and Indexing. The American University -- Center for Technology and Administration, Washington, D.C., May 15-17, 1967. To be published.

[16] F. Tate, Chem. and Eng. News, 45, No. 4, 78 (1967); and numerous other papers in Chem. and Eng. News, and in J. Amer. Doc. by Dr. Tate and other members of the Chemical Abstract Services staff.

[17] G. K. Springer, "AGISAR System for Processing Digitized Pictorial Data", Ph.D. Thesis, Pennsylvania State University (1970).

[18] D. Hillman, "Negotation of Inquires in an On-Line Retrieval System", Inform. Stor. and Ret., 4, 219 (1969) and numerous other papers by Prof. Hillman and other members of the Lehigh University group.

APPENDIX

MIS COPENHAGEN 70 - Program Committee

Harald Josefsen, Chairman
    Senior Consultant, Parsons & Williams,
    Copenhagen, Denmark

Bengt Ahrfelt,
    Director, The Swedish Office of Organization
    and Management,
    Stockholm, Sweden.

Birgit Johansen,
    Office Manager, The Danish Edp Council,
    Copenhagen, Denmark

Erik Johnsen,
    Professor, The Copenhagen School of Economics and
    Business Administration,
    Copenhagen, Denmark

Jakob Krarup,
    Senior Lecturer, The Technical University of Denmark,
    Lyngby, Denmark

Sjir Nijssen,

    Manager Industry Planning, Control Data Europe,

    Brussels, Belgium

Ole Stangegaard,

    Director, ØK-DATA,

    Copenhagen, Denmark

THE BOARD OF DANISH IAG

Th. Herborg Nielsen, President

    Professor, The Århus School of Economics and Business

    Administration,

    Århus, Denmark

Mogens Boman, Director, The Danish Edp Council,

    Copenhagen, Denmark

Ole C. Nord,

    Director, Parson & Williams,

    Copenhagen, Denmark

Willy Olsen,

    Director, I/S DATACENTRALEN af 1959,

    Copenhagen, Denmark

UNIVERSITY OF RHODE ISLAND

3 1222 00690 9140

NO LONGER THE PROPERT
OF THE
UNIVERSITY OF RI LIBRARY